Applied Drama

Theatre and Performance Practices

General Editors: Graham Lay and Jane Milling

Published

Christopher Baugh	*Theatre, Performance and Technology*
Greg Giesekam	*Staging the Screen*
Deirdre Heddon and Jane Milling	*Devising Performance*
Helen Nicholson	*Applied Drama*
Michael Wilson	*Storytelling and Theatre*
Cathy Turner and Synne K. Behrndt	*Dramaturgy and Performance*

Forthcoming

Deirdre Heddon	*Autobiography in Performance*
Philip B. Zarrilli, Jerri Daboo and Rebecca Loukes	*From Stanislavski to Physical Theatre*

Theatre and Performance Practices Series
Series Standing Order
ISBN 1–4039–8735–1 hardcover
ISBN 1–4039–8736–X paperback
(outside North America only)

You can receive future titles in this series as they are published by placing a standing order. Please contact your bookseller or, in case of difficulty, write to us at the address
below with your name and address, the title of the series and the ISBN quoted above.

Customer Services Department, Macmillan Distribution Ltd
Houndmills, Basingstoke, Hampshire RG21 6XS, England

Applied Drama

The Gift of Theatre

HELEN NICHOLSON

palgrave
macmillan

First published 2005 by
PALGRAVE MACMILLAN
Houndmills, Basingstoke, Hampshire RG21 6XS and
175 Fifth Avenue, New York, N.Y. 10010
Companies and representatives throughout the world

PALGRAVE MACMILLAN is the global academic imprint of the Palgrave Macmillan division of St. Martin's Press, LLC and of Palgrave Macmillan Ltd. Macmillan® is a registered trademark in the United States, United Kingdom and other countries. Palgrave is a registered trademark in the European Union and other countries.

ISBN-13: 978–1–4039–1645–7 hardback
ISBN-10: 1–4039–1645–4 hardback
ISBN-13: 978–1–4039–1646–4 paperback
ISBN-10: 1–4039–1646–2 paperback

This book is printed on paper suitable for recycling and made from fully managed and sustained forest sources.Logging, pulping and manufacturing processes are expected to conform to the environmental regulations of the country of origin.

A catalogue record for this book is available from the British Library.

Library of Congress Cataloging-in-Publication Data
Nicholson, Helen, 1958–
    Applied drama : the gift of theatre / Helen Nicholson.
       p.   cm. — (Theatre and performance practices)
    Includes bibliographical references and index.
    ISBN-13: 978–1–4039–1645–7 (hard.)
    ISBN-10: 1–4039–1645–4 (hard.)
    ISBN-13: 978–1–4039–1646–4 (pbk.)
    ISBN-10: 1–4039–1646–2 (pbk.)
    1. Theater and society.   I. Title.   II. Series.
    PN2049.N53 2005
    792'.01—dc22   2005047456

10   9   8
14   13   12   11   10   09

Printed in China

Contents

v

Acknowledgements

As research in applied drama is sensitive to the contexts in which the practice takes place, there are inevitably many people to thank. Firstly, formal acknowledgements are due to the AHRB and to Bloodaxe Books, for permission to reproduce Jackie Kay's poem 'In My Country', which was first published in *Other Lovers* (1993). Parts of Chapter 5 were recycled from 'The Performance of Memory', in *Drama Australia*, 27: 2 (2003), and I am pleased to acknowledge their permission to include aspects of the paper in this book. I am also grateful for advice I have received from Adrian Jackson, who kindly read parts of the manuscript, to series editors Jane Milling and Graham Ley, and to Kate Wallis at Palgrave Macmillan who steered the book forward with much tact and diplomacy.

I am especially indebted to Penny Bundy, Sharon Grady, Andy Kempe, Louise Keyworth, Sally Mackey, John Somers, James Thompson and Ruth Williams, all of whom shared their practice, insights and ideas with much generosity and good humour. The last thanks go to my mother, who first taught me to love the arts and showed me the value of community. This book is dedicated to the memory of her many gifts.

HELEN NICHOLSON

General Editors' Preface

This series sets out to explore key performance practices encountered in modern and contemporary theatre. Talking to students and scholars in seminar rooms and studios, and to practitioners in rehearsal, it became clear that there were widely used modes of practice that had received very little critical and analytical attention. In response, we offer these critical, research-based studies that draw on international fieldwork to produce fresh insight into a range of performance processes. Authors, who are specialists in their fields, have set each mode of practice in its social, political and aesthetic context. The series charts both a history of the development of modes of performance process and an assessment of their significance in contemporary culture.

Each volume is accessibly written, and gives a clear and pithy analysis of the historical and cultural development of a mode of practice. As well as offering readers a sense of the breadth of the field, the authors have also given key examples and performance illustrations. In different ways each book in the series asks readers to look again at processes and practices of theatre-making that seem obvious and self-evident, and to examine why and how they have developed as they have, and what their ideological content is. Ultimately the series aims to ask questions about what are the choices and responsibilities facing performance-makers today?

Graham Ley and Jane Milling

1 An Introduction to Applied Drama

Radical Directions

In her autobiography, theatre director Joan Littlewood tells a story about the plans for *The Fun Palace*, an ambitious and visionary project that aimed to create a 'playground of learning' in the deprived East End of London during the 1960s. Her article in *The New Scientist* described an acting area which would, Littlewood wrote, 'afford the therapy of theatre to everyone'. For shop and factory workers, participation in theatre would counteract the daily boredom of unsatisfying working lives. People would be able to escape their drab routines and find psychological pleasure in enacting aspects of their own lives through which, she hoped, they would develop a 'critical awareness of reality' that might lead to their engagement in social research.[1] In practice, *The Fun Palace* never materialised. Plans were quashed by bureaucratic councillors who were more concerned with curbing vandalism than developing entertaining approaches to lifelong learning. Littlewood was undaunted. Although Littlewood's East 15 Theatre, near to the proposed *Fun Palace* site, had been repeatedly looted by thieves whom the local authorities described as 'young savages' and 'unsavoury elements', she invited these young people into the safe space of the theatre, and encouraged them to find ways of telling their own stories behind the security of locked doors. By 1975, Littlewood remarked caustically that 'our savages' were organising festivals for themselves.[2]

It is an optimistic story, bearing witness to the power of drama to affect social and personal change. It is also a story which is familiar to those who work in community arts – it has been told and retold many times, about many different people, in many different social contexts.

1

What this story identifies is the relationship between theatre practice, social efficacy and community building. Joan Littlewood, a socialist theatre director who did much to shake up the British theatre establishment in the mid-twentieth century, saw no distinction between these modes of cultural practice – for her they were all part of the same political project. By working with young people, and listening to their stories, she enabled them to find their own forms of artistic, cultural and theatrical expression.

This book is an investigation into the value and values of drama, theatre and performance that take place in community settings and in educational contexts. It is about theatre-making in many different and sometimes rather unglamorous places – in, for example, care homes for the elderly, hostels for the homeless, schools and prisons – led by practitioners who have experience in facilitating drama with community-based participants. In this introductory chapter I shall begin by considering how the terms 'applied drama' and 'applied theatre' are generally used, and how they are related to the histories and practices of community-based theatre. I hope to raise questions which will be addressed later in the book, and to map some of the debates and discussions that permeate the field.

What is Applied Drama/Theatre?

The terms 'applied drama' and 'applied theatre' gained currency during the 1990s, finding particular favour with academics, theatre practitioners and policy-makers who have used them as a kind of shorthand to describe forms of dramatic activity that primarily exist outside conventional mainstream theatre institutions, and which are specifically intended to benefit individuals, communities and societies. Included in the port-manteau of applied drama/theatre are practices as diverse as, for example, drama education and theatre in education, theatre in health education, theatre for development, theatre in prisons, community theatre, heritage theatre and reminiscence theatre. Each of these forms of theatre has its own theories, debates and highly specialised practices which often are rather different from one another. They also draw on research in different branches of philosophy and the social sciences, notably cultural studies, cultural geography, education, psychology, sociology and anthropology, as well as contributing to research in drama, theatre and performance studies. In other words, applied drama and theatre are interdisciplinary and hybrid practices. Drama practitioners have been working in educa-tional, therapeutic and community settings for many years, but the emergence of the terms 'applied drama', 'applied theatre', and sometimes 'applied performance' signals a renewed interest in the professionalisation of these fields and in reviewing common theoretical and political concerns which accompany their various practices. Because applied drama and applied theatre are relatively new terms, there is no real consensus about how they are used. Descriptions of higher education courses in applied drama and theatre reveal different inflections and interpretations. The Central School of Speech and Drama in London describes the practice of applied theatre as 'intervention, communication, development, empowerment and expression when working with individuals or specific communities'. This tone is echoed by the Drama Department at the University of Manchester, where there is a further emphasis on the politics of space and dispossession in their commitment to apply theatre to 'non-traditional spaces and marginalised communities'. In Australia the international online journal *Applied Theatre Researcher* is more politically eclectic, describing applied theatre as 'theatre and drama in non-traditional contexts – theatre in the community, theatre in business and industry, theatre in political debate and action, theatre in lifelong education and learning'. The New Zealand Ministry of Education is more policy-driven, claiming that applied theatre is 'part of the wider discipline of Drama in Education' and that it involves work 'in business, corporate and community settings'.[3] What is evident here is not only the different values and aspirations of the institutions and practitioners involved in applied drama, but the wide range of dramatic practices with which they are accompanied.

One of the common features of these many different facets of applied drama/theatre is, as Judith Ackroyd has pointed out, its intentionality – specifically an aspiration to use drama to improve the lives of individuals and create better societies. Ackroyd, who includes both process-orientated and performative practices in her description of applied theatre, helpfully sums up the common beliefs of many different practitioners in the field.

They share a belief in the power of the theatre form to address something beyond the form itself. So one group use theatre in order to promote positive social processes within a particular community, whilst others employ it in order to promote an understanding of human resource issues among corporate employees. . . . The intentions of course vary. They could be to inform, to cleanse, to unify, to instruct, to raise awareness.[4]

The idea that theatre has the potential to 'address something beyond the form itself' suggests that applied drama is primarily concerned with developing new possibilities for everyday living rather than segregating theatre-going from other aspects of life. What are considered to be 'positive social processes' or what values are to be understood by newly empowered 'corporate employees' do, of course, change over time and are variously construed in different local and global contexts.

The distinction between applied *drama* and applied *theatre* is similarly moot. Philip Taylor, an academic and practitioner working in New York, makes a distinction between applied drama, which he sees as process-based, and applied theatre, which he describes as performance-based.

While there are similarities with applied drama, what one tends to find in the latter is a dependency on conventional British drama in education strategies to teach about issues, events, relationships. Applied theatre is powered by a strong sense of aesthetic education and is usually centred on structured scenarios presented by teams of teaching artist–facilitators.[5]

This sounds very like an extension of the kind of distinctions made between British drama in education (DIE) and theatre in education (TIE) during the 1970s and 1980s, where DIE was primarily regarded as a teaching methodology across the curriculum, and TIE involved teams of actor–teachers working with students in participatory performance programmes.[6] Taylor has offered an illuminating definition of the difference between applied drama and applied theatre in relation to his own practice, but I have not found this distinction in common use elsewhere. Furthermore, in many of the applied drama/theatre practices discussed in this book there is a reluctance to make a neat separation between process and performance-based work, and I have found that many practitioners acknowledge a productive consonance between the two. Not only does this raise questions about how 'performance' might be defined in the field, it also suggests that the terms 'applied drama' and 'applied theatre' are often used quite flexibly and interchangeably.

If applied drama and applied theatre are hybrid genres, my choice of 'applied drama' as the title of this book, and my invoking 'theatre' in the sub-title, is not intended to be a major point of controversy. There are no specific ideological, pedagogical or methodological reasons for this, except that I am trying to be as inclusive as possible, and offer equal weight to both terms. The etymology of both 'drama' and 'theatre' are significant to the values of applied drama/theatre. Drama derives from the Greek word *dran* (meaning 'to make or do') and theatre from *theatron* (meaning 'viewing place'), which, when combined, seem to indicate the process of action and reflection which lie at the heart of applied drama/theatre praxis.[7] But if the title of this book appears to emphasise 'drama' rather than 'theatre' it is because I have been swayed by the argument that many people outside the theatre business tend to associate 'theatre' with specialist buildings, lights, costumes and so on, rather than the more diverse and less showy practices often associated with applied drama/theatre. Plumping for both terms in the title signals my attempt to recognise the importance of all forms of theatre practice and performance as they are applied to specific contexts and different audiences. In this book, however, I usually use the shorthand 'applied drama' to suggest the range of theatrical and performative practices which constitute the field. For ease of reference, I have also decided to call workshop leaders or facilitators 'practitioners', and those who take part 'participants'. This is not intended to be hierarchical but simply to use this terminology to suggest the divisions of labour which I have observed in practice.

In many ways I am ambivalent about categorising any work as either applied drama or applied theatre, and I would be very concerned if the convenience of this collective noun reduced a rich diversity of theories and artistic practices to a single homogeneous discourse. The application of drama to different institutional or community settings illuminates fundamental questions about the role and significance of *all* theatre practice to society, and about how theatre-making articulates and challenges contemporary concerns. For me, therefore, interesting debate lies not in whether different forms of performance practice are labelled as 'drama' or 'theatre', nor in creating strict definitions of what applied drama or applied theatre might be, but in raising questions about what is meant by the word 'applied', to what or whom drama and theatre might be applied, and for what reasons, and whose values the application of theatre-making serves and represents.

Pure and Applied Drama

One way to begin to address questions about the roles and functions of applied drama/theatre is to analyse how it relates to, and contrasts with, other cognate disciplines and artistic practices. I find it interesting that other academic disciplines that customarily use the preface 'applied' often contrast it with 'pure'. In mathematics, for example, pure mathematics is abstract and theoretical, whereas applied mathematics is concerned with using theoretical models to solve practical problems. Most practitioners working in applied drama are motivated by individual or social change and there is, therefore, a similar interest in the effects and usefulness of the work. With its roots in the libertarian practices of twentieth-century drama education, community theatre and alternative or political theatres, there is both radicalism and an instrumentalism about applied drama.

The term 'applied drama/theatre' is intensely problematic if it is seen to stand in opposition to drama/theatre as an art form, particularly if this implies that its production values and status in the academy are diminished. Bjørn Rasmussen, speaking at the inauguration of the Centre for Applied Theatre Education and Research in Brisbane, was concerned with the different places occupied by applied theatre and 'not-applied' theatre in the cultural hierarchy.

> I never found the expression 'applied' drama or theatre quite sound, because I always found it somewhat downgrading, implying that the applied stuff is second best, not quite as genuine as the essence. . . . I thought the concept of 'applied' amplified a low status position in the power play.[8]

Although it is interesting to note in this context that applied science has a higher status in the academy than pure science, Rasmussen is surely right to point out that creating a new set of binary oppositions between 'applied' and 'not-applied' drama risks emphasising the utilitarianism of applied drama at the expense of its artistic and aesthetic qualities. All forms of drama and theatre practice, he argues, rely on aesthetic engagement for their power and effectiveness, and applied drama is no exception. This means that, whatever its objectives, the quality of the work in applied drama needs to be high, and it should not rely on an impoverished or limited artistic repertoire. There is, however, another element which I would add to Rasmussen's analysis – the values attributed to the ideal of the 'pure' aesthetic.

Pierre Bourdieu's sociological study of the 'pure' aesthetic as a mark of the 'distinction' of taste offers a useful analysis of the social inequalities associated with the arts. Bourdieu argued that since the eighteenth century the aesthetic has been regarded as personally and socially transformative, with the consequence that the arts came to be thought of as a new faith, imitative in some ways of religion.[9] This elision of goodness and beauty did not, however, have the effect of democratising either aesthetic appreciation or artistic practice. On the contrary, the distinction of taste was thought to depend on highly cultivated individuals who possessed hearts and minds which were sufficiently pure, disinterested and unencumbered by everyday matters to make aesthetic judgements. Artists became increasingly sanctified and professionalised, with the Romantics claiming for themselves a special kind of disposition, and unique powers of perception and imagination. This meant, Bourdieu concluded, that aesthetic judgements acquired a social distinction that contributed to a specific form of political economy in which the bourgeois dispositions of artists and intellectuals were valued as the moral guardians of a liberal polity. Bourdieu described this as the 'politics of purity', where standards of taste became divided along class lines, and the aesthetic sense became increasingly harnessed to – and was believed to legitimate – dominant class and hegemonic values.

This returns the debate to questions of power and cultural production, where the ideal both of artistic production and of aesthetic appreciation has acquired symbolic capital. In relation to applied drama, Bourdieu's sociological account of the politics of purity has particular resonance. Practitioners in applied drama have often distanced themselves from 'mainstream' theatre practices and spaces, which have been considered the preserve of the middle class. Drama educator Jonothon Neelands, for example, recalls this iniquitous tradition when he describes the 'restrictive art of theatre' as a 'literary and private aesthetic'.[10] Baz Kershaw has also written movingly of his early encounters with Western theatre culture, from which he felt excluded by virtue of his class background. Drawing on Bourdieu's idea of theatre as 'a miracle of predestination', Kershaw describes mainstream theatre as not so much a space for free speech and creativity, as 'a social engine that helps to drive an unfair system of privilege'.[11] In this configuration, theatre becomes a place of bourgeois self-righteousness, only really available to traditionally educated, middle-class audiences who passively consume hegemonic values. For Bourdieu, this uncritical readership of 'high art' was historically linked to the *detachment* and disinterestedness associated with contemplation of aesthetic 'purity' whereas, by contrast, popular taste was linked to *involvement* and participation in the arts. He argued that displays of enthusiasm by spectators have been treated with suspicion in the academy; entertainment which appealed to 'collective participation' rather than 'formal exploration' has been thought to be inferior.[12]

Twenty or more years on from Bourdieu's analysis of class divisions in the arts, the academy has a far wider recognition of popular theatre forms. His analysis of the social implications of judgements of taste has also been rightly criticised for being too fixed around stable notions of class. Western theatre practitioners and their audiences have also enjoyed a long tradition of social criticism, and there is ample evidence that theatre can be a place where it is possible to imagine the world to be different. As an audience member, I find it difficult to imagine more disturbing and moving theatrical experiences than seeing Edward Bond's *Saved*, Sarah Kane's *Blasted* or Caryl Churchill's *Faraway*, all of which were first performed in London's Royal Court Theatre – a radical theatre, but none the less a conventional performance space. None of these plays would be considered to be 'applied' theatre, but all offer a powerful social critique. In setting an agenda for the political efficacy of theatre, the playwright Tony Kushner has argued that art is not simply concerned with passively reproducing cultural values, it may also be actively engaged with cultural and social change. According to him, 'Art is not merely contemplation, it is also action, and all action changes the world, at least a little.'[13] For contemporary practitioners in applied drama this emphasis on action rather than contemplation is important. Although Bourdieu's modernist divisions between high art and popular culture may still have resonance, it is approaches to theatre-making which emphasise involvement, participation and engagement which are of particular significance to the values of applied drama.

Where Did Applied Drama/Theatre Come From?

Contemporary practitioners in applied drama are indebted to their radical predecessors in twentieth-century theatre, and to pioneering educationalists who aimed to democratise processes of learning. There are three interrelated theatre movements that have made significant contributions to twenty-first-century applied drama: theatres of the political Left, which have been variously described as political, radical or alternative; drama and theatre in education; and community theatre. Taken together, they offer a powerful legacy which links social and personal change to dramatic practice, and articulate a commitment to using theatre to break down social hierarchies and divisions. What these traditions share is an interest in working in clearly defined contexts, with and for specific audiences, and in furthering objectives which are not only artistic, but also educational, social and political. Although differently inflected, all practitioners in applied drama are in some way indebted to these complementary histories.

The history of political, radical and alternative theatres has allied applied drama to cultural activism. Although politics has long been associated with theatre, their relationship was energetically reconfigured during the twentieth century. The century saw an explosion of artistic practices designed to rally political activism through performance-making, and the development of processes of working which questioned the rigid divisions of labour and social hierarchies in commercial theatre and beyond it. At the centre of many debates that contributed to the political and artistic changes, which began in the 1920s with the Workers' Theatre Movements and lasted for much of the century, were questions about the social purpose of theatre and its political philosophy. Throughout the changing political landscapes of the twentieth century, theatre held an enduring appeal to social and political activists, and particularly to those in civil rights movements. Theatre offered an immediate and visible platform for public debate and for the performance of protest, and it was thought to be a powerful way to reach the hearts and minds of its intended audiences. Often linking political protest with popular culture, these were forms of theatre which generally aimed to encourage social action and grassroots mobilisation.[14] Although in many instances the politics and aesthetics of activist theatre have changed, the application of theatre to social problems and to direct action is indebted to this performative tradition.

There are two strands of pedagogy that have influenced applied theatre: one derives from the Brazilian Marxist educator Paulo Freire, and the other from European models of progressive education. Freire, whose work is discussed in more detail in Chapter 3, was committed to overturning traditional teaching methods based on the hierarchical transmission of knowledge, and advocated approaches to learning which placed the learner (rather than the teacher) at the centre of the pedagogic process. Freire was particularly concerned with adult literacy, and his work had a profound influence on theatre director August Boal, who remains a powerful figure and a strong presence in applied drama. Progressive education shared a similar interest in learning by doing, and drama and theatre in education were thought particularly well placed to contribute to the child-centred approaches to learning that became embedded in many educational practices during the 1960s.[15] One of the legacies of this educational movement is the use of dramatic play, improvisation and role-play as a learning medium. In contemporary practice, these two pedagogical strands are often interwoven, and have led to questions about where knowledge is situated and whose cultural experiences are reproduced in theatre-making. The legacy of both these movements has subjected the negotiation between power, learning and knowledge to critical scrutiny.

Community theatre (sometimes also called grassroots theatre) has been variously articulated and construed in different parts of the world. There are connections with both theatre pedagogies and radical people's theatre, and it is characterised by the participation of community members in creating a piece of theatre which has special resonance for that community. As Eugene van Erven has pointed out, community theatre tends to emphasise the dramatic potential of local or personal stories.[16] The influential British practitioner Ann Jellicoe famously denied that her work in community theatre had an explicit political agenda, but there is none the less a concern for social inclusivity and community-building through the process of making theatre. As I discuss in Chapter 5, the concept of community in itself is controversial and problematic, and community theatre is not exempt from debates about who is included or excluded from specific community groupings. Whatever its limits and limitations, however, community theatre remains an important form of artistic communication that continues to influence practitioners in applied drama.

There is considerable overlap between these different traditions and, historically, there has been a strong tradition of robust debate and collaboration between practitioners across these different fields. One of the central legacies of these three cultural practices that permeates the broad field of applied drama/theatre is an emphasis on activity and involvement with theatre-making rather than passivity and uncritical consumerism. In applied drama, processes of working are embodied and involved rather than passive and detached, as participants are invited to engage physically and emotionally with the work by professional practitioners with special expertise in developing community-based practice. One of the priorities for those working in applied drama is often a political concern to demystify the arts by encouraging people from many different backgrounds and contexts to participate actively in drama and theatre, whether as reflexive participants in different forms of drama workshops, as thinking members of theatre audiences, or as informed and creative participants in different forms of performance or theatre practices.

Contexts and Audiences

The shift in terminology to 'applied drama/theatre' is significant, I think, because it does not announce its political allegiances, community commitments or educational intent as clearly as many forms of politically committed theatre-making which were developed in the last century. Applied drama has emerged in a period of cultural change in which the long tradition of the arts being seen to have inherently transformative and universally redemptive qualities has been troubled by new insights into the cultural production and representation of knowledge. It is significant that the emergence of applied drama as a field of study and praxis coincided with a period which Baz Kershaw has described as a 'new world disorder' in the 1990s. In this period of social change, political theorists and cultural critics have been renegotiating and re-envisaging Western democratic traditions following the collapse of Cold War dualisms and the subsequent fragmentation of the political Left.[17] The social and material circumstances in which Joan Littlewood came to regard theatre practice as an antidote to the alienating effects of industrial capitalism have changed, and the impulses which motivated such work have become subject to radical review.

For applied drama, a sense of political uncertainty has strong practical implications. Practitioners often work with people in the most vulnerable of situations and frequently see the casualties of this new world disorder at first hand – working with, for example, refugees, asylum seekers, the displaced and the homeless. Others may be involved with 'empowering' members of an increasingly mobile and globalised workforce by encouraging active decision-making and affective involvement in work processes. Globalising processes are of central importance to applied drama, not least because they threaten to erode local, national and regional cultures through the spread of homogeneous transnational corporations. Equally significant is the impact of migration – one of the contemporary consequences of globalisation – which has forged new social identities in which members of diasporic communities feel connected to different places and environments. The stable identities associated with belonging to a bounded place are re-imagined and re-configured as it is recognised that many people have multiple cultural affiliations, and that relationships between the local and the global are complexly interwoven.

The conceptual metaphors associated with social change within this new world disorder emphasise the politics of (dis)location – difference, alterity, mapping, hybridity, liminality, borders and margins – all of which draw critical attention to the way place and space articulate diverse cultural and political meanings. As the term 'applied drama' emphasises the *application* to specific settings, contexts and audiences, this greater focus on spatial metaphors is important, in relation to identity, particularly as applied drama often takes place in situations which are troubled. There is often a messiness about work in applied drama, focusing on interrogating what Victor Turner has called the 'contamination' of context, which makes the 'flaws, hesitations, personal factors, incomplete, elliptical, context-dependent, situational proponents of performance' visible.[18] Applied drama is, in Turner's terms, always contaminated by context, and is intended to be sufficiently fluid to address the concerns of local audiences and participants. This accepts that practices in applied drama are both intimately connected with the social and cultural contexts in which they take place and symbolise experience of diasporic spaces.

The metaphor of social and personal change that I find most appropriate for the interplay between place and space, thought and action in applied drama is not one of 'transformation' but of 'transportation'. Richard Schechner has offered a distinction between these two aspects of performance practice. 'Transformation', he argues, affects a permanent change which is often, but not always, associated with ritual. In such cases (as in marriage or a bar mitzvah ceremony, for example) transformation is intended to be lasting, and the outcome is immediate, predetermined and predictable. It is led by experienced social actors whose expertise affords them the necessary status to lead the performative event or to initiate the ceremonial rites. 'Transportation', however, is less fixed – performers are 'taken somewhere', actors are even temporarily transformed, but they are returned more or less to their starting places at the end of the drama or performance. In the long term, this process does not preclude more permanent transformations because, Schechner argues, 'a series of transportation performances can achieve a transformation'.[19]

Although I recognise the power of theatre-making to touch people's lives, I remain rather uneasy about using the term 'transformation' to describe the process of change afforded by practising drama. This is partly because I feel uncomfortable about making such grand claims for the effects and effectiveness of my own work as a practitioner, but also because it raises bigger political questions. If applied drama is socially transformative, is it explicit what kind of society is envisioned? If the motive is individual or personal transformation, is this something which is done *to* the participants, *with* them, or *by* them? Whose values and interests does the transformation serve? Seen in this light, the idea of transportation suggests greater scope for creativity and unpredictability than that of transformation. Should transformation occur, it is a gradual and cumulative process, the result of learning and negotiation with others, a progressive act of self-creation. In the process of transportation, the outcomes are clearly focused but not fixed, and change may take place gradually, a collaborative and sustained process between participants and often in partnership with other supportive agencies. It is about travelling into another world, often fictional, which offers both new ways of seeing and different ways of looking at the familiar. As British theatre director Tim Etchells has said, performance is about 'going into another world and coming back with gifts'.[20]

Making a Difference

At the heart of this book there lies a struggle, an attempt to straddle an irresolvable tension – between the overarching ideal of a radical, just and inclusive democracy for all and a respect for local circumstances, the social contexts of the participants and cultural differences. Making a difference is a struggle, as Brecht understood, and it depends on breaking old certainties and creating new artistic methods to represent changing social circumstances:

> Methods become exhausted; stimuli no longer work. New problems appear and demand new methods. Reality changes; in order to represent it, modes of representation must change. Nothing comes of nothing; the new comes from the old, but that is why it is new. The oppressors do not work in the same way in every epoch. They cannot be defined in the same fixed fashion at all times.[21]

Applied drama is intimately tied to contemporary questions about the politics of context, place and space, and this means that working in drama often brings into focus questions of allegiance, identity and belonging. In turn, this prompts a series of questions about how conceptions of citizenship, culture and community might be constructed and understood. What are the implications of globalisation for applied drama? What ideas of humanity, identity and selfhood are assumed by drama practitioners working in educational and community contexts? What is meant by community? Given its libertarian history and its interest in democratic action and universal human rights, how might practitioners in applied drama negotiate different world-views in their work? Is there a balance to be struck between equality and difference? How might we approach community contexts which are characterised by plurality and cultural dissonance? This book offers an investigation into these complex practical and theoretical questions.

One of the principles that underpins this book is that theory and practice are not separate processes or modes of thought, with one based on action and another on reflection. They are interdependent and constantly in flux. It also seems to me that applied drama and theoretical debate often share similar aims – to imagine the world to be different. I am reminded here of bell hooks, who argues passionately for a way of thinking about theory as social production. She describes how she saw in theory a 'location for healing', a way of looking at the world differently, a focus for asking risky questions.[22] Neither thought nor action is without a theoretical foundation, hooks claims, however implicit, and theory can be as creative as more obvious forms of practical action. Theory is about the ways in which we look at the world, and in these terms it informs our everyday lives and actions. Seen in this light, social critique and the critique of practice are impossible without theory. All critical judgements are based on some theory of value – it just depends on how far these values are acknowledged or articulated.

I have considerable sympathy with hooks's view. There are times when I have found myself defending both theory and practice, and I think the best way to do this is to say how they are related and mutually sustaining. Theory finds a point of connection between 'why' questions (such as why is drama important in educational and community contexts?) and 'how' questions (as in how do people structure and organise their practice?). As a practitioner, I often find that it is difficult to know which comes first – the theory or the practice. There are times when I am devising theatre or facilitating workshops when I find that theoretical reading provides valuable insights into where to go next. At other times I want to use the flexibility of practice to test out or illuminate theoretical ideas. Both become integral to the drama, as a practical embodiment of theory. Gilles Deleuze, in conversation with Michel Foucault, has identified the relationship between theory and practice:

> At one time, a practice was considered an application of theory, a consequence; at other times, it had an opposite sense and it was thought to inspire theory, to be indispensable for future theoretical forms. . . . The relationships between theory and practice are far more partial and fragmentary. . . . Practice is a set of relays from one theoretical point to another, and theory is a relay from one practice to another. No theory can develop without eventually encountering a wall, and practice is necessary for piercing this wall.[23]

From the point of view of applied drama, I find this way of thinking extremely helpful. Without theory, I have found that even the most reflexive of practice gets stuck and becomes repetitive, just as theory can become bafflingly abstract without practice. Rather than rooting debate in a modernist polarity between theory and practice, there can be a more fluid continuum between the two. Deleuze describes this continuum as 'theoretical action' and 'practical action' and this gives theory a performative function.[24]

In writing this book, I have tried to recognise the continuum between theory and practice, and to acknowledge that theory has a performative dynamic. My intention is not to limit applied drama to a particular set of ideas or practices, but to interrogate some of the theoretical assumptions on which practice is based, and to subject practices to theoretical scrutiny. The book is structured in three parts. The first part raises questions about citizenship and pedagogy, addressed in two separate chapters, and this analysis of two of the central concepts that underpin practice in applied drama offers a framework for subsequent discussions. Taken together, these chapters locate the central arguments of this book – that applied drama is fortified by a robust understanding of the politics of cultural difference, in which questions of citizenship, pedagogy and praxis are neither individualised nor privatised, but acknowledged as both a positive attribute of contemporary society and as a site of struggle. Chapter 2 examines different models and practices of citizenship, and suggests that drama has a part to play in encouraging participants to *act* as citizens. Chapter 3 explores the challenges presented by globalisation to pedagogies and praxis in applied drama. It builds on the discussion of citizenship by investigating the potential for relationships between pedagogy, praxis and performance, arguing that there is a continual need to exercise vigilance over how learning is defined and how knowledge is constructed in applied drama.

Part II offers a discussion of narrative. The two chapters in this section are built on the premise that practice in applied drama is poised at the intersection of different narratives – of selfhood, community, culture – which means that the narratives of fictional and lived experience are in continual negotiation. Chapter 4 offers an investigation of how fictional narratives might impact on creating narratives of selfhood. Chapter 5 questions ideas of community, and explores how making dramatic narratives based on lived experience might contribute to the process of community-building. Part III examines theories of creativity and social justice. Chapter 6 examines different ways of thinking about the relationship between creativity and social intervention, and Chapter 7 pays specific attention to the implications of furthering a human rights agenda in and through dramatic practice. The final chapter returns to the idea of the gift, asking questions about how this political metaphor might serve as an ethical basis for practice in applied drama.

Throughout this book I have chosen examples of practice that illuminate and challenge some of the theoretical issues raised. The examples are eclectic rather than representational, and there is no attempt to provide a survey of practice, which is so rich and varied it would be impossible in a book of this length. Researching applied drama raises many ethical questions, both in terms of research method-ologies and in the representation of the voices of the participants. It is perhaps paradoxical that applied drama, arguably the most democratic of theatre practices, often takes place in private spaces and places where vulnerable participants can feel safe. It is not the role of the researcher to invade this privacy, nor to abuse the participants' trust, and this sensitivity to context has meant that I have had to rely on three major sources – reflection on my own work as an insider in the process, as is customary in our field; on analysing the work of practitioners with whom I have developed sustained professional relationships; and on accounts of practice that have already been published or made public through performance or video documentation. The methodology has included participant observation, and often interviews or discussion with participants, but my critics will no doubt note that I have not presented case studies which include a detailed analysis of the partici-pants' voices; even what might be called 'my' practice actually belongs to the participants just as much as me and, unless I have their permission, I have not discussed it here.

My aim in this book is not, primarily, to offer a fixed and detailed description of what applied drama *is* in all its various different guises, but to raise questions about what it might be *for*, and what its values might be. Applied drama/theatre is perhaps most helpfully regarded not as a new academic discipline nor as a specific set of dramatic methods but as a discursive practice – as a way of conceptualising and interpreting theatrical and cultural practices that are motivated by the desire to make a difference to the lives of others. This book is intended to raise some theoretical, political and ethical issues which might be applied to a number of different situations and practices, and it is on these terms that it invites you to share some of my experiences and thoughts, however partial and incomplete the story may be.

Part I
Participation and Praxis

2 The Practice of Citizenship

Drama as Citizenship

The vision of a popular theatre that unites thought, feeling and action remains a powerful symbol of social democracy. The idea that the arts have the potential to illuminate contemporary concerns, articulate dissent and offer personal solace is deeply embedded in the popular imagination and is seen by many as an essential attribute of a liberal polity. Theatre, as the most public of art forms, has a particular part to play in the collective exploration of ideas, values and feelings – as a space and place in which society might be reshaped through the imagination. The North American director Peter Sellars describes this impulse in theatre-making as 'a question of civil rights rather than public relations', which contributes to the process of building democratic communities and encouraging active, participant citizenship.[1] This focus on creating a society of equals through artistic practice means that applied drama, with its particular emphasis on the social, personal and political impact and effectiveness of theatre, is part of a wider cultural ambition. Applied drama and applied theatre may be the most recent names for community-based, educational and interventionist approaches to theatre-making, but it belongs to a much longer tradition of cultural efficacy.

The problem with asserting that applied drama is related to citizenship is that the concept of citizenship is highly contested – even in Western democracies – and its interpretation in practice belongs to different ideological traditions, commitments and disputes. Theorists who have followed Marx have been sceptical about ideas of citizenship, arguing that social freedom is gained through equal access to the means of production, and the liberal ideal of the free and independent citizen simply disguised the real conflicts and inequalities lying in the economic structures of society.[2] Questions of what citizenship might mean in the post-Cold War era have been further compounded by contemporary concerns with balancing social cohesion with cultural diversity both in the context of international agendas for human rights and within pluralistic democratic societies. As a response to these changing world circumstances there has been a recent revival of interest in citizenship, and the assumptions associated with the concept have been challenged by the proliferation of political discourses aimed at resistance and social inclusivity – identity politics, post-colonialism, the politics of the body, gender and sexuality, for example – which have forged a reassessment of where the margins of rights and power are drawn. One of the effects of this 'new promiscuity of the political', as Baz Kershaw has dubbed it, has been the recognition that public issues and private lives are not separate forms of social engagement, with the one focused on civic matters and the other on the domestic sphere, but complexly and intimately interwoven. What it means to be a good citizen in pluralist societies is fraught with ambiguities and contradictions, requiring a revitalised political vocabulary and a renewed concept of radical citizenship.

In whatever way it is construed, an interest in questions of citizenship remains a central tenet of many aspects of applied drama. Citizenship education has become yet another element of formal education in England – as elsewhere in the Western world – and there is a well-intentioned belief that drama is a good place to raise difficult issues and to debate moral action. Although I am sure this approach has its place, there is something which leaves me uneasy about linking drama to officially sanctioned versions of citizenship education. The aims of the British government's campaign for citizenship education seem laudable enough – tackling apathy, stimulating debate, promoting awareness, encouraging political literacy – but it seems to me that the relationship between citizenship, drama and performance has always been rather more creative, unpredictable and subversive than this official discourse implies. It is hardly surprising that when British schoolchildren protested publicly against the war in Iraq in 2003, the Head Teachers' organisation treated their absence from school as truancy rather than as a practical illustration of the active citizenship they were charged with promoting.[3] The practice of citizenship does not always generate conformity and consensus – on the contrary – and the imaginative and performative protests of environmental activists, anti-globalisation demonstrators and AIDS campaigners have demonstrated that active forms of citizenship can mean spectacle, carnival and direct action as well as more sober forms of debate.[4]

In this chapter, I am interested in exploring how far a renewed concept of radical citizenship has the potential to draw attention to the many different ways in which practitioners and participants in theatre construct experience and perform *as* citizens in different local, regional and global contexts. There are three particular strands of the citizenship debate that are particularly germane to this discussion. The first part of the chapter is concerned with an analysis of *participant* citizenship (as well as a system of legal rights and responsibilities), and this provides a theoretical framework through which to view examples of practice in applied drama. With this in mind, I hope to find a way of thinking about how the passion of performance articulates with political citizenship. The second major debate is concerned with the more social and domestic aspects of citizenship, where I begin to explore how social networks built on altruism and care impact on applied drama. This leads me to reflect on tough questions about how the good intentions of practitioners in applied drama might be interpreted. The final element of the discussion begins to draw together some thoughts about the ethos of citizenship in a world where the traditional boundaries of nation-states have been challenged and eroded. The debate turns on how theatre practice might articulate the interconnectedness of social networks, including the balance of power between global politics and the particularity of emotional relationships, local traditions and beliefs. Citizenship has a strong ethical dimension, which means that challenging practice in drama always involves negotiating its various inflections.

Citizenship as Participation

Chantal Mouffe has argued that a radical, democratic citizen 'must be an active citizen, somebody who *acts* as a citizen, who conceives of herself in a collective undertaking'.[5] This conception of citizenship as participation, she suggests, is a response to the limitations of liberalism, which has reduced citizenship to a legal status. This has had the effect, Mouffe argues, of focusing on the statutory rights of the individual rather than on more collective forms of identification and social action. If citizenship is about *acting* as a citizen, with all the implications of performance that this phrase entails, how might practising drama encourage people to become active participant citizens?

To begin to answer this question we have to try to understand the historical distinctions between civic, political and social citizenship, a debate which also takes account of how the public and the private spheres have been differently construed and constructed. The touchstone for many sociological discussions about citizenship is the work of T. H. Marshall, whose influential essay 'Citizenship and Social Class' was published in 1949 during a particularly optimistic period of the British Labour movement. Marshall categorised citizenship into three distinctive stages and entitlements: civil citizenship (constructed in the eighteenth century to protect individual liberty, freedom of speech and the right to justice); political citizenship (a largely nineteenth-century phenomenon, which was concerned with the entitlement to participate in the exercise of political power); and social citizenship (which was developed in the twentieth century, to provide social welfare, education and the right to a full share in the social heritage).[6] Marshall observed that citizenship became increasingly formalised during the historical period which also saw the rise of capitalism, and that it represented an idealistic vision of social equality in an economic system riven with inequality.

Despite the many objections to Marshall's taxonomy, his vision of a social citizenship remains a potent symbol of policies and practices which have regarded citizenship as a collective undertaking rather than an expression of self-interest. That Marshall is now rightly accused of ignoring issues of gender and race, of creating an evolutionary model of citizenship which pays scant attention to cultural citizenship, and of ignoring the effects of economics on citizenship, is a testament to the ways in which conceptions and practices of citizenship have changed since 1949 rather than a wholesale repudiation of his utopian intent.[7] There are still things we can learn from his analysis, particularly in relation to the tensions he found between citizenship as a concept and citizenship in practice. Marshall identified that as a *concept* citizenship is fundamentally equitable, as 'those who possess the status are equal with respect to the rights and duties with which the status is endowed'.[8] In *practice*, however, he argued that both civil and political formulations of citizenship had contributed to social and material inequalities because they emphasised the individual at the expense of the social. Whilst civil and political rights are intended to constitute a formal – and universal – legal status of the individual, social citizenship is more concerned with the collective, and especially with the needs of the poor and socially disadvantaged.

By linking applied drama to citizenship I am following the argument that citizenship is not simply a collection of legal rights and obligations, which are not easily changed, but it is also a more fluid and pliable set of social practices. Writing from a sociological perspective, Bryan Turner has commented that the phrase 'social practices' indicates the 'dynamic social construction of citizenship', and recognises that conceptions of citizenship are contingent on their historical and cultural contexts.[9] In other words, the ways in which citizenship is practised have changed in the past and will doubtless change in the future. If citizenship is a social practice, subject to a continual process of re-negotiation, it has relevance to the more ordinary and everyday activities of life as well as the bigger political issues of the day. Participant citizenship involves more than accepting one's statutory rights as an individual – however important they may be – and invites questions about the contribution we are each making to the process of social change. Reconciling the legality of civil citizenship with the collective responsibilities of social citizenship requires, as Chantal Mouffe has argued, a new articulation between the public and private spheres.

Chantal Mouffe is concerned to develop a theory of participant citizenship that does not regard it simply as a legal status with little impact on the everyday lives of law-abiding citizens, but as an *identity*. She argues in favour of an 'embodied citizenship' in which individuals *act* as citizens within a wider framework of personal, political and ethical associations. Borrowing an insight from psychoanalysis, she suggests that all identities are constructed through processes of identification which, as 'an articulation of an ensemble of subject positions', both challenge and affirm a person's sense of selfhood.[10] It is through identification with a range of identities, discourses and social relations, she argues, that individuals might recognise their allegiances with others as well as their antagonisms or differences. This acknowledgement of difference is important to Mouffe, who also argues that a shared sense of identity *as citizens* is vital for democratic politics. She recognises, however, that political interpretations of citizenship will always be characterised by conflict and division as different communities and interest groups seek to address its exclusions and redefine its limits and parameters. This citizen is not a passive recipient of rights, but demonstrates a commitment to the ideal of citizenship by making an active contribution to creating a more equitable society. Mouffe's vision of radical democratic citizenship acknowledges that identity is built on collective forms of identification, common struggles, shared principles and dependent social networks which are not simply enshrined in law, but extend to all aspects of social life.

If there is, as I am suggesting, a relationship between citizenship and applied drama, it is not because there is one definitive theory or set of practices which command universal agreement. There are, however, recurring themes in applied drama which resonate with Mouffe's vision of radical democratic citizenship. Drama is a good way for people to extend their horizons of experience, recognising how their own identities have been shaped and formulated and, by playing new roles and inhabiting different subject positions, finding different points of identification with others. The idea that drama can take people beyond themselves and into the world of others is deeply rooted in the values of applied drama, and this chimes particularly well with a vision of social citizenship as a collective and communitarian undertaking. In their recent books on applied theatre, both Philip Taylor and James Thompson stressed the role that drama might play in opening cultural assumptions for critical scrutiny, providing an opportunity for participants to work 'towards ambiguous or incomplete moments' (Taylor) and, in Thompson's terms, offering a 'break with certainty', enabling participants to think, feel and see things differently.[11] Active and creative participation in performance practices that dislodge fixed and uneven boundaries between 'self' and 'other' is, in many ways, the subject of this book. It is this aspect of citizenship which, I am suggesting, has most relevance for applied drama. It is a way of theorising citizenship which includes the visible and public acts of citizenship exercised as civic duty or as political protest, but it also extends to the more domestic practices of care, trust and community support.[12] These interrelated ways of acting as citizens have particular significance for practice in drama, where strong emotional bonds between participants are often created, and which also takes its responsibility for the wider social world very seriously. Of course, drama does none of these things automatically. Performance is not in itself politically radical, relationships between participants and practitioners are not automatically trusting, and theatre is not necessarily an instrument for change. It depends on the spirit in which these things are used.

Political Citizenship and Popular Theatres

Political activism is motivated by passion. In articulating this insight, Chantal Mouffe is highly critical of 'Third Way' politics which seek to eliminate antagonisms, arguing that its emphasis on political consensus creates apathy and disaffection. A 'well-functioning democracy', she argues, 'calls for a vibrant clash of democratic political positions'.[13] Theatre has a long history of articulating social dissent, and popular theatre in particular has been used to protest, to stimulate debate and provoke questions, thus enabling people to become emotionally engaged with political issues. Throughout the twentieth century activists of the political Left, influenced by the work of Meyerhold, Piscator and Brecht, found that forms of theatrical expression which were familiar to their target audiences were effective tools for social mobilisation.[14] Brecht defined the relationship between activism and popular theatre in the following terms:

> Our conception of the 'popular' refers to the people who are not only fully involved in the process of development but are actually taking it over, forcing it, deciding it. We have in mind a people that is making history and altering the world itself. We have in mind a fighting people and also a fighting conception of 'popularity'.[15]

Marxist interpretations of popular theatre, to which Brecht of course ascribed, would recognise only forms of expression that conform to a vision of social change based on the class struggle. More recent experiments in popular performance have been more ideologically eclectic, however, and indicative of different forms of political citizenship. In this section I shall consider two examples of the many ways in which popular forms of theatre and performance have been newly applied to an activist, political citizenship.

One form of popular theatre that explicitly demands a 'vibrant clash of democratic positions' is known as 'legislative theatre', and was developed by the Brazilian theatre director Augusto Boal. Boal is possibly the most influential of contemporary theatre practitioners – his reputation has been built on his work in disadvantaged communities across the world, and his influential book *The Theatre of the Oppressed* has been widely read since its first publication in English in 1979. Boal is indebted to Brecht's analysis of the potential political dynamic between actors and target audiences, and he has sought to develop Brecht's construction of the 'popular' by encouraging audience members to take over the stage in a 'forum' – or performed debate – as part of the performance itself.[16] During his period of office on Rio de Janeiro's City Council from 1992 to 1996, Boal famously established a system of working which aimed to integrate political citizenship with theatre practice. Gathering together special interest groups or members of particular communities, Boal aimed to encourage increased participation in the legislative process by using a range of drama strategies designed to elicit opinion about the issues of the day, to stimulate political debate and to find practical solutions to everyday problems. He described this process as 'making theatre as politics rather than making political theatre' and he intended to use his elected power to 'transform desire into law'.[17]

The strategies Boal used to increase citizens' participation in civic politics are well documented in his book *Legislative Theatre* (1998). As a form of cultural production, Boal's legislative theatre is explicitly interventionist, with the intention that 'each oppressed person should try to gain an understanding of the oppression experienced by others and show solidarity with them'.[18] Boal's enthusiastic rhetoric is seductive, and it is sometimes difficult to discern how far his ambitions were realised by reading his accounts of this aspect of his work. Paul Dwyer has pointed out that although Boal is a good storyteller – clearly part of his skill as a theatre practitioner – his stories change over time, and this suggests that his summary of his political activities is inevitably partisan.[19] What I find intriguing here is Boal's use of the formal structures of power, and the ways in which he used his civic role as a politician to further his constituents' sense of identity as political citizens. Certainly, new laws were introduced, and Paul Heritage's description of the excitement generated by the demonstration of some of the strategies of legislative theatre at the Seventh International Festival of the Theatre of the Oppressed illustrates the necessary link between passion and politics which, Mouffe argued, is central to the practice of a radical democratic citizenship.[20]

As a professional theatre practitioner and experienced political activist, Boal had significant expertise and resources to draw upon in conducting his experiments in legislative theatre. Because at the time he was working within the framework of government, this element of his work is primarily concerned with extending political involvement in civic citizenship. A slightly different articulation of political citizenship and theatre is extended by activists and protesters who operate outside established structures of power. Rather than harnessing theatre to already established political structures, these artist–activists use creative acts of protest and performative gestures as direct action. A good example of the use of popular performance for this kind of subversive intervention has been documented by John Jordan, an activist himself, whose analysis of the campaigning (dis)organisation 'Reclaim the Streets' offers evidence for the link between creative resistance and political citizenship. 'Reclaim the Streets' evolved in Britain from imaginative campaigns against road building in the 1990s, where activists developed a form of 'DIY culture' which was designed to draw attention to the ways in which global ecosystems and local environments are being destroyed. Jordan describes the playfulness of artist–activists who built elaborate tree houses to halt road building, filled houses with earth to prevent demolition, and held parties on motorways to stop the traffic. In terms which echo Boal's criticism of the straitjacket of his term of office in local government, Jordan comments that:

> Direct action introduces the concept of play into the straight, predictably grey world of politics.... The playfulness of direct action proposes an alternative reality but it also makes play real; it takes it out of western frameworks of childhood or make-believe – and throws it in the face of politicians and policy makers.[21]

The street party has remained an important weapon and symbol in this political armoury, with regular (but unregulated) parties in major cities across the world advertised on the internet (www.reclaimthestreets.net). Streets are 'liberated' from the traffic and turned to carnival, a chaotic and exuberant popular protest which lays down a direct challenge to the sobriety of official culture. It is, Jordan remarks, a form of action which 'calls for a society where the personal and the political, the passionate and the pragmatic, art and everyday life, become one'.[22]

Both these examples illustrate the inadequacy of contemporary political systems and their failure to inspire the kind of vibrancy and debate which are essential attributes of a radical society and democratic citizenship. In each instance, though differently inflected, theatre and performance are intended to offer ways of extending the boundaries of democracy, providing a cultural response to the political problem of apathy and disillusionment. The new political aesthetic of performance has been well theorised by Baz Kershaw, who sees it as evidence of a newly emergent form of democratic pluralism.[23] If this is the case, the application of the playful unruliness of performance to serious political commitments will help create a dynamic and troublesome form of political citizenship which those in authority cannot easily ignore. Whether this form of disruptive social action is *good* citizenship, however, rather depends on your political perspective and point of view.

Good Intentions, Altruistic Motives

So far my discussion has been informed by the idea that citizenship is a dynamic social practice, an identity that is constructed through networks of identification, open to change and renewal, rather than a fixed and immutable legal state. An emphasis on citizenship as an embodied social practice not only implies that it is revitalised by public debate and political action, it also draws attention to the ways in which people support each other and take responsibility for others as well as for themselves. In this section I am interested in interrogating how practice in applied drama facilitates the relationship between private motives and feelings and the more public elements of citizenship. In particular, I hope to find ways of thinking about the implications for organising and facilitating applied drama, and how the good intentions of those who practise in the field cohere with an active, ethical and social citizenship.

Projects in applied drama are often organised by professional practitioners, usually with a background in theatre, and frequently working in partnership with other agencies including funding bodies (such as charities or government agencies) and in the setting of host organisations (a specified community group, a school, prison or hospital, for example). In these contexts, the values of the practitioners obviously have a major impact on the processes of working, and they are very often motivated by a desire to make a real difference to the lives of others. This is not, however, an easy role to negotiate, particularly where practitioners are regarded as cultural outsiders. Writing about theatre in Bangladesh, Syed Jamil Ahmed has expressed a level of unease about the presence of 'an invisible Subject' (the practitioner) who assumes that a particular society 'needs to be transformed'.[24] Ahmed is particularly concerned with the potential imbalance of power between non-indigenous practitioners and local participants in theatre for development, and it is not uncommon for practitioners to express similar reservations about being regarded as 'cultural missionaries' when working in contexts or communities with which they are unfamiliar. There is sometimes an interpretative gap between the good intentions of the practitioners and how they are initially perceived by the participants, which can be very troubling. And this is entirely justifiable. Assumptions that drama is 'good for you', however disguised, are likely to meet with resistance. I vividly remember working in a hospital with a group of people who had sustained head injuries, who began just about tolerating the interventions of the drama practitioners as a necessary part of their rehabilitation and therapy but who, frankly, given the choice would rather have had their old lives back.

In a very different setting, James Thompson has described his work in situations of war and conflict as 'ugly, unglamorous and dirty', and has raised questions about the limits of work with vulnerable people and his ethical responsibilities as a drama practitioner.[25] In spite of the many rewards of the work, I have often wondered what motivates practitioners to seek out 'ugly, unglamorous and dirty' situations and how, as practitioners, we might reflect on what this implies about our values, our sense of responsibility and understanding of citizenship as a social practice. Ahmed has called into question the 'ostensibly altruistic motives' of practitioners in applied drama, and this challenge suggests that the issue might be illuminated by a theorised understanding of the relationship between citizenship and the politics of altruism.

The history of the word 'altruism' is a useful starting-point for this discussion. It was first coined by Auguste Comte, a French philosopher whose major works were written between 1830 and 1842, to mean the opposite of egoism. Comte was a positivist, which means that he was interested in developing a rationalist (rather than theological or metaphysical) systemisation of society. He believed that the highest human faculty is the intellect, and part of his project was to find ways of achieving human betterment through creating a society based on rationalist principles and a clearly defined social order. In his later work, Comte became increasingly concerned with moral education, and it is at this point that altruism became integral to his social vision. He argued that altruism, rather than egoism, would bring about social harmony, because altruism would ensure that everyone would work for the common good. What is interesting, however, is that Comte linked altruism not only to public virtue but to economic patterns of labour. In his social system, labour would not serve private enterprise but would be integral to state economics.

> [A] new system shall have taught all men that there is public utility in the humblest office of co-operation, no less truly than in the loftiest function of government. Other men would feel, if their labour were but systematised, as the private soldier feels in the discharge of his humblest duty, the dignity of public service, and the honour of a share in the action of a general economy.[26]

Comte particularly favoured the utilitarianism of industry, and his collective enterprise was based on rigid divisions of rank and status. Altruism provided a moral justification for industrial capitalism, and altruism rather than egoism was explicitly intended to support a hierarchical social and economic system.

The history of the concept of altruism suggests a less equitable political dynamic than more recent interpretations would imply. Altruism is generally regarded as a positive attribute of society, but it is often used rather loosely. In his discussion of the ethics of altruism, David Miller provides a definition of an altruist as 'anyone who goes to the rescue intending to help'.[27] In this description, altruism is more closely associated with the motivation of the altruist than the effects on the recipient, which – like a gift – may or may not be welcome. Furthermore, Miller points out, it is more likely that altruistic gestures are offered to those whom the 'altruist' regards as deserving in some way – either morally, politically or ethically – and there is significant evidence to show that altruists are selective about who they help. In a slightly different vein, Neera Badhwar argues that self-interest and altruism are not opposite poles, but interrelated. Altruistic acts are socially and psychologically beneficial to the giver, Badhwar suggests, because altruism is itself a significant part of his or her self-identity.[28] On both counts, the politics of altruism are rather ambiguous. In Miller's description, the altruist presupposes that someone needs rescuing for a particular reason – whether they have asked for help or not – and assumes that the recipients' lives will be enhanced as a result of this intervention. Badhwar's interpretation recognises that altruism has specific benefits for the giver and that, however benign, the self-regarding motives of the altruists are always implicated in other-regarding acts.

Perhaps most significantly for practitioners in applied drama, both Miller's and Badhwar's research confirms that there is still an uneven balance of power between altruist and recipient, with the uncomfortable implication that, however well-intentioned, some acts of altruism may have the effect of keeping 'other' people in their place. Because practitioners often work in contexts in which they are outsiders, for all kinds of reasons their good intentions about 'helping' others in 'need' may be construed as patronising or authoritarian, contributing to keeping 'others' on the margins rather than taking centre stage. Although this would be very far from the intentions of egalitarian practitioners, the concept of marginality has become the cause of resentment. This well-meaning attitude is beautifully dramatised in the play *I Have Before Me a Remarkable Document Given to Me by a Young Lady from Rwanda* where the poet Simon, who is employed to 'help' refugees with their creative writing, misinterprets Juliette's behaviour towards him. He makes the assumption that Juliette, a Rwandan refugee, is in awe of him, whereas she is actually disappointed that he does not live up to her expectations.

Juliette: I thought he would be a proper writer. A man of letters. Not a man with a stain on his trousers. And there were no books in his room. I thought I would see rows of his books. Some in the drawer he said. Why hide them in a drawer. What was that new word... scribble? I'll write that down. It doesn't sound too nice. He's a scribbler that man.

Simon: Well, that was short. Sweet girl...bit naïve...shy. Probably looks up to me: 'The Writer'. Well, I'll have to do something about that at our next meeting, make her more at ease.[29]

This play offers a salutary reminder that, when working in applied drama, good intentions to be good citizens are not always good enough. This point is particularly well expressed by James Thompson, who has described the bewilderment he has experienced as a practitioner, and the state of uncertainty resulting from the 'positive effect of amazement, fascination and doubt', which he finds to be the 'stimulus for critical and questioning research'.[30] As a practitioner working in a cultural context different from his own, Thompson suggests that a level of uncertainty and humility about the effect and effectiveness of this work is extremely productive. What an analysis of altruism offers to this debate is another way of theorising this uncertainty by finding points of connection between acts of altruism and self-interest, and recognising that they operate as a continuum rather than as binary opposites. Once the reciprocal relationship between self-interest and other-regarding acts is acknowledged, I think there is the opportunity for a more optimistic interpretation of the relationship between altruism and social citizenship.

I am convinced that the affective dimensions of theatre provide a good way to negotiate a productive consonance between altruism and self-interest. An interesting example of how this takes place in practice is provided by Anne Tanyi-Tang's research into how indigenous women in a region of Cameroon applied drama to their domestic problems. She described two performances devised by women in the Mundemba Sub-Division of Cameroon who used theatre 'not as a weapon' but as 'a means of appealing to men's consciences'.[31] The first performance she witnessed was primarily directed towards civic officials who were threatening to punish many villagers for tax evasion. A group of elderly women, using popular forms of performance, demonstrated the problems they experienced in transporting cash-crops and purchasing tax coupons because of poor transport conditions and the appalling roads. They also used the performance to show the uneven division of labour in their community, with women undertaking all the farming and the domestic responsibilities whilst their husbands remained idle. Given that in this society women were prohibited not only from taking an active part in politics but also from speaking publicly in the presence of men, theatre was one of the few ways in which they could make themselves heard. The effects were significant and lasting. The officials built a road so that the women could sell their cash-crops, and this enabled the men to purchase tax coupons with less financial strain. On a subsequent visit to the region, Tanyi-Tang witnessed women in the Christian Women's Fellowship (CWF) perform a play that was highly critical of the way in which their husbands tried to prevent their membership of this organisation, having persuaded their menfolk to sit together wearing home-made uniforms for the event, so that their presence in the audience was highly visible. The play, which used the form of a parable to demonstrate the inequities of domestic life, appealed to their husbands' consciences. As a result, Tanyi-Tang observed, their attitude towards the activities of the CWF changed and they agreed to fund future activities, showing their remorse for their former selfishness by buying examples of the women's handiwork at inflated prices.

These examples illustrate the ways in which theatre provides a means whereby domestic issues might be brought into the public arena. The Cameroonian women used their experience of social citizenship to enhance their own status as civic citizens in the wider community, and this effectively reversed the trajectory of Marshall's (Western) taxonomy of civic, political and social citizenship. They used theatre to raise awareness of their situations in ways that both showed their altruistic concern for the general welfare of the community as well as serving their self-interested desire for practical assistance and emotional support in their daily lives. Watching their performances led the target audience to see things from a different perspective, in turn challenging their self-interested positions, a process which enabled members of the audience to behave more generously towards the women. Altruism, as philosopher Keith Graham has identified, encourages self-development through a process of 'broadening of horizons beyond the personal, even though as a matter of fact the person is not left behind'.[32]

Whether practitioners are cultural outsiders or local performers, practising drama has the potential to bridge the ethical division between civic citizenship and social citizenship, and between citizenship as a legal status and the more personal and interpersonal dynamics of social citizenship. This observation takes me back to Chantal Mouffe's description of citizenship as a process of identifications, a 'collective undertaking' in which a plurality of identities are recognised and legitimated rather than being ignored or privatised. Acknowledging that there is a reciprocal relationship between altruism and self-interest, between practitioners and participants, performances and audiences, has the potential to disrupt social hierarchies and to displace individualism with forms of citizenship that are more overtly social and collective. At its most generous and altruistic, theatre practice encourages just such collective forms of social citizenship, a process of self-identification with others which Graham has described as 'irreducibly plural'.[33]

Ecological Citizenship

Both drama and citizenship are creative practices, and both are concerned with the values, needs and aspirations of individuals, communities and societies. Citizenship is an evaluative term and, whilst I am not arguing for placing applied drama at the service of citizenship education, I am suggesting that theories of citizenship offer a productive way of conceptualising the dynamic between social networks, personal relationships and altruistic practice that lies at the heart of applied drama. The issues surrounding practice in both applied drama and citizenship are, however, intensified by globalising pressures generated by the erosion of the nation-state, the inequities of global capitalism and the compression of space and time through digital technology. As a conclusion to this chapter, I shall focus on how a concept of ecological citizenship, as one response to globalisation, might impact on thinking in applied drama.

Ecological citizenship is a metaphor that suggests the complex, interdependent, interactive and often uneven relationships between local and global interests in the practice of citizenship, and it is also a literal description of an important environmental movement. It seems to me that, although it is obviously outside the remit of this chapter to engage in a detailed discussion of the politics of ecology, an ecological citizenship is a way of conceptualising a number of different themes that have emerged in this chapter – the dramaturgy of civic citizenship; citizenship and political activism; altruism and social citizenship. At its most literal, ecological thought asks questions about the relationship between private actions and public responsibility, about values and practical action. It is a way of thinking about daily actions – do I drive or walk to the shops? – which places the ordinary and everyday in the context of global issues. Ecological citizenship involves imagining how the future might be, and acting to change it. To tease out the parallels between ecological citizenship and applied drama a little further, I shall focus on one example of how drama offers participants the opportunity to grapple with their identities and responsibilities as citizens in this complex and interdependent world. The theatrical experience imprinted on my mind that captured the ethics of global citizenship most acutely for me was, literally, about ecology.

The performance took place in a village near Batticaloa, a town in the Tamil district of Sri Lanka which had suffered particularly badly during the twenty-year civil war. At the time of my visit in summer 2003 the curfew in the area had recently been lifted and there was cautious but growing confidence in the peace process. This village bordered the lagoon, and there was heavy dependence on its fish stocks for the local economy. As part of a conference on community theatre, the local children of the village had devised a performance about the waste materials that had begun to litter the fertile fishing grounds nearby. The play was performed in Tamil entirely by the children, so my understanding of the dialogue was inevitably limited. Nonetheless, sitting watching the play on the sandy ground which bordered the lagoon I found that the power of their message was very clear. The play opened with two girls dressed as Westerners symbolising the mess of waste, their jeans and shirts heavy with plastic bags and bottles, and they scattered litter across the round stage in their wake. Fishermen bemoaned the demise of the fish stocks as their families went hungry. Children dressed in brightly coloured costumes represented fish and sea creatures, who withered and died as a result of the pollution. As the fishermen cleared the contaminated water, a more optimistic and colourful new life was illustrated by the arrival of birds and butterflies, performed in song and dance. On the surface, it was a straightforward morality play.

In this community, pollution and litter were both a real problem and a theatrical metaphor for globalisation. The cease-fire in Sri Lanka had brought much speculation about the economic future of the area and traditional livelihoods were threatened by encroaching multinational corporations. In terms of this drama, I had not been able to see the devising process and it would be easy for me to make simplistic and romanticised assumptions about how the children had worked towards the views the performance illustrated. What I did witness, however, was an interesting negotiation between the local context of production, the dramatic content of the play and theatrical form. The physical geography of the performance space and the landscape represented in the play merged and informed each other. The polluted lagoon was clearly visible to the audience; its presence was a reminder of what Slavoj Žižek has called 'the hard kernel of the Real' which can be perceived in fictional images and dramatic narratives.[34] The message of the play was unequivocal. The children represented the destructiveness of the West on a literal level – as litter and pollution – and located themselves in direct opposition to it. But theatrically, the imagery could be interpreted more ambiguously. The boy who played the elderly fisherman was a powerful theatrical presence, his painted moustache, weather-beaten hat and sarong indicating his age and status as a character. His performance style invoked the sweeping gestural languages and strong vocal timbre of Kouththou, a traditional form of performance indigenous to the area. This sense of a cultural ecology of performance was underlined by the fact that the play took place on a low circular stage which was partially prepared for the eight-hour performance of Kouththou which was to take place that evening. By contrast, the girls who personified the litter were not only wearing Western dress, they also sang songs which adopted the beat of Western pop music. As performers, the girls seemed to be enjoying themselves, and I was told that the clothes they wore were their own. The juxtaposition of these two performance styles suggested continuity between the past and the present, between the real and the fictional. These children were not playing themselves, but by using different performance styles succeeded in positioning themselves in relation to two dissonant world-views. It was a semiotic reminder that these children would need to negotiate both local and global perspectives and interests in their lives.

The interweaving of ecological citizenship, geography and theatre in this performance created a powerful aesthetic, and the unity of purpose was enhanced by the dynamic interaction between the performance text and its context. The children's performance seemed to have captured a moment of resistance, in which they acknowledged through their choices of performance styles that they were not insulated from the semiotics of globalisation, but they also invoked local cultural traditions as a way of symbolising the need to maintain threatened systems of labour. Taken together, the alignment of context and text indicated the networks of social responsibility and the multiple layers of identification which are inherent in the practice of both citizenship and drama. There was an altruistic and ethical care for the environment – an abstract concept for many Western children whose food comes packaged from supermarkets – informed by the self-interested imperative to protect a major source of food. From my point of view, a cultural outsider, the performance made me conscious of the dissonant and antagonistic pressures faced by these children, and how the global continually asserts itself into the local.

I am not claiming that this performance represented an ideal or idealised model of citizenship. On the contrary, my reading of the performance occupies what Žižek has called 'the shared space of understanding between different cultures', and is part of a process of intercultural dialogue which he insightfully described as an 'infinite task of translation, a constant re-working of one's own particular position'.[35] As Rustom Bharucha has pointed out, the interculturalist is an infiltrator and not 'a free-floating signifier oscillating in a seemingly permanent state of liminality and in-betweenness'.[36] What I am suggesting here is that both performers and audience were engaged in a process of reworking their own position in relation to others, whether across cultures or within them, and this is integral to the practice of citizenship. This is not confined to the more obvious negotiations between industrialised nations and the developing world, but includes contexts which are culturally diverse but are in close geographical proximity.

An active performative citizenship is concerned with the ethics of how people interact with each other and with their environment. It suggests that fixed boundaries cannot be drawn between the public and private, between self and other, altruism and self-interest. These concepts are not oppositional, but are experienced as an interdependent social system. This way of thinking is based on the understanding that identity is sedimented through a multiplicity of relationships and iden-tifications. There is also a risk that the idealisation of independence and autonomy leads to a denial of the individuals' own vulnerabilities and feelings. Psychoanalytic theory suggests that it is easy for such feelings to be projected onto others, casting them as weak, vulnerable or needy people.[37] By contrast, the conception of citizenship I am proposing is one in which individuals acknowledge their own vulnerabilities and limitations, and recognise that their dependence on a network of social relations is emotionally, culturally and politically productive.

The points of connection I am finding between conceptions of radical citizenship as social practices and applied drama is that both involve networks of collaboration and offer multiple ways of identifying with others. The place of drama in this construction of an active, participant citizenship lies in experiencing moral dilemmas, inhabiting different narratives and examining life from a range of perspectives. The feminist writer Selma Sevenhuijsen has offered an analysis of social responsibility in relation to citizenship that has rich dramatic potential:

> Moral deliberation is not concerned primarily with solving or eradicating moral dilemmas, but with making them productive, by looking, for example, at an issue from different perspectives and taking conflicting moral reactions and moral idioms as sources of morally relevant knowledge.[38]

The dialectic of theatre fits well with this model of citizenship because the process invites participants to give shape to the conflicts and ambiguities inherent in different dramatic situations and to explore their limitations and possibilities in the practice of everyday life. Such 'sources of morally relevant knowledge' may be both strange and familiar to participants in drama, taking them beyond the world they already know. In this sense, acting as citizens involves recognising the unpredictability of context, the messiness of emotional relationships and the political significance of dialogue as well as more abstract conceptions of citizenship as a collection of legal rights.

3 Pedagogies, Praxis and Performance

Mapping Pedagogies

Applied drama has strong ties to education. Advocates of applied drama in its different guises have regarded its participatory, dialogic and dialectic qualities as effective and democratic ways of learning in many formal and informal educational contexts. This interest in the processes of learning is generally described as *pedagogy*, a term which, as feminist educationalist Patti Lather points out, focuses attention on 'the condition and means through which knowledge is produced'.[1] Of course, it has long been recognised that the production of knowledge is highly complex, and emancipatory models of education have, for a century or more, emphasised the centrality of the learner in the pedagogic process. Pedagogies designed to encourage interactivity and collaboration have been seen to be in direct opposition to authoritarian and didactic approaches to learning and, as a collaborative art form, drama has been particularly well placed to contribute to such an educational project. Drama and pedagogy are both *activities*, contingent on the cultural contexts in which they take place, and the process of bringing them together has been regarded as a powerful way of encouraging creativity and challenging passivity.

The questions of where knowledge is situated, what forms of knowledge are valued, and how knowledge is shared, remain a major preoccupation in the range of practices which constitute applied drama. Moreover, as applied drama is a global phenomenon that operates in many different cultural contexts, there is no one pedagogical method that might be universally effective, or universally appropriate. Any approach which advocates a 'one size fits all' learning policy is likely to ignore local dynamics and the concerns of particular interest groups. Nonetheless, there are, if not general trends, recurring pedagogic principles in applied drama which are both exchanged through global networks and re-interpreted in specific local contexts. As a practice, it is generally understood that knowledge in drama is embodied, culturally located and socially distributed. This means that knowledge is produced through interaction with others, and that this reciprocity between participants generates new forms of social and cultural capital. 'Reciprocity', Lather argues, 'implies give and take, a mutual negotiation of meaning and power'.[2] Pedagogy is primarily concerned with how this negotiation and exchange happens.

This insight leaves open the central question of what kind of culture and society practitioners and participants in applied drama wish to promote. Lather suggests that in order to address this methodological gap, pedagogy needs to be linked to *praxis*. Or, put another way, there is a need to bring together 'how' questions with 'why' questions in order to establish a clear rationale for practice. Lather's definition of praxis as 'the self-creative activity through which we make the world' is illuminating.[3] Applied to drama, praxis does not denote a linear model of learning, but a cyclical process in which practice generates new insights and where, reciprocally, theoretical ideas are interrogated, created and embodied in practice. Praxis, therefore, is built on a circularity of thought, feeling and action. In this discussion I am hoping to re-open debates about the triangulation of performativity, praxis and embodied pedagogies, and to consider how this process of learning might enable participants to map new possibilities for meaning-making.

The metaphor of the map is a useful way of conceptualising the connections I am making between narratives of space, place and time in applied drama.[4] You would follow a map in order to undertake a journey, to be transported (in Richard Schechner's terms) from one place to another. On this journey, paths might collide or your direction might change to take in new vistas and perspectives. You might encounter barriers, dead-ends or summits that force a change of itinerary, a new track or an unexpected route. A pinnacle might be reached, the landscape thrown into relief, and a new journey begun. A map shows that there are many different ways to reach the same vantage point, but although a map allows you to plan your route, each journey is different and the experience is unpredictable. The map is based on journeys which have already taken place, but it also offers a guide for those who have yet to start. It offers an imprint (but not a fixed image) of the 'in-between spaces' which Homi Bhabha has characterised as a space of emancipation.[5]

A map indicates activity; it needs to be interpreted and inhabited before it can be turned into a story. It names histories and alludes to local legends. It also suggests the affective and aesthetic dimensions of a journey, marking places which are beautiful and difficult, but not noting their significance nor offering clear solutions about how best to approach or encounter them. Because applied drama operates at the points of intersection between culture, community and identity, the metaphor of the map indicates the negotiation between local circumstances and global realignments which is acutely relevant to its pedagogic practices.

This chapter is based on the premise that if pedagogical practices in applied drama are to be effective, they need to be negotiated, planned and focused according to different contexts and situations. The chapter is structured in four parts. The first section will examine theories of praxis and pedagogy which are orientated towards emancipation, specifically focusing on the work of the twentieth-century Brazilian educator Paulo Freire and the related concepts of border or critical pedagogies which have gained popularity in North America.[6] The second section takes the idea of performative pedagogies as its starting point, and raises questions about the political equations between efficacy and efficiency, liminality and transgression. In the third section I shall consider the relationship between knowledge, creativity and language, and in the conclusion I identify some implications for an embodied pedagogy in applied drama. Taken together, these three central concepts of pedagogy, praxis and performativity provide an opportunity to investigate political constructions of learning and knowledge in applied drama, and to further a theoretical framework with which to analyse learning in the context of uncertain pedagogical journeys in an increasingly globalised world.

Crossing Borders: Pedagogies of Location

Dwight Conquergood has argued that the study of performance is located at the intersection between two domains of knowledge – the map and the story. The map is 'official, abstract and objective' whereas the story is 'practical, embodied and popular'.[7] Using this analogy, Conquergood draws attention to the history of Western thought, which separated theory from practice and which cast rigid boundaries between critical analysis and creativity. In this Enlightenment project, he argues, objective scientific knowledge is privileged over local, vernacular and community-based 'know-how', and this then forges hierarchical distinctions between officially sanctioned forms of knowledge and ways of knowing which are more 'active, intimate, hands-on participation'.[8] Pedagogies in performance studies, he suggests, can travel between these two domains of knowledge by finding points of connection between creativity, critique and citizenship and by opening up the possibilities for local stories and community participation in academic inquiry. There are obvious parallels between Conquergood's activist version of performance studies and applied drama.

Conquergood is writing from the perspective of his North American academic culture, and his concern is to erode the boundaries between different forms of disciplinary knowledge. My own interpretation of the metaphor of the map is similarly intended to diminish the space between theory and practice, albeit in slightly different terms. Whereas Conquergood sees maps as primarily bureaucratic, my emphasis on the provisionality of maps recognises that they are also intimately connected to local history, legends and autobiographical stories, and that not all maps carry official or objective information (as the visual representations of journeys of Aboriginal Dreamtime in Australia clearly illustrate). But Conquergood's analysis of the political status of maps and, by extension, the politics of location helpfully illuminates the pedagogical debate. He points out that maps become 'crisscrossed by transnational narratives' as people migrate, and that stories are transported and exchanged as diasporic populations travel across official borders either voluntarily or through economic or political necessity. Crossing borders is a political act, he suggests, where some people are excluded, searched and interrogated and through which others can travel easily and freely. Borders indicate the interplay of movement and fixity, and this has repercussions for the meanings attached to places. He described the local as a 'leaky, contingent construction', and location is 'imagined as an itinerary rather than a fixed point'.[9] If this is the case, it means that in many contexts across the world it is impossible to talk about the 'local' without some implied reference to the global. This is both literally a physical experience and a metaphor for pedagogy. There are two ways of looking at this. A bounded sense of place may offer a secure basis from which to speak, to defend local, communitarian or territorial interests. Alternatively, borders are a way of keeping people in their place, of excluding others, or of ensuring that people living within a particular territory maintain their power or continue to be marginalised. Either way, politically and pedagogically, location is about the exercise of power.

The re-negotiation of cultural geographies has been recognised in educational and cultural discourse. Spatial metaphors such as 'border crossing' (Giroux, 1994) and 'speaking from the margins' (Spivak, 1987) suggest the complex signification of actual movement and location in the development of world-wide cultural dynamics. If applied drama appears most at home in the borderlands, it is because it is envisioned as a flexible and radical alternative to forms of pedagogy perceived to be instruments of disciplinary authority and social control. The Brazilian educator Paulo Freire, whose work *Pedagogy of the Oppressed* (1970) continues to inspire practitioners in applied drama, extended the idea that pedagogy could act as resistance to political oppression. Freire followed Marx by arguing for active models of pedagogy in which authoritarian approaches to learning are inverted, and where learners are encouraged to share their ideas in dialogue with others. He was critical of what he described as 'banking education', in which students listen, receive and memorise information given to them by teachers. Freire observed that this experience of powerlessness led people to internalise their oppressors' view of them as 'sick, lazy, and unproductive', an identity which he suggested might be challenged through problem-posing pedagogies.[10] In classic Marxist terms, this process of '*concientizacao*', or critical consciousness, is an approach to learning which Freire sees as leading to collective engagement in the class struggle. Freire's political pedagogy takes account of personal feelings as well as material circumstances, and it is partly his emphasis on the 'real' that has resonated with drama practitioners working with marginalised groups across the world.

There are numerous examples of practice in applied drama that have been inspired by Freire, not least because of his profound influence on Brazilian theatre director Augusto Boal. The example I have chosen to illustrate Freire's political pedagogy is not Boalian, but an adaptation of active learning strategies devised by the charity Action Aid to encourage adult literacy in the developing world. The technique, known as *Reflect*, takes the local environment as a basis for learning rather than prescribed literacy 'primers'. Local 'literacy circles' begin with participants representing their experiences graphically, drawing maps, charts and diagrams of places and events which are important to them in locally available materials such as leaves, sticks and beans or rice. Constructing these graphics encourages stories to emerge and discussions to take place, a creative process on which the facilitators build when the group is ready to move into making their own written texts. The process enables participants to use their own local knowledge as a starting point for literacy development, inviting them to generate a vocabulary around a theme or a place which is significant to them. Reading and writing activities are developed from this starting point, a strategy which places the experiences of the learner at the centre of the pedagogical process. They are also designed to encourage dialogue and exchange, and to foster networks of care and support both within local communities and beyond. *Reflect* strategies lend themselves well to dramatic exploration, as participants represent aspects of their autobiographies in symbolic form. For example, at the beginning of the devising process a group of refugees were asked to map their experiences, placing the symbol of a paper heart on the place in the world where they felt most at home, and then tearing it into small pieces and then placing the segments on the map to show all the places in the world where they felt they had left parts of themselves. This action – and many others in which participants similarly charted their experiences visually and physically – prompted reflection on stories of enforced migration and diaspora. Working through this process enabled them to use a range of languages to tell their stories, starting with their first languages as well as English, and moving easily into the symbolic, embodied and visual languages of drama. In common with Freire's approach to adult literacy, the project provided a supportive context for participants to extend their ability to communicate in spoken English. As its name suggests, this pedagogic strategy encourages reflection on lived experience, but the process also offers the participants control over what they want to say and what they wish to withhold.[11]

Reflect is Freirean in that it connects thought and action, an essential attribute of his praxis. The process also values the vernacular, and the existing knowledge of the participants is central to the learning process. Where strategies such as *Reflect* often depart from a strict Freirean pedagogy, however, is in their politics. Freire's praxis is indebted to Karl Marx's politicisation of the term, a term which has its conceptual roots in Hegelian philosophy.[12] Praxis, in Marxist discourse, is not just any relationship between theory and practice, but a creative and politically interventionist strategy, consistently orientated towards socialism. For Marxists, including Freire, praxis is regarded as an active process of critical engagement with experience aimed at disrupting established power relations, on both a material and intellectual level. Praxis was an important revolutionary strategy, appropriated by twentieth-century theatre activists who aimed to disturb the complacency of naturalised bourgeois sensibilities by awakening the masses to the reality of their oppression. For Freire, whose Marxist pedagogy adhered to well-defined battle-lines between oppressed and oppressor, good and evil, self and other, praxis actively involves the oppressed in critical dialogue about their material circumstances as part of their struggle for liberation. Like many of his contemporaries, Freire assumed that 'authentic praxis' based on 'true reflection' on a 'concrete situation' would automatically lead to Marxist politics.[13]

In considering how Freirean pedagogies have influenced contemporary educational debates, US applied theatre practitioner and academic Sharon Grady has pointed out that the critical pedagogies of Henry Giroux and Peter McLaren reproduce a neo-Marxist politics of education. Does following these theories in applied drama make practitioners into 'accidental Marxists', she asks? The question is apposite. Freirean-inspired critical pedagogy is a transgressive pedagogy in which, Grady suggests, 'teachers are asked to be revolutionary agents' whose role is to 'empower' their students to work against (or transgress) the hegemonic forces of capitalism.[14] It assumes, as I have pointed out, that there is a critical vantage point from which a transparent 'reality' might be clearly visible. When allied to the transgressive politics of theatre-makers such as Brecht and Piscator, this way of thinking about learning has provided practitioners in applied drama with a powerful political agenda.

There has been, however, a paradigm shift in Western artistic practices from transgressive to resistant politics in recent years. In his analysis of this change in the intellectual and cultural climate, Hal Foster argued that transgressive politics was derived from the modernist avant-garde, where it was assumed that art-making made it possible to stand outside, transcend or transgress contemporary social realities in order to critique them. Resistant politics, by contrast, recognises that all knowledge is contextually bound. It accepts that, although power is unevenly distributed, the idea that there are clearly identifiable social structures which might be transgressed is no longer an adequate representation of the complexities of capital in the era of globalisation. The role of the political artist in this context, he suggests, is to challenge dominant representations by investigating 'the processes and apparatuses which control them'.[15] This leaves a political conundrum. According to Foster, all cultural action and production – including drama and theatre – is contingent on context, and although political art is resistant to dominant cultural formations, it is, by implication, also parasitic on them. This gives rise to a central and problematic question, which Baz Kershaw has identified: 'How can performance, in being always implicated in the dominant, avoid replicating the values of the dominant?'[16] For applied drama, Kershaw's question is central to formulating a new conceptualisation of praxis which both recognises and challenges its contextual limits.

Spatial metaphors for politics and pedagogy signify the impact of globalisation on contemporary thought, and images of borders and margins are often intended to suggest an interest in disrupting dominant regimes of knowledge. But all borders are arbitrary constructions, all embody specific narratives and all require policing. This does not, however, preclude participants crossing borders, resisting guards or reaching new and unexpected places. On the contrary, when learners cross into new territories they will leave something of their 'old selves' behind as they begin to identify with different positions and perspectives. This experience is often deepened in drama when participants simultaneously occupy two worlds – the actual world of the workshop or rehearsal, and the imaginative or fictional world of the play. Kate Donelan, working in Australia, has explored the way in which drama offers young people a positive opportunity to develop intercultural understanding, in which they are invited to share their experiences and to explore the cultural narratives of others. Interestingly, she suggests that understanding is facilitated when intercultural boundaries are mapped, challenged and rewritten through the process of theatre-making.[17]

The emphasis on spatial metaphors means that questions about who controls the crossings are continually implicated in constructions of pedagogy and, because creativity is restricted by strict disciplinary borders, a more equitable praxis allows for more fluid and imaginative constructions of knowledge and location. As the *Reflect* exercise demonstrates, it is possible to be geographically located and belong to one place but simultaneously to imagine and identify with social practices in other space/time configurations. This negotiation between different locations effectively redefines the pedagogic map. According to educationalists Richard Edwards and Robin Usher, this process draws attention to the 'place' of the learner, to how and where knowledge is located and performed:

> As location is simultaneously a dislocation from other positions, pedagogy therefore becomes a process of constant engagement, negotiation and encounter. . . . Here, what is central is not the fixed position (a state of being) but the active and open state of becoming.[18]

These dynamic learning processes require open-handed guardianship of the ethical borders of applied drama as well as continual vigilance about where its political limits might be drawn. Praxis is informed, therefore, by the creative and contingent mapping of different narratives – cultural, personal, social, political, artistic – and learning is negotiated and choreographed as encounters between the artistic practices of drama and theatre and the vernacular know-how of the participants. Although these pedagogic processes are always recognised as incomplete, they have the potential to dislocate and change the location and structures of knowledge. This means that radical pedagogies, continually orientated towards 'an open state of becoming', are also *performative* pedagogies.

Performative Pedagogies: Efficacy or Efficiency?

The idea that pedagogy is a performative encounter, rather than a meeting of fixed positions, turns attention to how constructions of performance in different disciplinary fields might illuminate learning matters in applied drama. This concern is amplified by the fact that drama is in itself a performative act, even when the work does not lead to a conventional theatrical performance. In all its manifestations, questions of power and knowledge have been central to discussions about the politics of performance, and surface in many different guises. The two interpretations of performance I am particularly interested in exploring in relation to pedagogy in applied drama derive from *performance studies*, which analyses performance as cultural practice, and from *performance management*, which was generated in the corporate sector and is concerned with accountability and achievement. The differences between the two uses of the term appear difficult to reconcile. Performance studies looks to the margins, to local cultural practices, the dispossessed and the diasporic, whilst performance management looks to the global, to standardisation, homogenisation and to uniformity. One is associated with efficacy, the other with efficiency. They seem to emphasise very different, and incompatible, ways of articulating the performance of knowledge and power.

On the face of it, pedagogical approaches to applied drama have little to do with the language of performance management and are closely allied to performance studies. The emphasis on borders, margins and liminality in applied drama as a *leitmotif* for its pedagogical practices is based on the assumption that if learning shifts from the traditional centre to the radical margins, and surveys the world from the shifting vantage points of the borderlands, it will be emancipatory. Dwight Conquergood emphasises the relationship between performance studies and the politics of location:

> Performance privileges threshold-crossing, shape shifting, and boundary-violating figures, such as shamans, tricksters and jokers, who value the carnivalesque over the canonical, the transformative over the normative, the mobile over the monumental.[19]

There is, however, a risk that this very emphasis on marginality becomes domesticated and forms a new educational orthodoxy. In response to pedagogical questions about social exclusion and inclusion, Jon McKenzie's analysis of performance studies is illuminating. McKenzie argued that in performance studies liminality has become the norm and the dominant conceptual model. It is an interest in transgression and performance efficacy, he suggests, that defines performance studies and thus an emphasis on marginality lies, paradoxically, at the centre of the discipline. As a further challenge, McKenzie invokes Victor Turner's anthropological research to show how liminal performances which begin as transgressive rituals aimed at disrupting social norms often mutate over time, and eventually become conservative reinforcements of the status quo.[20] A good example of this is the Notting Hill Carnival, which is held annually in London. It began in 1964 as a resistant protest against racism and an assertion of Caribbean culture and, although the carnival itself maintains its radical roots, by 2002 carnival performers were also content to lead the Queen's Golden Jubilee procession staged (and commodified) as a show of national unity. The emphasis on marginality in drama education and applied drama has not, by and large, taken account of the potential slippage of liminality into conservatism, nor of how quickly theatre practices and pedagogies once regarded as 'alternative' become absorbed into the mainstream.

Whatever the cracks and fissures of transgressive pedagogies, practitioners in applied drama have maintained a continual commitment to the democratisation of learning. Performance management seems diametrically opposed to this. If performance studies has emphasised the liminal, focusing on performative practices which are 'in between' spaces and times where social conventions are challenged, management studies has focused on the norms, standards and elements of performance which signify achievement or competence. The political differences between the two disciplines seem huge, and the relationship between power and knowledge inverted. Applied drama, with its interest in border pedagogies, decentralisation and deterritorialisation of knowledge, seems distant from the discourses of efficiency associated with management studies. Performance management has, however, introduced a new language into commerce and industry, emphasising the importance of creativity and intuition in the workplace. Employees and managers are expected to be flexible and adaptable, to take initiative, operate as part of a team and be affectively engaged in their work. Jon McKenzie has offered a summary of the paradigm shift from manager/employee roles

The Changing Role of Management

From	To
Risk-taking avoided	Innovation encouraged
Directive	Participative
Control of people	Enabling control of product
Inform if need to know	Inform if want to know
Commitment to boss	Commitment to purpose
Competitive	Collaborative

The Changing Role of Employees

From	To
Dependent	Empowered
Passive	Assertive
Childlike	Mature
Cynical	Optimistic
Competitive	Co-operative
Distrustful	Trusting
Ignorant	Informed
Unskilled	Skilled
Assumed lazy	Motivated

FIGURE 1   THE CHANGING ROLES OF MANAGEMENT AND EMPLOYEES

based on models of people as machinery to those based on systems theory[21] (see Figure 1).

This way of thinking about workplace relations has a remarkable resonance with the language of the kind of participant pedagogies with which applied drama has been associated. Substitute the words 'teacher', 'practitioner' or 'facilitator' for 'manager', 'participant' or 'student' for 'employee', and these lists would not look out of place in many drama education/applied theatre texts, where they might serve to summarise the differences between traditional and radical pedagogies. Performance management's drive for efficiency and productivity has appropriated Freire's argument that an oppressive society naturalises characteristics such as laziness and ignorance, and turned them into a system which supports a capitalist economy. By inverting the dialectic, this approach to management seeks to ensure greater commitment from 'human resources', a process which is in turn expected to lead to greater commercial profit.

Performance management is based on the ideal of an active subjectivity, where employees are created who have people skills, the ability to adapt to new situations, and are committed to self-improvement. Seen in this way, some of the 'unfixed' qualities of performance, valued in performance studies and in applied drama, are also evident in performance management. Designer employees or active, participant citizens? In one interpretation, following Foucault, performance management means that the self becomes an enterprise, representing yet another attempt to 'govern the soul' through creating self-regulating citizens.[22] An alternative reading is that this kind of reflexive modernisation is benign, creating increasingly flexible and egalitarian work practices. However construed, applied drama cannot escape this debate. For some people working in applied drama, performance management has made corporate commissions a palatable option, and many drama programmes aimed at team-building, creative thinking or countering workplace harassment have proliferated. The website of the British theatre company Drama for Training, who specialise in corporate work, for example, advertises a range of courses in anger and stress management, talent development and so on. One of the aspects of this work that is particularly intriguing is that they use the dramatic strategies of the Marxian practitioner Augusto Boal, despite the fact that the company uses theatre-making to maximise corporate efficiency and competitiveness within a global marketplace. Their website states that they use Boalian methods to construct 'fully interactive training workshops, individually tailored to suit the HR needs of organisations across the globe'. The webpage about managing change is particularly revealing in this respect:

Every company needs to change. Without change – we stand still and our competitors leap to the fore.

Managing change ensures

- managers and staff are totally committed to proposed changes
- managers and staff drive the change which ensures success
- the costs for 'driving change' are in proportion to positive results
- an environment where acceptance of change exists
- a culture where creativity, openness, honesty and integrity exist and drive success
- changes are less stressful for all involved which in turn reduces absenteeism and recruitment costs thus increasing productivity.[23]

Each of these bullet points shows the relationship between change and individual commitment, and implies that personal qualities such as honesty and integrity are not values in themselves, but measures of 'success' and 'positive results', which will increase productivity. Similarly, their advert for drama workshops on equality and diversity, which use Boal's technique of forum theatre, emphasises staff recruitment and retention rather than any political or moral reasons for creating an equitable working environment. The languages and practices of performance management are, moreover, not confined to the corporate sector. Despite their different motives and intentions, aspects of performance management have crept into the kinds of organisations on which applied drama depends for its funding or in which it takes place – such as charities, educational institutions, hospitals and voluntary organisations. Professional practitioners across the globe have become skilled in writing grant applications in which criteria and performance indicators are identified, learning is clearly structured, and evaluation is expected.

Both performance management and applied drama are allied to performative pedagogies, as in each case learning is embodied and understanding is shown in practical situations. Both have an expectation that skills and insights learnt in rehearsals or workshops will be transferable into other situations and contexts. Edwards and Usher have identified this as a trend in education, suggesting that learning is not valued for its own sake, but for its usefulness or efficacy:

> [t]he performativity of knowledge can take different forms because of its location in different social practices. This means that its efficacy may vary. For instance, it can enhance self-knowledge and lifestyle through personal development opportunities made available through the consumer market. In critical practices, it can be a pedagogy of performance which moves beyond a Western form of rationality and its preoccupation with the written word (the book) to embrace diverse forms of cultural learning across the globe.... [O]ther than its efficacy for realising different socially constructed aims, knowledge no longer has a single canonical referent.[24]

From the point of view of practice in drama, it is interesting that Edwards and Usher emphasise that a pedagogy of performance recognises cultural diversity, and that it takes account of forms of learning which are not confined to the written word. The central point, however, is that 'efficacy may vary'. The destabilisation of canonical forms of knowledge implies that no pedagogic practices will, of themselves, generate a specific form of social change. In the language familiar to both applied drama and performance management, performative pedagogies might be 'empowering' but in very different ways. What is learnt depends on how drama is used, on the educational aims of particular projects, the narratives of the participants and the specific social locations and cultural contexts in which the work takes place. This is both pedagogical and profoundly political, making the need for a clear rationale for practice – a praxis – even more acute.

Dramatic Literacies and Differentiated Knowledge

My reading of performative pedagogies implies that similar dramatic strategies may be effective in contexts which have very different educational aims and political agendas. This would contradict Freire's utopian vision that an educated population would use their learning not to adapt to an unjust society, but to bring about political change and overthrow oppressive social structures. Once this faith in the political consequences of learning had been broken, commentators have tended to emphasise how the democratic processes of his pedagogy might be applied to different emancipatory discourses rather than used to reach specific learning outcomes.[25] From the point of view of applied drama, however, it is also important to remember that Freire's praxis was not solely concerned with emancipatory pedagogical processes, but with developing adult literacy. It was important to Freire that illiterate adults learnt to read and write in order that they might take an active part in society, and his progressive pedagogy was a means of achieving this end. In order to encourage effective literacy learning, Freire's teachers were not asked to deny their own specific expertise or pedagogical intentions, but to build on the expertise and knowledge of the learners, which they might not themselves share. In other words, Freire's dialogic pedagogy was based on an exchange of differentiated knowledge.

The idea that literacy, power and social equality are intimately linked, a significant Freirean insight, remains particularly important to applied drama as the process of theatre-making also relies on communication between participants. Freire stressed the relationship between language, thought and human agency, describing literacy as 'word-and-action' rather than 'mere vocabulary'.[26] For Freire, literacy is 'an act of knowing', and he encouraged learners to assume 'the role of creative subjects' as part of the process of becoming literate. In order to facilitate this learning, teachers were urged to respect participants' existing cultural knowledge and experiences, but also to encourage them to develop new ways of thinking. Increased powers of literacy not only extend learners' confidence as thinkers and speakers, Freire argued, they also lead them to new conceptual horizons. In terms that are reminiscent of Wittgenstein's famous dictum 'the limits of my language are the limits of my world',

Freire recognised that it is only through language that learners extend their cognitive abilities. According to Freire, literacy develops a capacity for 'critical knowing' in which education is a creative process of 'constant problematising'.[27] It is this relationship between creative participation and critical reflection which has become central to pedagogies in applied drama.

Although it is generally agreed that language is required for creative and critical thought, one of the central debates in literacy education is concerned with the social values placed on different forms of language. Freire recognised that some forms of language use have been legitimated by the establishment, and he understood that the language of official discourse is often alienating to those who are illiterate and socially disadvantaged, whom it renders silent. My guide for these tricky political and pedagogical debates is Lisa Delpit, an African-American educationalist who has written extensively about literacy and cultural conflict. Delpit argues that black children are socially disadvantaged if they are not taught to communicate effectively in a range of linguistic registers. It is not a matter of replacing the vernacular with standard English, she argues, but of ensuring that the cultural codes of different forms of spoken and written language are made explicit in order that they might be used to best advantage in different contexts. In terms reminiscent of Freire, she links the acquisition of communication skills with creativity and critical thinking:

> Students need technical skills to open doors, but they need to be able to think critically and creatively to participate in meaningful and potentially liberating work inside those doors. Let there be no doubt: a 'skilled' minority person who is not also capable of critical analysis becomes the trainable, low-level functionary of the dominant society.... On the other hand, a critical thinker who lacks the 'skills' demanded by employers and institutions of higher learning can aspire to financial and social status only within the disenfranchised underworld. Yes, if minority people are to effect the change which will allow them to truly progress we must insist on 'skills' *within the context of* critical and creative thinking.[28]

Delpit is critical of those who advocate the improvised and unedited 'process writing' at the expense of forms of literacy learning which make the cultural codes of communication explicit. She argues that debates about process and product have been unhelpfully polarised, and that a more equitable pedagogy finds a constructive negotiation between the two positions. Her aim is not to obliterate language diversity; on the contrary, her pedagogy is directed towards ensuring that young people are able to use a range of 'languages' in order to become active citizens in a global community.

Translated into drama, the idea that literacy is not a set of isolated skills but encourages creative and critical thought draws attention to the different 'languages' which are available to actors as a means of communication and expression. In drama, communication is embodied and meanings are created and read through the body, aurally, visually and kinaesthetically. As such, drama is a form of literacy – you can think, feel and represent ideas and experiences with your body as well as with your mind. But the body is not a neutral space, which means that Delpit's arguments about the social implications of literacy and the cultural hierarchies of language also apply to the practice of drama. So what are the implications of her approach to pedagogy for applied drama? What resonates with my experiences in applied drama is Delpit's insistence on the teaching of skills in context, as a way of extending the linguistic and cultural repertoires of the participants in order to increase their potential to participate as citizens. This also has an impact on how practitioners see their roles in different pedagogical encounters.

As a form of learning which aims to be as inclusive as possible, there have been debates in drama education and in other forms of applied drama about how far to introduce forms of theatre which have symbolic capital within the establishment (writing from a British perspective, Shakespeare is an obvious example here), or whether practice should primarily focus on forms of cultural expression which are perhaps more immediately accessible, such as those based on improvisation. Delpit's argument about the process/product dichotomy is apposite here. If, as she suggests, creative pedagogies encourage a multiplicity of readings of texts and contexts, practitioners would not expect participants to follow a single line of enquiry nor a single linguistic register, but would invite them to experiment with a range of possible alternative interpretations and readings. This approach would apply equally to a reading of *Hamlet* and to the improvisation of a scene in which the situation is directly familiar to participants. A good example of how practitioners have encouraged multiple interpretations of established plays might be found in the work undertaken by the late Murray Cox, who ran projects on Shakespeare in Broadmoor, a secure psychiatric hospital in England which cares for some of the most dangerous and disturbed patients in the country. Cox took performances of Shakespearean tragedies to the hospital as part of a therapeutic programme, and he found that the plays provided the necessary aesthetic distance for patients to identify with characters and situations on stage. It was not the symbolic capital of Shakespeare which interested the audiences, but a more personal relationship with the stories. The actor Brian Cox recounted the reaction of one patient to his performance of *King Lear*:

> A consultant came and told me that three of her patients . . . came quite separately to her and said, 'I did so envy the ability of Cordelia and her father to have a farewell . . . it made me think about my own situation, particularly before I murdered my parents.'[29]

Even allowing for an actor's tendency to sensationalism, this testament suggests that the patients were encouraged to bring their own experiences to their interpretation of the play, a process which had psychological benefits. Therapeutically and pedagogically, the success of the process relied on various forms of differentiated knowledge coming together – including that of the patients, the therapists and actors. In this context and in others, working flexibly and creatively with scripts or other tools of cultural expression can enable participants to think and perceive dramatically, to use the aesthetic distance of theatrical metaphor to confront difficult issues and to find new forms of identification with others.

It is particularly in the context of dramatic improvisation that the political metaphor of the 'voice' becomes a literal and physical presence. An education which enables the voices of participants to be heard is a powerful antidote to more authoritarian forms of learning. Delpit qualifies this position, however, by suggesting that the good intentions of liberal teachers can appear patronising unless this aspiration is accompanied by an understanding of the cultural norms of oral communication in children's homes. This extends to what is communicated through facial expression, body language, intonation and gesture, all of which are part of the body's cultural inscription. This is relevant to a range of contexts to which drama is applied. Prisoners and young offenders often develop their own forms of linguistic communication to denote 'insidership' (literally, in this case) to a specific institution; street gangs often have their own oral codes, and many professions have some form of jargon specific to them.[30] To take away this language is to deny part of that person's identity. But identity is not fixed, and all of us belong to many different communities. Part of this process of change, as Delpit has pointed out, is to learn new forms of communication. A less threatening way for young people to try out voices which are not their own, she suggests, is through drama, both improvisation and scripted plays. This is familiar territory to drama educators, who have long understood

that drama is a powerful means of literacy learning in b
and informal education sectors.[31]

The objection to what Freire described as a 'banki\
to education is that it is intent on transmitting canon\
knowledge rather than encouraging interpretation, creativity \ ....que.
Drama is particularly well placed to contribute to approaches to learning
which counter this authoritarianism, not only because it offers the
opportunity for dialogue between teacher and learner (as advocated by
Freire), but also because drama relies on interaction and exchange
between the participants themselves. This raises questions about the
role of the teacher or practitioner, and what kind of knowledge is
needed for such fluid educational encounters. Freire is unambiguous.
In terms indebted to Gramsci's concept of the organic intellectual, his
pedagogue is a 'knowing subject', a 'specialised educator' who does
not perpetuate the symbolic capital of dominant culture, but regards
education as a dynamic process of coming 'face-to-face with other
knowing subjects'.[32] This raises complex questions about what kind of
expertise practitioners in applied drama require. Writing from the
perspective of formal education, Delpit, like Freire, is clear that children
should be 'allowed the resource of the teacher's expert knowledge'
whilst also being encouraged to value their own forms of expert knowledge. North American feminist educator Elisabeth Ellsworth has described
this negotiation of different forms of knowledge as a 'pedagogy of the
unknowable' because it is never possible to 'know' fully the social
experiences of others.[33]

This balance between the known and the unknown is particularly
significant to applied drama, where practitioners need to gain an understanding of the contexts in which they work as well as the various skills
in facilitating drama. What practitioners need to know to facilitate
successful projects will depend on the context in which they are working
as well as the objectives and scope of the practice. In order to develop
their understanding of the community setting or client group, many
drama practitioners work in close partnership with related professionals
(such as teachers, social workers, probation officers and psychiatrists)
and develop interagency projects in which the participants themselves
may act as consultants. There is a related debate here about whether
applied drama projects always need to be run by drama specialists, or
whether client-support groups, prison officers or the police, for example,
can develop some skills in drama facilitation. Perhaps most significantly,
working in drama often requires a change in institutional culture, a shift
in thinking from the idea that professionals control the situation

(because of their expert disciplinary knowledge) to a recognition that client groups have specialised knowledge of their own situations, and experiences which are central to the work.[34]

Most practitioners in applied drama are eclectic, using many different forms of improvisation extensively in their work, but also finding appropriate places for other forms of cultural performance. Setting rigid boundaries between process and product, and between improvisation and script, is often counterproductive, and frequently an inadequate representation of the experiences of both practitioners and participants. The Broadmoor patients continued to process their experiences of seeing *King Lear* long after the performance, for example, with the support of the psychiatric consultants who worked with them. This example is perhaps unusual in that the patients were audience members rather than participants in the drama, but it does make the point that, when drama is part of a therapeutic or pedagogical process, it is not always helpful to make a sharp separation between the experiences. Similarly, many drama workshops productively combine script and improvisation as part of the process of exploring ideas, roles and situations. Patti Lather has drawn attention to the networks of pedagogic practices which might be used to probe constructions of knowledge, a process which is more likely to illuminate the ambiguities and contradictions inherent in knowledge formation than to provide clear-cut answers.[35] This approach to applied drama relies, therefore, on a synthesis of differentiated knowledge, achieved through dialogue between practitioners and participants, which is intended to enable all those involved to negotiate and cross borders which had been previously closed to them.

Embodied Pedagogies

So far I have argued that whatever the different values of the practitioners and participants, the efficacy and effectiveness of the work depends on the formulation of a praxis – the embodied synthesis of theory and practice – rather than a particular battery of drama strategies, forms or techniques. Practitioners in applied drama use many different forms of theatre and performance in their work, and any recommendation of one particular set of dramatic practices over another would be restrictive. What makes drama 'applied', however, rather than just 'drama', is not only the educational, institutional or community contexts in which it takes place, but also the pedagogical processes, however broadly defined, in which participants are invited to engage. On an entirely practical level, drama is composed of material elements, of bodies and voices in space, and the physical embodiment of knowledge and understanding is integral to the art form itself. The metaphor of bodies is important in relation to pedagogy – the location of knowledge, border crossings, the local/global nexus, intellectual and imaginative journeys and so on – but so is the literal presence of bodies in the practice of drama. In this, the final section of the chapter, I shall consider some of the implications of the body in dramatic pedagogies.

To support this move from the abstract into the concrete, I shall begin by reflecting on the kinaesthetic and the physical elements of my own practice. Some practitioners tend to start workshops with discussion and gradually move into practical work, but I have usually started the other way round. This is simply a matter of preference, but what often works for me is to begin by engaging participants physically in the drama, and then to spend time reflecting in different ways on how and why particular ideas and feelings have been embodied. This is not a hard-and-fast rule, but it is based on the simple principle that drama is unlike many other forms of learning because it has an aesthetic dimension and, as the aesthetic is a discourse on the body, it engages all the senses. In a project that I recently directed with a group of children with various learning and physical disabilities, the potential for somatic learning in drama was demonstrated very clearly. The project was supported by Creative Partnerships, an educational initiative in creative learning in England which fosters productive collaborations between creative practitioners and education providers.[36] In this contribution to the programme, local children worked with a group of undergraduate students, all drama specialists. The work was planned with the children's teachers and the students intended to work alongside the children as fellow artists. The project aimed to extend the participants' powers of physical expression and, in particular, to encourage the children to work beyond the literal and into the world of the imagination and metaphor. Because the children had very different abilities and disabilities, the students planned to introduce a range of approaches to learning, focusing on the kinaesthetic languages of drama – including movement, sight, touch and sound – so that children with different abilities might all find points of entry into the drama. The collaborative elements of the work meant that the children and students could pool their abilities, and where they experienced physical difficulties they were encouraged to rely on each other's senses as part of the dramatic aesthetic. They made a scene based on a play by Lin Coghlan, *A Feeling in My Bones*, which tells the story of a boy, Sean, who is threatened with eviction from his home in the Cumbrian hills so that his house can be turned into a profitable holiday cottage.[37]

Using their bodies and large pieces of fabric to symbolise contrasting landscapes, the participants explored the feelings evoked by places where you feel at home, and those where you feel strange and uneasy. In early workshops, the children found it difficult to move beyond very naturalistic representations of people and situations. This was fine but rather more one-dimensional and talk-based than we had hoped. When the students used physical theatre to model more abstract representations of place, the children's work began to take on far greater emotional and intellectual depth. For example, in an exercise in which the children and students became the kitchen appliances in Sean's house, ideas burst into life. Two children created inventive stories from a wise old kitchen table who could barely move she was so creaky, whilst others created the gabble and chatter of a hyperactive washing-machine whose repetitive movements showed that he was sick and tired of cleaning the evidence of Sean's mysterious adventures. The collage of movement and sound they created was extremely atmospheric, capturing Sean's moods and anxieties in a dramatic moment of pathetic fallacy. Aspects of this work were developed into the final performance, perhaps most inventively when one of the girls, a wheelchair user who had found it difficult to control her hand and head movements at the beginning of the project, became the energetic engine of the train which came to take Sean to the city. Their engagement with Sean's story was embodied in the practice itself, and their reflections showed that they had generated new insights and skills through the interplay of aesthetic, intellectual and emotional sensibilities.

What I learnt from these children was that their learning was enhanced when they used their kinaesthetic imaginations, and whereas their work in the more abstract physical languages of theatre was inventive and expressive, their naturalistic work in role was often stilted and predictable. I had seen this many times before in other contexts, but the power of somatic learning was all the more evident because many of these children had physical disabilities. What surprised me most in my observations was that the children were far more familiar with the limits and possibilities of their bodies than most apparently able-bodied children of their age and, as their competence grew, their increased confidence enabled them to make the transition from the physical representation of ideas and feelings into spoken and written language. It reminded me of a project I was involved in creating for children of little or no sight in collaboration with the Botanical Gardens in Cambridge. In this site-specific performance,

I witnessed how a similar integration of the physical and the cognitive impacted on children's learning. The work was designed to enable these children to 'see' *The Tiger in a Tropical Storm*, a painting by Henri Rousseau, through senses other than sight. The group of student artists who executed the project created a sensory experience of the painting in a damp hot-house of tropical plants and, by literally walking into the space and touching the dripping leaves and the fur of a model tiger, the children were able to use their sharpened senses of touch, smell, movement and hearing to create a sense of the image in their minds. In both cases, children were encouraged to speak in a range of different aesthetic languages, using the physical vocabularies of movement, image, sound and touch as well words as modes of dialogue, as means of communication. Penny Bundy described the process of aesthetic engagement with theatre-making as an intimate experience, in which there is both a connection with ideas stimulated by the work and a heightened awareness of the worlds in which they find themselves. This is not found haphazardly, she contends, but is more likely to be experienced when the creative process is carefully structured.[38]

Terry Eagleton has pointed out that the aesthetic is always a discourse on the body.[39] I have suggested that, because drama involves multiple channels of communication, interaction between participants is often physical as well as verbal. This means that establishing dialogue as an embodied pedagogy requires considerable sensitivity and awareness of issues about personal space, physical contact and appropriate boundaries. There is an intimacy about bodies, and how people feel about touching each other or using their bodies expressively is fraught with complications, particularly as the body is representative of wider cultural and social values. This means that physical interaction in the process of making drama is not always a matter of simply being sufficiently sensitive to individuals or establishing a level of trust within the group, though this is clearly important. Just as spoken and written language carries social meanings, so does the body, a point that has been clearly articulated by black, feminist and post-colonial scholars. The body is a discursive category, a site of struggle. Describing the racism she suffered, Atvar Brah has described how painful experiences of prejudice gradually become embodied and internalised as 'realities'.[40] Pedagogies which are embodied, therefore, involve a more complex understanding of how the body is culturally and socially constructed and experienced by different members of each drama group, and how discourses of the body might be enacted, interpreted and re-interpreted in the process of the work itself.

Part II
Narratives and Narrativity

4 Narrative and the Gift of Storytelling

The storyteller is the figure in which the righteous man encounters himself.

Walter Benjamin, 'The Storyteller', 1992, p. 107

Changing the Story

This chapter is an exploration of some of the ways in which narrative is set and experienced in applied drama. Throughout this book I suggest that applied drama is concerned with how narratives are constructed and how they might be deconstructed or challenged. Drama is in itself a narrative art, of course, and theatre-making is a good place to explore and represent narratives of selfhood, culture and community. There is often an oppositional quality to this work, and many practitioners in applied drama have a particular commitment to ensuring that dominant social narratives are disrupted. Drama provides a powerful opportunity to ask questions about whose stories have been customarily told, whose have been accepted as truth, and to redress the balance by telling alternative stories or stories from different perspectives. It is this understanding that narratives can be changed that lies at the heart of practice in applied drama.

In 'The Storyteller' Walter Benjamin described the ethical implications of the change from a society built on oral narratives and shared experience to a culture in which information is received in short bursts, through images, photographs and news clips. Writing in the aftermath of the First World War, Benjamin's analysis of the social role of the story-teller ends with the claim that the storyteller is allied to goodness. The storyteller's gift, he argued, is to use experiences of life to offer practical wisdom, finding narratives and metaphors that make connections between life as it is and life as it might be. As a Marxist, Benjamin recognised that stories play an ideological role in society, and he differentiated between stories which disrupt dominant patterns of thought, and those which perpetuate the values of the powerful. For Benjamin successful storytellers are not those who report events or provide information, but those whose stories encourage people to share their experiences and stimulate moral discussion. This form of storytelling is a craft, which storytellers use to engage their listeners through the expressiveness of their bodies as well as with their words. Good storytelling, in Benjamin's terms, combines aesthetics and ethics, an act of generosity.[1]

However nostalgic Walter Benjamin's account of the master storyteller might be, this elision of narrative, ethics and aesthetics has continued resonance in contemporary social theory as well as implications for applied drama. Narrative theory provides a good vehicle for exploring the ways in which practising drama effects changes of understanding and generates new insights because, as Paul Ricoeur has pointed out, it is placed at 'the crossroads between the theory of action and moral theory'. 'Telling a story,' Ricoeur suggested, 'is deploying an imaginary space for thought experiments in which moral judgement operates in hypothetical mode'.[2] On this basis, working in the 'imaginary space' of drama enables participants to juxtapose different narrative perspectives, to fictionalise life as it is experienced and, conversely, to make the imaginary world of fiction tangible and 'real'. Conceptualised and practised in this way, drama becomes a place to explore the ethical gap between description and prescription, hypothesis and factuality.

All stories are read and created through the lens of social and cultural experience, and this means that narratives are inevitably interpreted in many different ways. Recognising that stories have multiple interpretations involves identifying the limits of one's own horizons, and an interest in seeing alternative perspectives. This approach signals an aspiration towards social equality, as Kathleen Gallagher has pointed out:

> The distinctive educative force of theatre, however – its dialectics – invites us to take up points of intersection *and* confrontation, so that our dramatic explorations do not simply calcify cultural and ethnic boundaries and limit our own and our students' abilities to affiliate with multiple cultural identities, productively manoeuvre across borders, and develop capacities for functioning in diverse situations.[3]

Gallagher is concerned to erode fixed binary division between self and other, identity and difference, and to encourage dramatic explorations of narratives which actively interrogate and contest these boundaries. In these terms, self-creativity is an explicitly political process. It is her challenge to find ways of working in drama that enable participants to affiliate with multiple identities which I should like to begin to explore here.

The idea that identity is a continual process of *becoming*, rather than a pre-given expression of *being*, has involved a reconsideration of the concept of narrative and its significance in everyday life. A narrative conception of selfhood recognises that identity is not constructed autonomously but in relation to others, through both language and other symbolic codes available in different cultural practices. Atvar Brah summarises the argument:

> Since identity is a process, what we have is a field of discourses, matrices of meanings, narratives of self and others, and the configuration of memories which, once in circulation, provide a basis for identification.[4]

The idea that the self is a narrative, continually created and re-created through interaction with others, does not, however, suggest that individuals are without agency, or lack the ability to think or feel for themselves. In describing the self as discursively or culturally constructed, I am suggesting that identity is uniquely layered through a historical sedimentation of events and experiences over which, as individuals, we have some degree of choice. Life is not itself a coherent unity nor a linear narrative, but a 'configuration of memories' and 'matrices of meanings' which become stories as experiences are retold, re-created, ordered and interpreted. This acknowledges that the aesthetics of self-production is built on the convergence and interplay of different narratives, and that constructing narratives of selfhood is both an ethical and a creative process.

If working in drama is to enable participants to manoeuvre productively across borders, to borrow Gallagher's words, practitioners will be alert to how different narratives – personal, cultural, social and artistic – converge in the process. This is not, of course, confined to dramatic forms which have an obvious narrative structure – a wider description of narrative would include the games, rehearsals or drama workshops which convey something of the messiness of reality and explore its incoherence, and to which participants bring the complexity of their experiences of life, however fictionalised and incomplete. In this chapter I will investigate the representation of 'real' issues as fictional narratives, and in Chapter 5 I shall continue the investigation of narrative by focusing more explicitly on narratives of community.

Fiction as Reality

One of the central arguments in this book is that fiction and reality, self and otherness, are not in opposition or isolated from each other but, as narrative constructions, they are interrelated and mutually embedded. Autobiography often blends the fictional with the real, and over time life histories are rehearsed and become fictionalised. Conversely, fictionalised narratives found in myth and legend are integral to narratives of selfhood and community. This is particularly relevant to applied drama, in which participants are often invited to explore matters of local interest and personal concern. This means that the divisions between fiction and reality are deliberately blurred in order to provide a safe space for participants to transform experiences into dramatic metaphor or to find points of connection that are presented theatrically. Changes of understanding or new ideas come about when narratives are contrasted or juxtaposed or, as Ricoeur puts it, 'meaning emerges through the interplay of identity and difference'.[5]

One of the practices familiar to both drama educators and drama therapists is the use of both fictional and autobiographical narratives to play with alternative constructions of selfhood, to frame experiences in order to view life from different places and perspectives. The focus of the work in drama therapy and drama education is very different, and any use of narrative will be differently inflected according to context. However, many forms of theatre-making in applied drama have an interest in how fictional narratives might illuminate lived experiences. Writing about her work in prisons, Sally Stamp has offered an insightful discussion of how participants in drama education workshops often create narratives which, whilst not explicitly autobiographical, are analogous with their own situations and experiences, and they will identify strongly with plays or films which reflect aspects of their lives.[6] In drama therapy, by contrast, as the work is intended to encourage participants to explore personal situations and feelings, all members of a group will establish a contract which clearly identifies the scope and boundaries of the work. This distinction is important, and I remember very clearly feeling cheated and hurt on one occasion when I had signed up to participate in a workshop for drama educators, but where I was expected to explore quite personal relationships within my own family with a group of people I had met only a few minutes previously. This clearly contravenes codes of professional practice in both drama therapy and drama education. However, the boundaries between a fictional narrative and autobiography can blur very easily, and in non-therapeutic settings sometimes the narrative is taken in unexpected directions by participants, and this may touch nerves or invoke particular feelings for individual members of a group.

My assumptions about the ethical implications of constructing fictional narratives in drama workshops were tested on a visit to Sri Lanka in July 2003. I have noticed before that working in a very different context from my own makes me acutely aware of how deeply my own cultural values and experiences inform my practice, often subconsciously, and this work was no exception. As part of a small international delegation to a conference, I had been invited to run a workshop which would take place in the village of Seelamunai near Batticaloa. I would be working with a group of conference delegates – including teachers, theatre activists, youth workers and NGOs – and, as I would be working under the trees, probably the local children would join in too. I was aware that many people taking part were working with young people who have been affected or traumatised by the war. Tackling the issue of war trauma directly would obviously be both insensitive and inappropriate in a workshop of only two hours, particularly when my understanding of the context was limited. But I was interested in developing a workshop that involved constructing a fictional narrative that I intended to be sufficiently ambiguous for the participants to interpret in many different ways.

I had chosen to adapt a workshop I had developed with Andy Kempe for an in-service course for drama teachers in Wales. The narrative had been stimulated by a particularly haunting image of a little girl's dress, apparently washed up on a beach. In Wales we began the workshop with no preconceived idea about what the story of the dress might be – just that it had been found on a beach. In the three days we worked with the group of teachers, they developed a powerful story about loss, guilt and collective memory, in which the back-story of a little girl's disappearance was always present, but never discussed or explained. The work had been particularly successful, and I was interested to see what happened when it travelled. I knew that the workshop plans would need editing, and that I wanted the work to be much lighter in mood. Rather nervously, I asked James Thompson and Irene Fraser, both highly respected for their applied theatre work in Sri Lanka, what they thought about starting by laying out a little dress on the ground, and leading various activities through which the group would construct their own story about the little girl who owned the dress. There was nothing in the activities to suggest that she had died or disappeared – she would simply be an imagined character. There was a pause. In the village where I would be working, they told me, children had been murdered and their bodies washed up on the lagoon. Something that seemed very remote and imaginary in Wales felt painfully close.

I had to think again. I wanted the imagined world of the dramatic narrative to provide participants with a safe space, but this workshop was primarily intended to share models of professional practice rather than explore anything more personal. I made the decision that the girl would be imagined rather than enacted, and I hoped that this ambiguity would enable the group to create the story they wanted to tell. If it were too close to reality, there would be no space for the imagination, and only one possible story – that the little girl had been murdered in the civil war. I decided to change the tense from past to future. I still used the dress, but told the group that it belonged to a girl who had grown out of it, and who was alive and well and living locally. The narrative focused on her future, beginning with a comic representation of helping a wriggling and unco-operative child struggle into a dress which was too small for her, and moving into adult gossip about her sense of mischief. But despite my intentions, I was surprised how quickly the participants chose to create her back-story, with one group turning what I had expected to be a light-hearted scene about a prank into a far more harrowing story of the beatings she had received during the war. This was the participants' choice. In response to the same activity another group devised a very witty scene complete with two children commenting on the girl's antics in scandalised tones from inside an imaginary television. Gradually, however, a picture was emerging of an unhappy child, and the group wanted to offer an explanation for what they portrayed as her bad behaviour. They did not seem interested in apportioning blame, and the atmosphere in the workshop did not seem at all tense, but I was concerned that the workshop was being taken in directions I had not anticipated and which might be inappropriate in this context. I made the decision not to intervene and this enabled the story they wished to tell to emerge. But by the end of the workshop it seemed important to think again about the future, and I put the little girl's dress back in the centre of the circle. Following their cues, I told the group that she had woken in the night with nightmares and that, in my country, there is a tradition of singing lullabies to children if they are scared. I joined the other two British participants in singing a lullaby in English, and the other participants followed with a song in Tamil, with each person in turn making a wish for her future, the dialogue underscored by the local lullaby. In that context, this moment was almost unbearably moving. The story the group had created was of a child who had been damaged and traumatised by the violence she had experienced and seen. This had not been my intention, but this was not my story. It was theirs.

What I had not anticipated was how closely the imaginary character of the girl and the fictional narrative of the drama would reflect reality, and how closely the participants would identify with her situation. As a cultural outsider, and particularly as someone who has never experienced war at first hand, I was very conscious that there was a huge gap between my life and those of the participants. For example, one group had used the drama to satirise the daily routines of confronting armed guards, meeting curfews and coping with military occupation, and this was received with a hearty laughter of recognition, but to me the scene brought home the reality of living in a war zone which was far more troubling. I had been open about the fact that I was offering a workshop similar to those I run in the UK, and it was offered in the spirit of intercultural dialogue and exchange of practice rather than anything else; the practitioners with whom I worked were perfectly able to discern which elements were useful to them and which were not, and the children ran in and out of the workshop as they wished. The content of the story was created by the group, but I had created a narrative structure for the drama which assumed that the girl's actions could be explained in terms resonant with Western models of psychology. I thought that all I had done was offer a structure for the workshop, leaving the work as open-ended as possible, but had I insidiously exported my own values and assumptions? In the workshop, the child was a trope, or in Ricoeur's words an 'imaginative space', who became the object of the participants' sympathy, and on whom they projected their own ideas and feelings. This was integral to the narrative structure. I had learnt that Western models of psychology were ineffective with traumatised victims of the war in Sri Lanka and, although it was not my intention to enter this territory, I wondered how far I had naturalised my own culturally specific ideas of the narrative construction of selfhood.

James Thompson has analysed a similar confrontation between fictional and real narratives in his work during the war in Sri Lanka, arguing that encouraging participants to see situations in the drama from multiple perspectives revealed his own ethical values. In the course of a drama about the occupation of the participants' town, he had asked a group to find imaginative sympathy with a soldier who was part of the occupying force. He described how 'he sought to complicate the single narrative' but in the process was concerned that he was 'also undermining the single-minded sense of direction that a community in struggle needs if it is to overcome virulent oppression'.[7] Similarly, my own concern with challenging fixed perceptions of identity and difference in drama, and encouraging multiple affiliations, seemed inappropriate and hollow in a context where the participants had their cultural identities systematically denied by a brutal occupying force.

On the same day as I ran my workshop, Sithmparanathan, a Tamil leader and theatre director, had argued that the liminal space of ritual is the 'theatre of liberation'. Through these local tools of cultural expression, he argued, 'deep feelings' might be released.[8] My point is that, however much a group seems to own a story, there are undoubtedly cultural assumptions – ideas of individuality, for example – hidden in the aesthetics of storytelling, embedded in different narrative genres and therefore structured into even the most open-ended workshops. Seen in this light, the narrative structures of workshops are never innocent; they lead the participants' imaginative journey. It would be good to think that my own workshop was part of a rich intercultural dialogue and exchange, and certainly the feedback I received suggested that many of the strategies I used would be effective in work with children in the Sri Lankan context. However, given the history of colonialism in Sri Lanka, I also thought that the generous participants who took part in my workshop would have been right to be suspicious of British people bearing gifts, even if they were wrapped as fictional stories in well-intentioned drama workshops.[9]

Identity and Identification

My reading of the workshop in Sri Lanka raises questions about the cultural politics of narrative, and the impact of working with narrative in drama warrants further theorising. Many forms of drama rely on the convergence of different narratives because participants bring a range of ideas and experiences to the drama. This means that, from the perspective of any one participant, there is always a triangulation between their own narratives of identity, the narratives of others and the narratives of the drama itself which needs to be negotiated. My suggestion is that an understanding of this negotiation between different narrative perspectives – both real and fictional – might be helped by an understanding of the concept of identification. I have already raised this concept in relation to debates about citizenship, where I have suggested that citizenship is not solely a legal status, but that active citizenship is based on collective forms of social identification. There are two ways of looking at identification which seem particularly germane to debates about selfhood and social action. The first builds on the work of Freud that has influenced subsequent thinkers in the field of psychoanalysis, and the second draws on Brecht's critique of 'identification' in theatre (a term he sometimes used interchangeably with 'empathy'). I am interested in whether it is feasible that it is identification with different narratives which offers participants in drama the opportunity to bridge the gap between self and other, identity and difference, and to mark points of contact between fiction and lived experience.

At the centre of Freud's writing about identification there is an ambivalence about how far it threatens or subsumes identity, and how far it acts as a more positive force for self-creation. His writing presents different and sometimes conflicting arguments about the relationship between identification and identity. My aim here is to use two of Freud's key texts on identification, 'On Narcissism' (1914) and 'Group Psychology and the Analysis of the Ego' (1921), to sketch some of the ways in which his thinking might be applied to drama. In his early essay 'On Narcissism' his account of the transition from self-love to love of others turns on the process of identification. Childhood, he argued, is a narcissistic phase in which identification with others is uncritical, purely mimetic, based on self-love rather than a love which recognises others as separate people. This primary identification is sometimes extended into adulthood, where love of others remains fixed at the narcissistic phase, based on an identification with an ideal and idealised other, invoking the all-consuming emotional attachments of childhood. At this point in his writings, identification was inextricably tied to narcissism or, conversely, to the other key theme in his writing, hysteria. In *The Interpretation of Dreams* (1900) Freud interestingly described the 'secondary identification' of hysterics as a theatrical metaphor. Hysterics, he argued, are able 'to suffer on behalf of a whole crowd of people and to act all the parts in the play single-handed'.[10] Taken together, these two ways of thinking suggest a double-bind; primary identification with others is associated with a narcissistic sense of self, where love of others is a regressive search for the lost Narcissism of childhood, whereas secondary identification is a symptom and cause of an unstable identity, where the hysterics' secure sense of self is threatened by fantasies about their over-powerful effect on others. Neither version is likely to be attractive to practitioners in applied drama.

Perhaps more productive for drama practitioners is the revision of the concept of 'secondary identification', both by Freud in his later writings and by subsequent psychoanalytic theorists. Loosened from its negative association with hysteria, secondary identification can be very enriching. The theatrical metaphor Freud used in 1900 to describe secondary identification already signified its social dynamic, and his emphasis on identification *with regard* to another person, rather than just *with* them, signified the significance of social relationships and emotional attachments between people. It is in 'Group Psychology and the Analysis of the Ego' that Freud qualified his earlier position by recognising that secondary identification allows for personal development, and that relationships with others can lead to 'new perceptions'.[11] Unlike primary identification, where individuals are unable to distinguish between themselves and others, this kind of identification has much clearer boundaries. Social relationships are entered into, and emotional attachments are formed on the basis of recognising that other people are *not* oneself, and that they have distinct identities of their own. It is from this position of self-awareness that individuals might learn to see identification not as a violation of identity, but as a potentially positive dynamic in the process of self-creativity. In this sense, identification both produces and destabilises identity.

A Freudian conception of identification, therefore, offers a way of thinking about the relationship between self and other which both recognises its potential for self-development and warns against a loss of identity. Although Freud was obviously analysing relationships between people, his discussion of identification also has implications for engagement with the arts. Hélène Cixous has articulated the relationship between identity and identification in relation to reading:

> One never reads except by identification. But . . . [w]hen I say identification I do not say a loss of self. I become. I inhabit. I enter. Inhabiting someone at that moment I can feel myself traversed by the person's initiatives and actions.[12]

This kind of identification relies on metaxis – a sense of being both in the world of the story and outside it. In these terms, identification with fictional narratives involves both a process of self-reflexivity and emotional engagement with others. Drama, which invites multiple forms of identification, is potentially a very good vehicle for extending understanding of oneself in relation to others. Physical embodiment of the narratives of others can be a particularly powerful way to 'become' another temporarily or to 'inhabit' another's story. Cixous also pointed out that because the process of identification may challenge or affirm patterns of identity, there is no guarantee that it is a consoling experience. There is an ethical ambiguity here. On the one hand, although challenges to fixed patterns of identity may feel threatening, they may also lead to psychological liberation through which new social identities may be formed. On the other, there is no guarantee that identification with others, however life-changing, will be for the better (regardless of how the term 'better' is construed).

In psychoanalytic terms, identification has an historical dimension, as identity is formed through a life-time of identifying with others. The question that Freudian theories of identification fail to address, however, is concerned with its social and cultural meanings. There is a political dynamic to any discussion of self and otherness, which has been particularly powerfully articulated by feminist and post-colonial theorists, whereby identification with a dominant 'self' has, historically, created a marginalised and objectified 'other'. In other words, there is no certainty that identifying with multiple narratives in drama, as elsewhere, leads to social equality. This is central to Brecht's objections to identification (and empathy) in theatre, which he regarded as essentially conservative. He argued that identifying with characters inhibits spectators' ability to contrast the circumstances of their own lives with those portrayed on stage. For Brecht, this kind of identification perpetuates a familiarity or sameness rather than prompting change – in Freudian terms, it is solely narcissistic. Brecht was similarly scathing about the concept of a coherent identity or ego, which he regarded as a bourgeois myth. In these terms, the comforting elision between identification and identity had no place in Brecht's theatre. However, in the *Appendices to the Short Organum*, Brecht showed his awareness of the theatrical power of disrupting spectators' identification with characters on stage, and pragmatically suggested that this device might be used to challenge their political assumptions:

> However dogmatic it may seem to insist that self-identification with the character should be avoided in the performance, our generation can listen to this warning with advantage. However determinedly they obey it they can hardly carry it out to the letter, so the most likely result is that truly rending contradiction between experience and portrayal, empathy and demonstration, justification and criticism, which is what is aimed at.[13]

It is clear from this that Brecht placed qualities of self-identification such as 'experience', 'empathy' and 'justification' in opposition to 'portrayal', 'demonstration' and 'criticism' – terms he associated with more radical forms of social inquiry. What Brecht does value, however, is the spectators' identification with the *performers*, and he expected that this would de-naturalise and unfix any bourgeois illusions which might arise from identifying with *characters*. In an interesting passage, he explained how spectators might observe and critique their own social positions through identification with the performers:

> The performers' self-observation, as an artful and artistic act of self-alienation, stopped the spectator from losing himself in the character completely, i.e. to the point of giving up his own identity, and lent a splendid remoteness to the events. Yet the spectators' empathy was not entirely rejected. The audience identifies itself as being an observer, and accordingly develops his attitude of observing or looking on.[14]

This elision of self-identity, self-observation and self-alienation suggests that, in Brecht's theatre, some forms of identification have interventionist potential. It is not Freud's 'affective identification', but a cognitive process whereby established social and cultural meanings can be recognised and historicised.

What is useful about the unlikely combination of Freud's and Brecht's conceptualisation of identification is that it focuses attention on both the affective and the cognitive, on the potential for both social change and psychological development. In different ways, both writers accept that identity is constructed through a sedimented history of identifications, a process which has the potential to either shore up established patterns – either social or personal – or to destabilise them. Both perspectives are informed by epistemologies based on modernist conceptions of the subject. Distancing herself from this essentialism, Teresa Brenan has pointed out that from a psychoanalytic point of view social identification with others is not in itself necessarily transformative. She conceded, however, that 'multiple identifications' with the narratives of others may produce 'a way of coming to terms with the images one receives from others', a process which 'permits different thinking'.[15] This implies that identification with a multiplicity of narratives in drama has the potential to wear away fixed narratives of self and other, identity and difference, and open the spaces in-between where new insights might be generated.

Empathy and the Social Imagination: Plays and Players

In this section I should like to tease out some of the implications of applied drama for identification with dramatic narratives as both performers and as members of audiences. Playing roles is experientially different from seeing plays, and the premise that breaking down theatrical illusion is socially liberating has been accepted in many different practices in applied drama. Practices in applied drama are frequently explicitly designed to erode divisions and hierarchies between performers and audiences – Boal's hybridised 'spect-actor' is the most obvious example. As applied drama always encourages involvement and participation, there are many ways of working which challenge the acute separation between performer and audience that exists in some forms of theatre. This impulse takes Brecht's exhortation for audiences to identify *with* the performers to its logical next stage, in which participants are asked to identify themselves *as* performers. It is this distinction I am interested in exploring in this section, and I want to ask some further questions about the concepts of empathy and identification in relation to the moral and social imagination.

The example I would like to use to explore these ideas comes from Theatre in Education, which is well known for its history of encouraging engagement with social and moral issues through and in drama. The play I have chosen to discuss is Alistair Campbell's play *Anansi*, which was originally written for professional actors to perform *to* a clearly defined target audience of young people, but since its publication in script form it has been available *for* young people to perform themselves. This gives me the opportunity to consider the differences between the empathetic responses of an audience to the play and the potential for the young people's learning when they identify themselves as performers. Another reason for choosing this play is because it addresses the social significance of the imagination directly, which in itself raises questions about the role of traditional tales in relationship to moral education.

The play tells the story of the slave trade, and the action takes place on a slave ship journeying from Africa to its destination in the Caribbean. Above the hold, the captain's son is on his first expedition, and is horrified by the way the cargo of slaves is treated. In the hold, a dying old woman tells traditional stories to a girl in the darkness. She tells the Girl stories of Anansi, a trickster spiderman from African folklore, who outwits danger and survives against the odds. Theatrically, there is a strong contrast between the bleak 'reality' of the ship and the colour, energy and humour of the world of the imagination, 'a forest full of stories'. This juxtaposition ensures that the audience is particularly receptive to the moral lesson within the traditional tales, and also underlines the brutal history of the slave trade. This clear dialectic between reality and fiction, slavery and freedom, cruelty and resistance gives the play an unambiguous moral message, and the audience is positioned to condemn the evils of racism and admire the power of the imagination to overcome human degradation.

The play demonstrates the moral function of traditional tales. By teaching her stories from the oral tradition of Africa, the old woman gives the Girl an emotional and moral strength which is not just a personal solace, but symbolises the spirit of her culture, which she can preserve in her memory. The old woman comments that stories 'are a treasure no-one can steal, even if they have stolen your body'.[16] The suggestion that traditional stories have the power to restore the soul in the face of oppression and physical abuse is central to the play, and the audience is not asked to question this view. Within each of the stories themselves, the audience (and the Girl) is invited to identify with Anansi as he repeatedly saves himself through a combination of mischief and cunning, outwitting bigger and fiercer animals. It is not difficult to see why children might identify with this trickster, nor why he symbolises resistance against oppression. This is a good illustration of the neo-Aristotelian philosopher Alasdair MacIntyre's view that traditional tales serve a moral purpose in society, providing an education in virtue. He expresses the moral importance of traditional tales in apocalyptic terms:

> Deprive children of stories and you leave them unscripted, anxious stutterers in their actions as in their words. Hence there is no way to give us an understanding of any society, including our own, except through the stock of stories which constitute its initial dramatic resources.... And so too of course is that moral tradition from heroic society to its medieval heirs according to which the telling of stories has a key part in educating us into the virtues.[17]

MacIntyre accepts, somewhat schematically, that lessons from stories will be assimilated into the practice of everyday life. In this, he has ignored reader-response theories which suggest that readers (or audiences) bring their own values to textual interpretation. Furthermore, he has assumed that traditional tales generally offer examples of contemporary notions of virtue, and that in turn children will accept the moral message largely without question.[18] In both form and content, an uncritical reading of Campbell's *Anansi* play would endorse this view. The play also chimes well with Walter Benjamin's ethical storyteller, and the dramatic function of the old woman is to offer exactly the kind of practical wisdom to the Girl which Benjamin advocated. What I am interested in questioning, however, is how the play delivers its central moral message and what political values or perspectives are embedded in the narrative structure.

On the surface, Campbell's *Anansi* is a good example of a theatrical essay on moral education. Written as a performance text for adults to perform to children, the narrative structure leads audiences to empathise with the black girl who is destined for a life of slavery, but it is the character of the white Boy with whom they are invited to identify. His role provides the bridge between the audience and the world of the play. His horror at the conditions of the cargo of slaves, and his small acts of kindness towards them, constructs the not unreasonable expectation that the audience will be similarly appalled and he gives their anxieties a theatrical voice. An interesting exchange between the Boy and a Sailor after he has seen the Girl in the ship's hold exemplifies the play's dialectic.

> *Sailor*:   Slaves are different . . . more like, beasts, or so they reckon.
> *Boy*:   It isn't true! I saw a girl today, down . . . down there . . .
> *Sailor*:   Your trouble is too much imagination. You think too much and some thoughts are dangerous.
> *Boy*:   But she wasn't a beast! She was just like me![19]

The idea that the Girl is 'just like me' indicates the play's liberalism. There is a clear opposition set up between being a 'beast' and being 'like me' which further confirms the audience's identification with the Boy. Not only do his words guide the audience's feelings about slavery, but it is through his character that they are given a vision of social equality which has more contemporary resonance. At this moment in the play, seeing a black character as 'just like' a white character is clearly intended to indicate racial equality. There is, however, a political distinction to be made here between the audience's identification with the Boy (they feel themselves to be in his place) and empathy with the Girl (they feel pity towards her situation). The audience is positioned to feel compassion for the Girl, to pity her situation, but to recognise themselves in the Boy, who has witnessed slavery and may be able to use his experiences to bring about social change. This reading would suggest that the play anticipates a white audience and that it was written from a white perspective.

It is this relationship between identification, empathy and the social imagination which I wish to tease out a little further as it has significant implications for practice in applied drama. In an essay entitled 'The

Risks of Empathy', Megan Boler cites Aristotelian ideas of pity to argue that empathy creates politically passive readers. Empathetic readings, she argued, may induce pity but not action, and she denies that the social imagination is educated into an understanding of difference or suffering through this kind of compassionate reading. Boler offered a critical reading of Martha Nussbaum's view that readers might 'know the other' and understand how others feel through empathetic engagement with their narratives. I have some sympathy with this view, and I remain sceptical about some of the grander claims, for example that drama enables participants to know what it was like to live in specific social circumstances. I don't believe, for example, that walking around for an hour with a blindfold enables me to know what it is like to be blind, although it may give me a little understanding of some of the ways in which I rely on my sight. Boler argued that passive empathy is too comfortably pleasurable; it shores up the status quo by allowing readers to 'consume' the other, exonerating them from blame 'through the denial of power relations' which produce social injustice. A socially responsible reading, according to Boler, is based on the idea of testimony, in which readers recognise the historical specificity of the narrative rather than its universality, and in which readership is a collective process which requires 'self-reflective participation' rather than individualised empathetic consumption.[20]

Boler and Nussbaum both focused their discussion on reading literary narratives, especially novels, and it would appear that Boler's conclusion advocates the kind of collective readership and self-reflective engagement with narrative which is intrinsic to drama as a multi-dimensional and collaborative art form. I think it is worth probing ideas of empathy and identification a little further, and to do this I shall return to the *Anansi* play for a moment. On the surface, this play could be read as a rather cosy narrative in which the audience is exonerated from any social responsibility for the history of British racism because they empathise with a character whose imagination and cultural traditions protect her from some of the worst conditions humanity can inflict. But this reading would not account for the audience's identification with the Boy, who is complicit in her captivity, but is disturbed by it. In this context it is empathy for the Girl which engages their emotions, which hooks them into the narrative, but it is their identification with the Boy which stimulates moral debate. I have seen skilful teachers take this opportunity to ask young people to take their identification with the Boy to its logical conclusion by asking what they would do in his situation, and how they would react to racist acts they might witness today. What Boler fails to acknowledge is that empathy and identification are not always the same thing. She is right to point out that empathy can induce a comfortable passivity because it relies on an understanding that the reader is not in the same situation as the character with whom she is empathising. She does not, however, take on board that identification with others can be a rather less comfortable affair because, if Freud is to be believed, it has the potential to challenge one's own sense of identity.

If empathetic responses to theatre were left unquestioned, I would probably agree with Boal that empathy can be a 'terrible weapon' in which 'the *man* relinquishes his power of decision to the image' (his italics).[21] But his view presupposes that the man is sitting passively in the audience rather than constructing the image for himself as a performer, or deconstructing the image as a critical audience member. It suggests, in other words, that empathetic responses are not off-set by any other forms of social identification. I am not, therefore, critical of plays that are written from particular perspectives on the grounds of political correctness. On the contrary, I am interested in the implications of inhabiting the dramatic narrative and embodying roles which may or may not be appealing, and which may represent values and ideas which may be personally or politically challenging. Boler also suggested that one way to disrupt passive readings is to analyse how empathy is produced 'within networks of power relations represented by reader and text, mediated by language'.[22] Extended to the embodied and physical languages of drama, this suggests that an understanding of how dramatic narratives are constructed and performed might illuminate *how* empathy is elicited from the audience. This opportunity for learning has been recognised by Andy Kempe, who has pointed out that 'to understand a play in terms of its potential in performance demands that its readers are aware of their own position in relation to the text'.[23] If young people perform *Anansi*, for example, they will inevitably have to consider how to portray the roles of the Captain or the Sailors, who have no redeeming features. This process is not intended to help them to know what it would have been like to work in the slave trade, nor to feel empathy for the traders, but to explore the dramatic function of role, and through this portray the brutality to which the play bears witness. This way of working is intended to trouble passively empathetic responses to the play by considering how ideas are constructed and represented. This dialectic, described by Kathleen Gallagher as the 'points of intersection *and* confrontation', derives from locating oneself in relation to others, through recognising the parallels and differences between one's own values, feelings and situation and those of others.

Embodied Narratives

From the point of view of practice in applied drama, one of the central elements missing from the various analyses of the effect and effectiveness of narrative offered by Boler, Nussbaum and MacIntyre is a concept of the performative. Performance always unfixes and, because narratives in drama are embodied and made in collaboration with others, their meanings are always multi-layered. One of the distinguishing character-istics of applied drama is that the focus of attention is on the experience of participants, and their ability to work together in different ways – both in and out of role – is often of central importance. Participants and practitioners will identify or empathise not only with the narratives of the drama but also with each other, and this is often seen as a powerful part of the process. This means that, as John O'Toole has pointed out, in applied drama the distinctions between identity, role, acting and performance are often complexly interwoven.[24]

Theoretical debates about acting, performance and dramatic role-play have become increasingly nuanced, particularly as questions about the formation of social identity have impacted on performance studies. It once seemed quite obvious to assume that acting was the job of actors and usually seen in theatres, and that performance was an event for which you could buy tickets. With these relatively uncomplicated descriptions firmly in place, dramatic role-play seemed the most flexible and democratic activity, spanning a range of activities including childhood play, spontaneous improvisation and other forms of role-taking often in fictional or fictionalised contexts.[25] Given this history, it is unsurprising that, as a methodology, working in role has had an enduring appeal for practitioners in many different aspects of applied drama, where it has valued its apparent authenticity, flexibility and immediacy over the artificiality and staginess sometimes associated with acting and performance. Challenges to assumptions about such distinctions between role, acting and performance have been many and varied. The onslaught has been led by philosophical readings of identity formation, where the Enlightenment ideal of the autonomous individual has given way to the idea that identity is constructed and deconstructed as a dynamic and interactive process of narration, performance and representation.[26] There are two interrelated points which I should like to extract from this debate. The first is concerned with the implications of social interaction between participants, and the second relates theories of role and performance to practice in applied drama.

Peggy Phelan has pointed out that social interaction in theatre is primarily a negotiation between cultural production and power. Much Western theatre, she argues, 'evokes desire based on and stimulated by the inequality between performer and spectator'. Phelan invokes Foucault's analysis of the authority of the spectators' gaze to suggest the locus of power is not with the performers, but with the audience. In many forms of Western theatre, she argues, the dramatic narrative is constructed according to a perception of the spectators' desires, and this controls the theatrical exchange between audience and performer. This creates a point of view that is clear and easy to identify, but it also assumes conventional values and perspectives. She concludes:

> Redesigning the relationship between self and other, subject and object, sound and image, man and woman, spectator and performer, is enormously difficult.[27]

My suggestion is that, although applied drama is often explicitly concerned with analysing how images and narratives are constructed and interrupting predictable and inequitable points of view, its practices are not exempt from this difficulty. There are, as I have already argued, cultural assumptions in the way in which drama workshops are constructed. There are further questions to be asked about the ways in which perceptions of another's desire govern other forms of social interaction, and in what ways these perceptions might be amplified or challenged when participants in drama work in role.

Performance has long been a metaphor for all kinds of social behaviour, and Phelan's observations about the construction and location of power in theatre have wider implications. The idea that people act and interact according to their expectations of others is not confined to theatrical production, and has been well theorised by social scientists and performance theorists alike. Amongst the earliest and most influential was Erving Goffman, whose theories of performativity demonstrated that everyday social encounters are shaped by people's understanding of their roles within given situations.[28] When this insight is combined with Foucauldian analysis of performative exchanges, it suggests that all interactions and social identities are built on a negotiation of power, which includes people's perceptions of themselves in relation to others. This interweaving of roles has the effect of defining everyone in the social encounter, and suggests that role-playing – either explicitly dramatic or in more everyday interactions – is always complicated by issues of power and social context. It certainly challenges the perception that naturalistic role play is the most successful way in which the 'real' or authentic voice of the participant might be represented, and further suggests that role-playing, acting and performance are on a continuum rather than being separate modes of activity.

One of the central arguments in this chapter is that drama is a good vehicle through which participants might experiment with different identities and test out new ways of being. Although I am sure that drama can make a contribution to the process of *becoming* by shaping autobiographies and changing social narratives, I have expressed some scepticism about claims that drama always transforms beliefs and attitudes for the better. This is based on the understanding that no social encounter – including drama workshops – is exempt from other social narratives and alternative perceptions of power. It is often difficult to gauge the social effects of drama immediately, and when I read that participants have expressed profound changes in attitudes I often wonder whether they have been complicit in following the script of the workshop, or whether their change of heart indicates a positive but temporary identification with a kindly practitioner whose point of view may not be actually expressed, but whose values are nonetheless clearly visible to them.[29]

The process of embodying narratives in drama has the potential to trouble inequitable boundaries between the real and the fictional, between self and other, subject and object. Replotting these relationships draws attention to the performative, and this extends applied drama beyond an emphasis on role and situation and creating new narratives by using the rich and varied traditions of theatre and innovations in the arts of performance. It suggests that changing stories involves looking not just at the narratives themselves, but at how they are constructed, where assumptions of power are made, and whose values they represent.

5 Community Narratives: Space, Place and Time

In my country

walking by the waters
down where an honest river
shakes hands with the sea,
a woman passed round me
in a slow watchful circle,
as if I were a superstition;

or the worst dregs of her imagination,
so when she finally spoke
her words spliced into bars
of an old wheel. A segment of air.
Where do you come from?
'Here,' I said, 'Here. These parts.'

Jackie Kay, 'In My Country', *Other Lovers* (1993)

Questions of Community

A sentimental picture of local communities as comfortable social systems has re-entered the popular imagination and has been much used by politicians in their rhetoric, with positive connotations of interpersonal warmth, shared interests and local loyalty. Jackie Kay's autobiographical poem would challenge this image. Kay's experience of her 'honest' local landscape in Scotland is marred by the hurtful suspicion of those who assume that she does not belong there, and with the racist implication that she, as a black woman, is not welcomed by the 'locals'. Communities, as Iris Marion Young argues, are idealised symbolic constructions that not only bind people together but which also act as powerful means of exclusion, separating 'us' from 'them'.[1] If this is the case, the construction and shaping of local communities, a recurring theme in applied drama, is not so much a matter of recovering or rediscovering the lost narratives of a homogeneous past, but of making a contribution to redefining their actual and symbolic boundaries in the present and for the future.

It is interesting that there has been a renewed emphasis on the ideal of community at a time when an actual sense of belonging has become increasingly problematic. It is tempting to believe that creating hetero-geneous local communities will come to the rescue of beleaguered and fractured political economies. Location does play a central part in the narratives of identity, and how people feel about where they live, where they feel they belong and their daily social interactions is an important factor in their psychological well-being. But there are many different types of community, of which communities of location are but one form. In terms of community-building, therefore, drama projects that focus on straightforward constructions of local identity, shared histories and ideological unity to the exclusion of difference and diversity, are likely to reinforce the more conservative images of 'otherness' sometimes associated with localism (as evoked in Jackie Kay's poem). In part, this conservatism surrounding images of localism explains the paradigm shift from communities of locality to communities of identity, where the ideal of community has been de-territorialised and allied to mobility rather than stability, to the possibility of multiple identities rather than those simply inscribed through geographical location. Building inclusive communities of location in a pluralist society would, therefore, challenge the ideal of a common culture. It would aim to take account of competing narratives of interest, identification and identity and to recognise the different values and perspectives with which they are accompanied.

The shift in emphasis from the idealisation of homogeneous local communities to more varied forms of collective identification is largely indebted to the work of Benedict Anderson. Since Anderson suggested that communities are 'imagined' by those who share interests and other forms of mutual identification rather than restricted to face-to-face interactions or locality, there has been an increased interest in how dispersed populations maintain a sense of a collective or shared identity. The idea of an 'imagined community', through which people maintain feelings of connectedness with those outside their geographical area, has effectively loosened the idea of community from its idealisation as a local and bounded set of practices and expanded the cultural field.[2] The work of Avtar Brah has extended this debate by taking the condition of diaspora as a basis for narratives of community. She argues that identity is a 'context-specific construction', an on-going process in which a sense of self is developed in relation to those in *both* local and imagined communities.[3] In broad terms, Brah stresses the positive attributes of social identities forged in multiple contexts. Politically, she is critical of essentialist ideas of difference and identity, arguing that immutable conceptualisations of communities, nationalities or identities are likely to be used to support cultural hierarchies or deepen social division.

Recently, however, the idea that communities are imagined, and sustained through a continual negotiation of difference and identity, has found its critics. Vered Amit's analysis of conceptions and practices of community concludes that a sense of belonging is more likely to arise from informal social groups and networks rather than ephemeral but deterministic social 'categories' (such as social class, religion, race, sexuality, gender, nation or ethnicity). She is particularly critical of the rhetoric of diaspora and multiculturalism, which invokes borderlands and marginality without acknowledging the social content of transnational movement, and the real sense of anxiety and suffering experienced by those displaced. 'The greater the claims for their revolutionary and empowering possibilities,' she argues, 'the more nebulous and metaphorical these representations of categorical difference become.'[4] Amit has pointed out that the actual construction of communities always needs rather more effort than deterministic categories of identity might suggest. She argues that social practice is rather more flexible:

> [T]he most common avenues for forming a sense of fellowship, of belonging and social connection are realised through modest daily practices that are not often marked by symbolic categorical identities. These are people and identities loosely known as friends, neighbours, workmates, companions in a variety of leisure, parenting, schooling, political activities. Many of these associations are limited in time and space to particular places and activities.[5]

Amit's argument rests on the claim that social groups and networks are fluid and temporal, based on everyday interactions and associations. Put simply, people make friends, form social groups or develop networks because they like one another and because they have experiences and interests in common at the time.

Amit's theoretical discussion of the workings of groupings offers an important reminder of the social significance of emotional bonds, a key concept in the feminist theory of the ethic of care. Although Amit recognises that relationships may strengthen or wane over time, she suggests that communities are built on personal networks forged in present situations rather than on identification with collective histories. Her analysis lacks a sense of the complexities of cultural histories, and she emphasises those social networks which are found in the immediacy of lived experience and which have short memories. By contrast, Brah places an emphasis on the significance of the interplay between collective and personal histories in identity formation. She argues that feelings of community may be created by those who have 'shared collective narratives', even though personal testament and collective memories may tell different stories, and these narratives may frequently unsettle or contradict each other.[6] How meanings are ascribed to these interwoven narratives of self and community becomes, therefore, not a search for an 'unmediated truth' but a more creative process of invention and speculation.

Despite differences of inflection, Avtar Brah and Vered Amit share an understanding that social relations are negotiated and redefined through dynamic processes of interaction, communication and shared experiences. In this chapter I shall interrogate different conceptualisations of community in relation to applied drama projects which aim to represent and interpret personal, historical and collective narratives. Theatrical experiments in rewriting local stories seem like a good place to start to dismantle the kind of fixed ideas of community implied in Jackie Kay's poem, and to examine the possibilities of creating positive social networks through drama. Following Brah, I want to explore how imaginative interpretations of history might intervene in the future by relocating past identities in the performative present. I shall also consider, following Amit, how drama might create a sense of belonging through the social networks and friendships fostered by working together.

Communities and Location

I should like to start by looking at applied drama in relation to communities of location, where networks are forged by people who live geographically close to one another. This is often considered to be an ideal, where people in the same locality share mutually supportive relationships. Deconstructive analyses of communities of location, however, tend to revolve around two basic perceptions. One common argument is that communities of location are often romanticised, harking back to an imagined era in which homogeneity, unity and shared values formed the basis of social interaction. A related position, developed particularly by feminists, is that localism has had the effect of keeping people in their place, of entrapping the poor and confining women to the sphere of the domestic. More positively, as Amit has pointed out, people often rely on their locality for day-to-day companionship, support, a sense of security and well-being. This double-bind has been recognised by feminist theorist Elspeth Probyn, who has analysed both the potential and the limitations of communities of location. She described the local as 'only a fragmented set of possibilities', which can be restrictive if they are fixed at a moment of time, but 'to take the local not as the end point, but as the start' has greater social potential.[7] My experience of working practically in communities of locality has led me to believe that they are often rather messy and imprecise places, which means that thinking about the local as 'a fragmented set of possibilities' serves as a useful idea with which to begin this analysis of practice.

The project I shall discuss was an intergenerational drama project based in a city secondary school. Schools can provide an important meeting place for local people, and significant social networks can develop from this focus. Few of us, however, escape experiencing complex and contra-dictory emotions when visiting local schools, especially if we attended them, and this had particular implications for the intergenerational theatre projects I directed in urban schools in the early 1990s. Schools are not neutral spaces. Former pupils often experience an ambiguous sense of belonging and not belonging, a strange and unsettling feeling of walking through a film set of their lives. Others may have feelings of exclusion from institutional cultures, or be constrained by self-regulation, feeling they should in some way 'behave themselves'. Empty schools, like empty theatres, are full of ghosts. Schools are not like grave yards, static monuments to past lives, but they are none the less haunted by expectation – memories of what generations of pupils hoped they would become. They feel like archaeological sites, restless with hundreds of shards of half-remembered stories. This means that community-based performances held in schools or other venues of local significance always have elements of the site-specific. The performance space may be transformed physically and aesthetically from ordinary school hall to theatre but there is always the ghost of the past haunting the place. Mike Pearson and Michael Shanks described this aspect of site-specific work as a balance between 'the host and the ghost', a negotiation between the contemporary and the historical in which 'no single story is being told'.[8]

The image of hosts and ghosts is particularly relevant for drama projects undertaken in a local context in which the 'host community' had not always been welcoming to outsiders. The dramatisation of oral histories, however, even within the relative confines of a school, ensures that private narratives enter the public domain, a process that means that contentious social 'issues' or community 'problems' are dissipated as they become associated with familiar people. In one project I ran in the late 1980s the process was intensified by the young people's sense of disaffection with their place in society and in the local area. Thatcherism had systematically destroyed local industries, adult unemployment was long term and high. One of my duties as a teacher was to check the colour of the boys' bootlaces – white laces signified membership of the National Front, a neo-fascist organisation that had gained strength in the white 'community' as a result of local poverty. There had been race riots in the city earlier in the decade, and although the area surrounding the school was ethnically mixed, there was little communication and few shared activities between families of different backgrounds, and interracial friendships forged in school had done little to overcome local prejudices.

The school had been built in the 1950s as part of the postwar comprehensive ideal, and it fiercely guarded its reputation for innovation and equality. A sustained period of industrial action by the teachers, however, had soured valued local links, perhaps most aptly symbolised by the fact that we were barred from the community centre at lunchtime (unpaid lunchtime supervision was a particular point of dispute), which meant that there were significant bridges to mend. The reminiscence projects began as part of a sustained programme of community liaison intended to develop a stronger sense of belonging and self-esteem for young people and a greater involvement of local people in education. By encouraging young people to work with people of different ages and from diverse sectors of the community, we hoped to provide opportunities for young people to extend the social space in which they lived and renegotiate its boundaries. Pedagogically, the project was multi-layered; it invited students to blur the boundaries between the factual and the artistic, and to consider how they negotiated questions of authority and authorship in relation to the theatrical construction of oral history.

The starting-point for the devised work involved the students interviewing people they knew – their grandparents and other elderly members of the local community – about events that had shaped their lives. For many young people, learning to listen presented real challenges, and I suspect that many covered their embarrassment about the potential emotional closeness of the situation by firing questions designed to elicit information rather than encouraging more personal reflections on experience. From the interviews the students conducted, however, two distinct narratives emerged. One concerned the experiences of those who moved to England from previously colonised countries during the 1960s, with one particularly lively account from Ahmed's uncle about pompous white immigration officials, lost children and bursting luggage providing the potential for strong characters and a good plot. The other story that captured the students' imagination was told by Lucy's grandmother, who had worked in the local cigarette factory during the Second World War, where flirtatious 'tobacco girls' put their names and addresses in cigarette packets destined to be sent to soldiers. Interestingly, both sets of stories were humorous. There appeared to be an element of self-censoring on the part of the people they interviewed that excluded more painful or difficult memories. As Portelli points out, it is often the silences and omissions in the stories that are most revealing: '[T]he most precious information may lie in what the informants *hide*, and in the fact they *do* hide it, rather than in what they *tell*.'[9]

It is possible to speculate about why more painful memories were hidden. Many interviewees had family relationships with the students, and they presumably selected aspects which they deemed appropriate to the context. More intimately, some stories were illustrated by treasured possessions: small, private momentos – an aeroplane ticket, a hat, a cigarette packet, immigration papers – which symbolised particular events. They also served to focus the students' attention on the content of the narratives, as visible signs of lived experience.

The process of editing and adapting the material into theatre form presented particular challenges. How are conversations interpreted? Whose stories are chosen for development in drama? Who controls the texts? Do the actors have the authority to fictionalise the stories? How are the narratives shaped? How is the work presented and received? Because I had not introduced the students to the idea that memories are continually revised in the retelling, they were concerned to tell the stories as 'authentically' and 'faithfully' as they could. However, I found this desire to *reproduce* events rather than *represent* them troubling. Some students expressed an understandable anxiety about misrepresenting the very personal stories they had been told, and responded to this by insisting on a dramatic form which was heavily dependent on naturalistic acting styles in linear and episodic dramatic structures. Their reluctance to experiment theatrically meant that their drama was limited by the confines of a form which, whilst it suited a rather simplistic retelling of events, did not really capture the ambiguity or emotions of memory. Conceptually, this suggested that the students had a partial understanding of the ways in which personal history is constructed in memory, accepting without question that everything that had been told was literally true. They were actively resistant to alternative readings, feeling with some justification that they should honour the personal narratives they had been told. This central dilemma – how to *both* validate the testimony of the original speaker *and* open the narratives for critical interrogation (or, in this case, creative interpretation) – has been theorised by oral historians. The Personal Narratives Group sum up the debate:

> When people talk about their lives, people lie sometimes, forget a little, exaggerate, become confused, get things wrong. Yet they are revealing truths . . . the guiding principle could be that all autobiographical memory is true: it is up to the interpreter to discover in what sense, where, and for what purpose.[10]

The idea that there are multiple interpretations of truth in autobiographical memory suggests that a dramatic style that relies heavily on naturalistic forms of representation is politically, as well as artistically, constricting. As Peta Tait convincingly argued, to represent social experience as a 'coherently ordered, stable pattern of reality' in theatre is implicitly to accept hegemonic values.[11]

To encourage the students to question the boundaries between the fictive and the real, I suggested that they asked to hear the stories again, this time listening particularly for *how* the speakers commented on past events, and to notice any differences in the details. The act of retelling personal experience creates, as Joan Sangster points out, a dialectical relationship between the past and present in which the speaker does not 'relive' events, but 'rewrites' them.[12] The students discovered that the description of past events was interwoven with new insights and explanatory comment, sometimes contextualising the moment, at other times pointing out how the events had influenced the tellers in later life. By acknowledging the similarities and differences between the past and the present, the students recognised how the storytellers situated themselves in the present whilst negotiating their relationship with the past. Observant students noticed how performative elements of the story-telling (use of voice, enactment and gesture, for example) suggested particular emotional connections with specific events; whilst the stories were not substantially different in content from the 'original', on second hearing it was noticeable that the interpretation and emphasis had often changed. They became aware of the rehearsed elements of autobiographical stories, where it was obvious from the 'performance' that they had been retold many times, and when the elderly people were recalling details of life events which they had not spoken about for many years.

The awareness that the tellers themselves moved between the past and the present, and between multiple 'realities', gave the students licence to break the pattern of linearity in their drama. Until that moment, the students had been searching, in Derridean terms, for the 'myth of origin' – for the single, unmediated presence of truth. The process of devising became more concerned with what Derrida described as *absence* rather than *presence*: the artefacts, tape recordings and other ephemera used as props symbolising the missing originators of the stories. This sense of absence weighed the participants down. Educationally it inhibited their development as theatre practitioners as they were reluctant to experiment with dramatic form. It also prevented them from trying out ideas spontaneously; they were not representing lived experience creatively, but were engaged in a form of ventriloquising. The process felt, and was, second hand. Furthermore, their insistence on accurate presentation of the material culture of the times, particularly in the form of props and costumes, had prevented them from asking more abstract questions about memory and the interpretation of the past in dramatic form. From the moment when they began to interrogate the stories more closely, they recognised the dialectic between past and present, and they wove this into their drama, using the comments they had heard to frame the dramatic action. This was used most interestingly by one group of students, who spoke in Urdu when representing the story of the past, and English for the contemporary commentary, fluctuating between the official and the domestic, indicating multiple identities symbolised in powerful dramatic moments.

The shift in emphasis from 'authentic' reproduction to dramatic representation moved the work from an unmediated and uncritical retelling to a popular theatrical aesthetic. By introducing a few Brechtian 'devices' such as montage and popular songs of the period, they succeeded in creating a dramatic atmosphere that, to borrow John McGrath's phrase, made the shows a 'good night out'. Some elderly members of the community had small walk-on parts and were sometimes seen at different ages on excerpts of ciné film (recorded before the days of video!), and audience members joined in the songs. The problem with the performance was the use of theatre form, as this proved quite limiting. The process of working had used standard drama education techniques designed to disrupt narrative closure, leading to moments of reflection and political comment in performance, but the effect of the devised plays was still nostalgic, celebratory and safe rather than challenging. There was also little in the form or performance style which included the artistic traditions or popular culture of elders in the south Asian families; it was almost entirely based on a Western performance aesthetic. Some of the stories recounted, albeit often humorously, major life events, and there was a risk that the difficulties became sanitised or sentimentalised in the process of retelling. Above all, the work still lacked a sense of the stories *as* memory. Despite disrupting the linearity of the narratives, the past still came across as logical, rational and ordered. The social realism of the plays led to an emphasis on the mind rather than the body, on representing material realities rather than more abstract expressions of feelings or ideas. There was no real questioning of how the future might have turned out differently, nor how the events contributed to constructing subjectivities and framing identities. In other words, the dramatic style led the students to accept modernist definitions of subjectivity as essentially stable, thus missing the opportunity to consider how the performance of memory can, in itself, work creatively.

Perhaps one of the most moving aspects of the performance was how it led to dialogue between the elderly members of different racial identities whose previous personal contact had been limited and sometimes strained. But its weakness lay in the fact that the work did not really capture the aesthetic of memory, its instability and its contingency. Baz Kershaw has written critically of the 'performance of nostalgia' in community theatre, where the struggles of the past are sanitised into a commodified heritage.[13] This was not quite the case in this project, and perhaps in this particular context a safe and celebratory evening of lively drama, with an engaged and integrated audience, represented good progress. It was not dissimilar to Bruce McConachie's experience of directing grassroots theatre in Williamsburg, Virginia, where he attempted to change the community's attitude to race. Although the project had many successes, his verdict on the performance was ambiguous:

> Local citizens probably felt better about themselves and their community when they joined in on the final chorus. I would like to be able to say that several spectators came to me afterwards and admitted that Christian faith, individualistic capitalism . . . could not create our ideal community of the future, but of course that did not happen.[14]

In this intergenerational community project I was similarly left with a sense that something was missing. In this case I wondered if there might have been more effective collaboration, and if a more resistant pedagogy would involve all participants discussing how the stories were represented and the cultural politics of form.

Although the psychological benefits of reminiscence work with the elderly were well documented and growing in popularity during the 1980s, this was not my main concern in this project. Retrospectively, I think I was naïve about this, and I think that we used the old people as a resource for finding out information. They were 'happy to help', and enjoyed the contact with young people I am sure, but I think I took them for granted. In part, this was due to my lack of theoretical reading. I only really stumbled across research on the significance of personal and collective memories to communities through working on the project, and a stronger theoretical understanding of this from the outset would have strengthened the work. What I did understand, however, was that the process of retelling personal stories exhumed them, relocating them in space and time and breaking down distinctions between the real and the imaginary. As Portelli points out, the process of retelling autobiographical narratives allows 'historical, poetical and legendary narratives' to be interwoven.[15] Carolyn Steedman describes the role of remembered narratives as 'an agent of social formation', where interpretations of the past illuminate and extend people's understanding of their current place within their social world.[16] The performance did focus the participants' attention on the kind of community we were becoming, and there was evidence in the evaluations that seeing autobiographical stories performed had enabled people to gain some insights into their neighbours' actual experiences. Perhaps equally significantly, by exchanging stories about themselves some local people also became, if not close friends, friendly acquaintances.

Communities of Identity

It is a conventionally held view that all dramatic practice captures some element of the collective – in Richard Schechner's words 'a community for the time being' – not least because it involves people actually meeting or working together.[17] But the idea that communities of locality provide an inadequate account of the complexities of contemporary social life has led to further categorisations of community, including those of interest and identity. Concepts of community have been rethought as a result of new cultural, political and economic realities in which generations of men and women have found themselves with a sense of belonging to more than one place, or feel kinship to people with whom they share styles of living or political solidarity. These descriptions are usually harnessed to ways of living in the atomised West, in which the boundaries between 'life style', political commitment and shared identity often seem rather blurred. Linking community to empathetic identification with like-minded others opens up the possibility of new ways of thinking about community, but it also begs questions about identity politics and how multiple identities might be narrated and understood.

Throughout this book I have followed the idea that identity is created and performed in dialogue with others. A deeper sense of belonging to a community, however, derives from shared interpretations of experience. Developing this theme, communities of identity are constructed when people recognise their own experiences in others, and share an understanding of each other's values or stories. In some contexts, strong communities of identity are built by those who feel that they share common struggles: new social movements, such as gay, black and feminist movements for example, in which a shared sense of collective identification is seen as politically oppositional. The term 'community' is, however, often applied rather loosely to identity politics; labels such as 'the gay community' may provide a convenient shorthand, but they can also have the effect of disguising very real differences between people, and missing the possibilities of multiple identities, such as being gay *and* black, for example. In other words, communities of identity are constructed on a balance between sameness and difference – on the acknowledgement that particular interpretations of experiences are somehow different from the experiences and understandings of others. Equally, however, they are also discursive categories, and thus open to change. In this section I shall focus on a play which both illustrated and troubled the participants' membership of a community of identity. It was devised and performed by three women in London, all of whom were refugees, all from different parts of the world with very different narratives of migration. Becoming a refugee was not an identity of choice but of necessity, and membership of the local south London refugee 'community' was forced upon them by global circumstances. Their practice raises some interesting questions about the temporality and historical contingency of communities of identity, and how dramatic interpretations of autobiographical narratives inevitably give partial accounts of lived experience.

A Woman's Place was billed as 'a play devised and performed by refugee women'.[18] This play had developed from a sustained period of work with refugee organisations, although the three actors who volunteered to take part in the project did not know each other before working together. I saw the penultimate performance of the play at The Albany in Deptford, an arts centre in one of the most deprived areas of London. Not for the first time, I was struck by the efforts made to create a sense of community through the use of that particular building – a whiteboard behind the box office showed that in addition to the refugee play, rooms were being used by a National Association for the Care and Resettlement of Offenders' drama group, a music group for adults with learning difficulties, and for the rehearsal of a company of black dancers. When I had booked my ticket, I had been told to arrive early for my free drink and to see an exhibition by refugee artists. Duly arriving in good time for my beer, I found that tables inside the auditorium had been arranged nightclub style to encourage conversation. The art exhibition around the auditorium was supported by information tables offering resources for refugees in the area, and a raffle was taking place to raise funds. Although the play was clearly the focal point of the evening, it was framed by other events. This layering of the evening suggested that the amateur performers were in a sympathetic environment. What was interesting about the context of performance was that it consolidated a feeling of belonging to a welcoming community *of* refugees and gestured towards the sympathies of the host community in a country in which refugees have been vilified by a shamefully hostile press.

The play centred around the autobiographical narratives of two women, one an asylum seeker from Rwanda and another an escapee from a Cameroon prison who had recently obtained what is officially termed 'Indefinite Leave to Remain in the UK'. Their stories were framed by a French performer, Fleur, whose own story of displacement remained largely untold. Her role was, however, crucial to the structure of the drama. Through direct address she opened the performance by inviting the audience into the world of the play, offering a bridge between the rather comfortable environment of the theatre and the harrowing stories the performers had to tell. At times Fleur also acted as translator, as parts of the stories were told in Olive's and Clarice's first language, French. As their stories unfolded, the actors were supported by the strong visual aesthetic of the performance, particularly by pools of light that seemed to envelop the performers as they enacted their stories of human rights abuse, escape and eventual arrival in London. The final moments of the play drew attention to the idea of 'home' as each woman in turn left the stage to take a seat in the audience, a symbol of belonging to a new local community (represented by the audience) and leaving behind her status as refugee. Projected above the empty stage was a video of the women at home in

London, each carrying out ordinary domestic routines. These images problematised the performers' identities as refugees by showing their multiple identities as mothers, wives, friends and active professional members of society.

The theatricality of this play protected the performers by creating an aesthetic distance between them as people and their own autobiographical stories. The use of non-naturalistic acting styles, poetry and particularly the lighting and projections enabled the performers to represent, rather than retell, their autobiographies. Olive, a Rwandan Hutu who had been in London for nearly seven months, agreed to be interviewed by me on condition that her full name would not be included in this book for fear of recrimination. Olive explained that she found her own story so distressing that she could only perform it by imagining that she was talking about someone else. She also told me that in the devising process she had edited her story significantly, selecting events that she felt capable of retelling in live performance and missing out aspects that were either too personally painful or, interestingly, which perpetuated a negative image of her country as a violent place. This begs the question about how these women constructed their role as performers, and how they negotiated their identities as refugees in this specifically performative context. Olive described the process in terms of behaviour, where for the duration of the performance she behaved as if she were someone else:

> I am thinking that this is about someone else. My story is so sad it makes me very, very emotional if I tell it as me so I behave like someone else. When I first started the devising I had not been in London long and I kept thinking, 'What are these white girls [the directors] asking me to do?' We were telling stories in ways I had never done before, using bits of string and maps and pictures. It is not like performances at home. I tell my story in my own words but I also tell it in new languages because I had not seen a play like this before. It was fun to learn it this way.

This short comment is particularly revealing. Olive found a number of ways to separate herself from her story, both as an actor in the performance itself and in the devising process. Not only did Olive try to find ways of acting that made her feel safe, she also made an interesting distinction between her 'own words' and the theatrical language of the play, which was culturally unfamiliar to her.

How might Olive's process of enacting her identity as a refugee be understood? For both Olive and the audience the performance was complexly layered. As a performer, Olive knew that she was telling her own story, that she was performing herself. However, she also recognised that her performance was, in Schechner's terms, 'not me – not not me', in which it is evident that the actor is 'himself [*sic*] but he is not himself at the same time'.[19] Schechner is particularly critical of Western actors who, devoid of a 'culturally elaborate theatrical system', take refuge in individualism, relying on clichés such as 'sincerity' and 'personal truth'.[20] This takes on a particular resonance in relation to *A Woman's Place*. In many ways the whole point of the project was the interpretation and representation of lived experiences, intended both to raise awareness of the experiences of refugees and encourage the actors to explore their feelings in a safe context. Whilst in performance Olive may have been able to distance herself from her experiences, it was nonetheless a 'personal truth' which she performed. Olive's description of this process has something in common with Schechner's view of performance as 'restored behavior' in which performers 'get in touch with, recover, remember or even invent' behaviour in performance.[21] Schechner's description does not, however, take full account of the interiority of the performer, as Baz Kershaw has pointed out, nor the importance of memory.[22] That Olive relied on managing her memories while she was actually on stage was important to her. She needed to keep her feelings under control. By maintaining an aesthetic, linguistic and cultural distance between her stories and herself, between the exterior world and her inner feelings, Olive was able to redefine her relationship with her past and separate her identity as torture victim and refugee from her present identity as storyteller and performer. In other words, it was the act of performing herself as a refugee that also enabled her to step outside this categorisation of her identity. This was also indicated by Olive's awareness of the social purpose of the performance: 'I am also thinking it is a good story for white people to hear as they don't know the real stories of people.'[23]

The supportive context of the performance was endorsed by the presence of the local Member of Parliament who, before drawing the raffle, commented on how the play had enabled her to see refugees as individuals, with different stories and families, rather than as legal cases awaiting adjudication. For the women themselves, working on the drama symbolised a transitional moment in their identity formation, from refugee to local community member. As Avtar Brah has pointed out, identities are contingent on time and place, and might be renewed or altered. Although communities of identity extend beyond the spatial plane on which the rooted traditions of local communities depend, they also suggest an interesting social dynamic based on interaction, dialogue and shared interpretations of experiences and memories.[24] As such, although Olive, Clarice and Fleur were cast – and cast themselves – as refugees in *A Woman's Place*, taking part in the project showed that identification with particular communities can be changed in time. Their sense of belonging to a community altered as a result of working on the drama.

A Phenomenology of Community

Vered Amit offers a sceptical account of theoretical constructions of community, arguing that actual relationships of intimacy and social bonds have been neglected in analyses of imagined communities and communities of identity. Although in principle these collective forms of identification are 'quite portable', a sense of belonging to communities beyond the immediate experiences of living often only lasts for the duration of actual emotional or familial ties, and becomes watered down over time.[25] Following Merleau-Ponty's phenomenological idea of 'being in the world', I should like to extend Amit's account of how social experiences can turn into personal intimacies and social networks, and make a case for the significance of the body in cultural constructions of community. This is intended to move the discussion of community-building beyond the idea that communities are either imagined or constructed through 'face-to-face' interactions, as if the rest of the body were somehow invisible. As an illustration, my aim is to examine narratives of ageing in order to consider how the actual social experience of community involves what Merleau-Ponty described as 'body-knowing', an embodiment of personal and collective histories.

What I am searching for here are ways of working in drama that respect the relationship between the body and the various communitarian narratives through which individuals formulate identities. Places and stories are inscribed on the body, and our physical experiences of being in the world contribute to the archaeology of identity, contributing to the 'historical sedimentation' of selfhood, to borrow Kate Soper's memorable phrase.[26] Elspeth Probyn sees the embodiment of locality as symptomatic of oppression.

> In conceiving of the local as a nodal point, we can begin to deconstruct its movements and its meanings. Thus, in thinking how locale is inscribed on our bodies, in our homes, and on the streets, we can begin to loosen its ideological effects.[27]

Boal extends this perspective, describing how the body becomes 'hardened by habit into a certain set of actions and reactions'.[28] Linking memory, emotion and the body, Boal claims that the habitual repetition of movement is personally and politically limiting. In certain contexts this is, of course, painfully obvious. I vividly remember a Tamil primary school-teacher in Sri Lanka showing me how his body had been irrevocably scarred by the beatings he had sustained at the hands of the 'peacekeeping' Indian army who had attacked him after a school football match. Boal's use of dramatic strategies to deconstruct how experience has been etched on the body is explicitly political; his drama is about 'de-mechanising, de-structuring, dismantling' the effects of daily life.[29] Philip Auslander makes the point that Boal, like Brecht, believes that the body is expressive of a life of oppressions and that actions and gestures are scripted and determined by ideological constraints. Boal's objective, Auslander explains, is to enable participants in the drama to liberate themselves from this physical oppression, but in the process he labours under the misapprehension that it is possible for the body to escape 'ideological encoding'.[30]

Whilst Boal's reading of the living body is an important reminder of how personal histories are carried physically, the idea that the body is marked by signs of oppression (rather than experience) does assume that life has been a rather negative experience. In many situations, embodied memory is less obviously damaging than Boal appears to allow. Pam Schweitzer, whose pioneering work with the theatre company Age Exchange has made a significant impact on working with elderly communities in applied drama, has suggested that uncovering 'oppression' may sound rather heavy-handed in work which takes place in relatively comfortable situations.[31] This view is shared by Anne Davies Basting, whose work with Alzheimer patients has explored the relationship between memory and storytelling, where she has found that the process of collective storytelling often reveals the participants' present-day concerns through surreal imagery.[32] There is often a communitarian aspect to the ways in which experience is embodied and enculturated. In a warm and moving essay, Andrew Dawson offers an anthropological reading of the social effects of the ageing body on the practice of community in a former mining village in north-east England during the 1990s. Dawson found that handicrafts, poetry writing and performance played a large part in sustaining a sense of community amongst the elderly, who measured 'ageing well' according to how mental and physical decline was controlled and managed through these kinds of activities. Interestingly, Dawson points out that the traditions of artistic creativity in mining communities are indebted to the early twentieth-century modernist intellectual élite who, not unlike their successors in applied drama, set up arts activities in miners' welfare associations as part of their social reforms.[33] By the end of the twentieth century, when mining had been decimated and the population was ageing, cabaret nights at the Old Age Pensioners' club specialised in self-parodies of old age. As an example, Dawson tells the story of Ida, Kate and Mary, female members of the OAP group 'The Evergreens', whose ironic performance of the CanCan revealed incontinence pads beneath their tutus. In part this was a veiled gesture of community solidarity to the incontinent 'Mr M', who was under threat of expulsion from the club by officials, but it was also an example of the kind of self-deprecating humour that characterises the social capital of many strong communities in deprived circumstances.

Perhaps most interesting in Dawson's account is his description of how good stories move from the individual to the community. I can't be the only person who has appropriated a good story if it is plausible that it could have happened to me (now is perhaps the right time to confess that I have never actually taught a boy called Russell Sprout, although one of my friends certainly did). Passing on anecdotes is also a mark of the longevity of family relations – I could, for example, tell you quite detailed stories about 'cousin' Lizzie Berry's mince-pies, baked sometime during the 1920s, without knowing exactly who Lizzie was nor how I am related to her. In Dawson's account, there are two instances in which personal narratives were relocated into specific community settings. The first concerns Hilda, the source of many salacious stories about goings-on in colliery houses. As her memory deteriorated through Alzheimer's, she was prompted in her storytelling by those who knew her anecdotes well. In time, her fading memory led other members of the club to take over her stories, with Hilda prompting them. Eventually her stories became integrated into the community, and continued to be told long after her death. Another account involved Jimmy, who took Dawson to different places in the area (his allotment, the library), in order to locate his life history in places that were meaningful to him. Dawson concludes that:

> As memory fades, responsibility for the construction of narratives of self and, indeed, possession of these narratives slip inexorably from individual to community. In essence, the experience through bodily ageing of a self that transgresses the boundaries of the individual body is a matter for celebration precisely because it becomes a basis for sameness, a merging of individual selves, integral to senses of community.[34]

This relocation of the narratives of selfhood into narratives of community stretches the boundaries of the past and the future, the living and the dead. Rather than focusing on the negative aspects of old age, it finds a more secure place for personal memories in the future life of the community.

If memory is sensate, and places and experiences become imprinted on the body, it follows that the physical act of interpreting personal narratives in drama is a process that may touch old wounds or uncover consoling memories. Any drama that draws on how the ideologies of experience and location have been internalised and embodied is likely to feel very personal to the participants, and may be uncomfortably intrusive. More productively, listening to stories in environments of trust can create moments of friendship and intimacy, in which faceless political situations or moments of history become personalised. In my own practice I have found it revealing to observe how stories were told, whether participants looked comfortable or distressed, and to notice how their physicality altered as their stories were told. I remember working with one elderly man in 1984, then in his eighties, whom we interviewed about his experiences in the trenches in the First World War. We could see his body visibly stiffen as he told his story, shoulders back, a military bearing, which relaxed and dropped when he told stories of his demo-bilisation and return home. This physical response is what Jeff Freidman, whose LEGACY project recorded the oral histories of dancers in the San Francisco Bay area, calls the 'meta-gestus of re-membering'.[35] In rehearsal for a community play based on local stories and oral history, the boys telling an old man's story followed his physical lead, and devised an almost unbearably moving scene in which one boy read out the roll of honour on the local war memorial – many family names still evident in the cast list of the young people. The meta-gestus of remembering was referenced in performance; the old man himself mounted the stage to take over reading the roll, and together he and the boys changed the dramatic atmosphere by offering an ironic comment on his homecoming in 1918.

Freidman argued that the disciplined body has encoded and embodied different forms of knowledge, all of which are forms of a cultural language. Freidman theorised his work on performed oral histories by focusing on Bourdieu's concept of *habitus*, a concept he uses to analyse how both oral communication and physical expression are 'embodied channels of communication' located in social practice. This way of thinking about the kinaesthetic imagination narrows the gap between the cognitive and corporeal, and offers a way of historicising the body by constructing a shared sense of social identity and agency. It does not, however, fully address the realities of living with an ageing body nor challenge discourses of deterioration with which ageing is often accompanied in the West. In planning intergenerational drama projects, I have been particularly concerned to find ways of theorising the ageing body with some sense of optimism, as it seems to me that, in the cult of fitness and youth which permeates Western societies, we often receive negative images of the physical deterioration that accompanies old age. I also remembered my grandmother's and my father's overwhelming sense of social uselessness as their bodies changed with age. This led me to question whether the psychological benefits of reminiscence theatre might be found not only in the cognitive aspects of memory, in what people say, but in the body. The projects were designed to specifically encourage elderly people to recognise and value their existing physical abilities, and this has meant that I have not found Boal's conceptualisation of the oppressed body particularly helpful in this context. Whilst there is no doubt that the marks of lived experience are carried in the body, I am sure that the elderly people I have worked with would have not taken at all kindly to even the remotest suggestion that drama would liberate them from the embodiment of their oppressions. The Boalian principle that a lost humanity will be restored to individuals and communities by freeing the body from social inscription similarly implies that life has not been a positive experience.[36] If intergenerational drama projects are to challenge negative perceptions of physicality, and recognise the contribution made by the elderly in the community, they need to be constructed according to different theoretical models.

The idea that the body is a site of cultural inscription is familiar, but can the body be theorised, not just through the iterability of its languages, but through its history and genealogy? In his essay 'Nietzsche, Genealogy, History', Michel Foucault links the idea of genealogy to the body. He challenges Nietzsche's notion of *Herkunft*, a term by which he describes the 'stock or descent' of a person, such as blood ties, tradition and as indications of race and social type, a way of thinking about ancestry which he describes as Nietzsche's 'dangerous legacy'. None the less, Foucault acknowledges that, unlike the idea of soul or selfhood that suggests integration and unification, *Herkunft* implies discontinuity and lost events rather than integrity and wholeness. In distancing himself from the political pitfalls of an essentialist reading of identity, Foucault argues that 'genealogy does not resemble the evolution of a species and does not map the destiny of a people'.[37] By attaching the idea of genealogy and descent to the body, Foucault acknowledged that the body both is imprinted by experience – which he calls the 'stigmata of past experience' – and by the immediacy of 'feelings, desires, errors'. As such, he argues, the body is a site of conflict between the past and the present.

> The body is an inscribed surface of events (traced by language and dissolved by ideas), the locus of a disassociated self (adopting the illusion of a substantial unity), and a volume in perpetual disintegration. Genealogy, as an analysis of descent, is thus situated within the articulation of the body and history. Its task is to expose a body totally imprinted by history and the process of history's destruction of the body.[38]

This theoretical discussion of genealogy adds to the discussion about the body in community-based theatre by suggesting that history is imprinted on the body, not only as a readable system of linguistic signs, but as a rather more blurred and contested site, as a layered and sedimented repository of the past that articulates with the present. As a genealogy, our bodies store the imprint of previous generations, but also point to the discontinuities between one generation and another.

What I find problematic about Foucault's analysis of genealogy is his emphasis on the deterioration of the body, which remains curiously unproblematised. For Foucault (as for Nietzsche), history is destructive to the body, and as cultural values are inscribed on its surface, it inevitably suffers and deteriorates. In relation to intergenerational reminiscence theatre, this has two interrelated problems. Firstly, I feel that it risks implying to young people that although old people's bodies might be a bit decrepit they have some great stories to tell if only the young would listen carefully enough. Secondly, I have found that negative perceptions of the deteriorating body are readily challenged through practice. In Girton, the village I lived in near Cambridge, I brought together elderly members of the community with local children in a day of reminiscence drama. As part of the work, elderly people shared their performance and craft skills with the children, and the dexterity with which they taught the children and some of their parents how to knit, whittle wood, make jam, ice cakes and waltz (with much hilarity) put pay to any pessimistic discourses on the inevitable deterioration of the ageing body. By what criteria might these skilful people be described as deteriorating? Not only did they possess the physical skills associated with their craft, but they also showed through their use of their walking sticks and wheelchairs that they had learnt to use their ageing bodies gracefully.

Working together on different forms of crafts and social dance provided a context for much reminiscence and storytelling. Unexpected stories are entrapped in buildings and places, and the rather shabby wooden Women's Institute hut in which the Girton project took place asserted its presence into the drama, whether we liked it or not. It had been a jam factory, a dance hall for American GIs and local girls during the Second World War, a 1950s youth club and a meeting place for young mothers in the 1960s. The combination of the place and the craft and dance activities unleashed a store of memories. Moving into drama felt comfortable in this context, and both young and old found ways to interpret their own and one another's narratives. The emotional impact was inevitably heightened and I remember one such moment with particular clarity. Some of the younger jam-makers had succeeded in making a rather sticky mess on an old scrubbed pine table, and were attempting rather half-heartedly to clear it up. The two elderly women organising the jam-making immediately looked at each other and were reduced to uncontrolled fits of laughter. It was not until much later that day, when the children had gone home and some of the adults had gone to the pub, that I heard their story. The cause of the hilarity, it transpired, was that one of them had had to explain to her mother, after a particularly sticky moment with a GI, why she had jam in her hair. Now an upright member of the village community, she said that it was the smell and feel of the jam in the girl's hair that had brought back that moment of excruciating teenage embarrassment so sharply. This is what social psychologists call a 'flashbulb memory', and which drama practitioners describe as 'emotional memory', in which vivid moments can be recalled in all their textures and emotional complexities. In this case, I was advised that the story might be dramatised on the strict condition that its source was not revealed. In such ways stories are passed on, and in this case the anonymity of the story enhanced, rather than diminished, its status in the collective memory of the community.

Rather than seeing ageing in negative terms, perhaps an alternative way to conceptualise the body is as an archive. This builds on Foucault's idea that the body bears 'the stigmata of past experience', but also allows for optimism by looking at how the body might be reinterpreted for the future. In his essay 'A Note on the Mystic Writing Pad', Freud conceptualised the archive as something static or fixed, recalling the past 'without distortions'.[39] This conceptualisation of the archive does not look very promising. However, in *Archive Fever* Jacques Derrida offers a challenge to Freud, arguing that an archive is not about fixing the past, but always looks to the future. For Derrida, an archive is elusive, a promise which is just beyond reach.

> It [the archive] is a question of the future, the question of the future itself, of a promise and of a responsibility for tomorrow. The archive: if we want to know what that will have meant, we will only know in times to come. Perhaps.[40]

Derrida briefly applied this way of thinking to the body, in which the marks given to the body (he cites circumcision) are a sign of belonging to a society or a community. For Derrida, the archive marks the boundaries between the known and the unknown, the past and the future. To extend this idea further, the archival body is not the site of the deterioration of the individual, but a mediating presence between past experiences and future lives. In this conceptualisation, the body archives our lives performatively, where emotions, experiences and expectations are (consciously or unconsciously) recorded and to which we can, or may, return. This is particularly the case in performed oral history, where actors inhabit the stories physically and emotionally as well as cognitively and verbally. As memories are recalled they are reinterpreted, and as they are performed, they are unfixed, and may be relocated and archived in another's body. Dramatically representing their own and others' stories is, therefore, to become an archivist, a process which draws on physical memories as well as those that are linguistic and cognitive. This invites a new way of thinking about the body in space and time. Inhabiting others' stories, and archiving them in the body through performance, is not about 'preserving', 'conserving' or fixing history, but about making it a part of a dynamic of lived experience. This is in line with the phenomenology of Merleau-Ponty who focuses on the living, moving body-subject. He argues that the body continually exhibits 'expressive movement', an aesthetics of movement, and also 'body orientation', which looks forward and knows where we are going. Together, they result in *inhabitation*, a phrase he uses to point to the centrality of the body in perception, knowledge and understanding:

> We must therefore avoid saying that our body is *in* space, or *in* time. It *inhabits* space and time. . . . I am not in space and time, nor do I conceive space and time; I belong to them, my body combines with them and includes them. . . . The space and time which I inhabit are always in their different ways indeterminate horizons which contain other points of view.[41]

In this configuration, the living body has a sense both of location, of belonging, but is not constrained by time, place and space. The body has indeterminate horizons and boundaries. This means that the body is a space of possibilities, effectively dissolving the limits of subject and object, self and other.

In intergenerational storytelling, narratives previously located in specific spaces and times come to belong to both generations, and it becomes unclear which generation is the subject or object of the work. This is apparent in both everyday life and the practice of drama, in which individualised narratives are relocated in place and time, and this memory may be corporeal rather than cognitive. The idea that physically inhabiting personal and community narratives opens new horizons lends an ethical dimension to practice in applied drama. As Derrida points out, an archive signals a 'responsibility for tomorrow', and to encourage this approach to dramatic practice aims to move the participants towards a more dynamic and practical ethic of care. As an alternative to Foucault's deteriorating body, the archival body is a storehouse of narratives that are both located in the present and might travel through time, so belonging to future communities. As such, narratives of community become physically imprinted on the body, as an imaginative, ethical and optimistic process of 'becoming'.

Part III
Creativity and Social Justice

6 Creativity and Social Intervention

Cultures of Creativity

Because applied drama involves making art, it is inevitably associated with theories of creativity. The idea of creativity appears to occupy an ambiguous place in contemporary discourse. Its close alliance with humanist notions of genius, originality and the visionary powers of the artistic imagination has meant that, as a concept, creativity has come under critical scrutiny alongside the wider theoretical contexts from which it emerges. There is a sense of unease about the social role of creativity evident in much writing on the application of drama, and particularly amongst those on the political Left. In contrast, however, the concept of creativity has recently been revived in the corporate sector and in some aspects of education. But whatever political reservations and interpretations there may be about the idea of creativity, there remains a belief that it is an important element both in artistic production and in the more general practices of living. This chapter represents an attempt to prise open further the debate, to consider the implications of debates about creativity for applied drama and, in particular, to explore the importance of creativity to narratives of social intervention.

Although many different activities are now described as creative, most popular conceptions of creativity have their roots in the idea of the artist, a legacy of the Romantic movement. Although seeing the 'artistic type' as isolated and melancholic was not new to Romanticism, what became accepted in this period was the idea of artist as visionary who expressed, in Raymond Williams's words, 'a higher kind of truth'. In the writing of William Blake, for example, the creative imagination emerged as a form of divine inspiration; for Coleridge the professional artist had a natural inborn genius, and Shelley famously described poets as 'the unacknowledged legislators of the world'.[1] Building on Kant's interpretation of the aesthetic faculty as the means through which moral laws are internalised, nineteenth-century Romantic artists saw themselves as instrumental to social change. This view was based on the premise that freedom and autonomy are intimately linked to democracy, and that the liberated imaginations of professional artists give them exceptional insights and visionary powers. This way of thinking about creative practice continues to resonate in liberal societies, where social commentaries offered by artists, however anti-establishment, are often taken as a sign of a free and healthy democracy.

Sceptical readings of how creativity has been articulated in the history of Western ideas have revealed its ideological underpinnings with, for example, Marxist critics claiming that some conceptions of creativity have naturalised the bourgeois subject, and feminist thinkers arguing that the ideal of the creative genius assumed masculine norms.[2] Most enduring, however, is the twentieth-century reinterpretation of Romanticism, where it became accepted that qualities formerly associated only with the specialised artist – sensitivity, originality and imagination – are universal aspects of human nature. If, the argument goes, the imagination is the inner voice of our own benign human natures – a common romanticist view – we should listen to it, and allow it freedom of expression through creative practice. This way of thinking had the effect of democratising Romantic conceptions of creativity, but in the process it also naturalised liberal individualism. Creativity, self-expression and freedom of the imagination have been regarded as not only positive for the individual, but also socially beneficial – an idealist view based on the liberal maxim that good citizens will create good societies.

Although there have been political challenges to the ideal of the creative artist, the idea of creativity remains an important concept within applied drama and in everyday life. There are creative breaks in social systems, as well as new forms of artistic communication, and new ways of looking at the world can produce new forms of social action. What I am searching for here is a theory of creativity that might be applied to drama which is not entirely individualised, but takes account of the social and cultural contexts in which the work takes place. Place and space are literally important to creativity in applied drama, not least because its practices are often specifically responsive to the site or location in which the work takes place, and also because it sometimes happens in pretty unprepossessing environments that may not be conducive to creativity. Such a theory of creativity would represent a shift away from the traditional vocabularies of miracles and metaphysics sometimes associated with creativity, to the earthier, more contextually located and spatial metaphors of geography.

In this chapter I shall explore how creative practice is articulated in different situations, recognising that creativity is about doing and making, about the material manipulation of form and content and that, as such, it always has a social and political dynamic. The chapter is structured into three main areas of discussion. The first part examines the idea of the creative individual, making connections between the idealisation of the creative artist and the newly articulated model of the creative employee. The second aspect of the argument examines creativity in relation to social change and, using Boalian practice as an example, tests out differences in materialist and idealist conceptions of creativity. The final part of the discussion is concerned with place and space, and with finding ways to think about creativity as environmentally constructed. Rather than searching for an ideal model of the creative process, I am hoping to place the discussion of creativity solidly in the rather messier, unpredictable and material world of dramatic practice.

Creative Individuals

Although the Romantics' idea of artistic genius has been widely refuted, their codification of the creative individual retains some contemporary resonance. Over time Romanticist myths have been softened and democratised, and creativity has come to be regarded as a faculty of mind that might be developed through certain types of training or education. The idealisation of the intuitive artist has been largely replaced by the more general idea that creative people possess specific personal and cognitive qualities, which are variously summarised as the ability to think divergently, to be spontaneous, to be flexible, to take risks, generate new ideas and so on. This form of creativity is not confined to the arts and, in the post-industrial West, creative people are valued for their contribution to the economy and are regarded as essential to successful performance in an increasingly globalised market. In this conceptualisation, the creative individual is thought to possess abilities which bring about innovation in whatever field they choose to practise. In this section, using Howard Gardner's influential work as an example, I shall raise some questions about the values which have become associated with the idea of the creative individual.

Howard Gardner is credited with the theory of 'multiple intelligences', which he developed during the 1970s and 1980s and has continued to revise.[3] As a cognitive psychologist, Gardner was concerned to recognise more forms of human intelligence than just those measured by IQ tests. He identified many different forms of intelligence not valued in traditional forms of education, such as spatial intelligence, bodily kinaesthetic intelligence and intrapersonal intelligence, all of which, he advocates, should be included as part of the pedagogic enterprise. An approach to learning informed by his theories has clearly more radical potential than rote learning, and his psychological categorisation of human intelligence extends John Dewey's familiar view that people learn best by doing. It is not within the remit of this chapter to discuss Gardner's theories of multiple intelligences in detail. Rather, I shall focus on the aspects of his work where he discusses explicitly the concept of creativity.

In his book *Extraordinary Minds* (1997), Gardner develops a new taxonomy of creativity that builds on his analysis of Freud, Virginia Woolf, Mozart and Gandhi, all of whom he describes as 'exceptional individuals'. He uses his case studies to distinguish four 'species' of creator: 'Masters', 'Makers', 'Introspectors', and 'Influencers'. Masters and Makers (Mozart and Freud respectively) work in specific domains or areas of interest, and their creativity is stimulated by the world of ideas. Introspectors and Influencers are more concerned with people, and their creative endeavours are either focused inwardly, towards their own worlds (Woolf), or orientated towards influencing others (Gandhi). Gardner claims that there are distinct differences between these categories, and different varieties of creativity are associated with different personality traits and autobiographical influences. For example, he separates scholars from performers, arguing that the former require years of patient research to solve problems, whereas the latter need the more immediate rewards afforded by an audience. In defining the species of genius, Gardner quotes Keats's categorisation of 'the poetic character' approvingly, in which Keats claims that the creative artist has transcendental powers, a form of inner freedom which completely takes over.[4]

According to Gardner creative people tend to adopt common processes and practices. He uses his insights into the extraordinary minds of these highly gifted individuals to make more generalised suggestions about the characteristics of the creative individual. These processes are here summarised by Anna Craft:

Reflection: making time to reflect, in a variety of ways.
Leveraging: picking out what they are good at and really pushing that.

Framing: the spin put on things that do not work out. Creative people neither ignore nor are put off by failure but instead ask: 'What can I learn from this?'[5]

Gardner's argument shifts, therefore, from notions of the transcendental genius to practical strategies for creative learning, and in part it is his attention to effective learning processes that have led to his work finding favour with educationalists interested in creativity.[6] Creativity, for Gardner, is primarily individualised, and it is interesting that nowhere in his account of 'extraordinary minds' does he locate the subjects of his study in their social or cultural contexts, nor does he reflect on how factors other than those associated with personal life histories might influence their learning or achievements. This means that his theories of the inner workings of the mind are privileged over more social concerns of how class, gender or ethnicity (for example) impact on learning. It is interesting in this context that Gardner described drama as a form of 'bodily intelligence' that is based on close and concentrated observation of life, imitation, and emotional engagement. Nowhere in this brief account does he grapple with issues of creative collaboration, nor how ideas are generated with others, nor the more cognitive or intellectual aspects of theatre-making. There is an awareness of muscle memory and the physical elements of learning in drama, but his analysis is built on the work of actors as individuals, who learn their craft by observing others but who develop their abilities outside the ensemble. Gardner is primarily interested in learning lessons from the work of those gifted with 'high potential in the area of bodily intelligence', citing Stanislavsky, Charlie Chaplin and Woody Allen as models of excellence.[7] Marxist educators Bill Roper and David Davies have analysed Gardner's theories of multiple intelligence in relation to drama education, where they point out that he has not taken account of the social dimensions of learning. Applied to creativity, this implies that his priority is the development of a particular kind of creative individuality with the consequence, they suggest, that his work has had an enduring appeal for the middle class.[8]

It is important to locate Gardner's theories of creativity in his North American context. His *Project Zero* aims to develop approaches to critical and creative thinking in education, and his *GoodWork* research project has the broad and utilitarian objective of identifying productive relationships between the needs of society, the professional classes and their employers.[9] This is a significant development that allies creativity to current economic needs. With the demise of manufacturing industry in the West, developing a culture of creativity in the workplace is regarded as one way of encouraging employees' affective involvement in their work, and their flexibility and commitment to their organisation, which is seen as leading to economic success. British educationalists Bob Jeffrey and Anna Craft recognise that this highly individualised 'empowerment culture' indicates a new way of thinking about social change:

> It switches the responsibility for social change from governments and large global forces back to the individual in whom dilemmas and conflicts of power within society are realised. . . . Empowerment is seen as essential to survival and the locus of creativity is once again seen as lying within the individual.[10]

This kind of creativity is primarily orientated towards workplace efficiency and to competition within a global marketplace. Some practitioners in applied drama have extended their brief to include corporate work or work in large organisations in the public sector (as I noted in Chapter 3), and they find their work fitting into an environment where employees are encouraged to take risks and use their initiative. Richard Florida, an American economist, takes this argument a step further. Florida claims that there is a newly emerging 'creative class' which is made up of an ideal type of creative individuals who are unconventional, passionate about their work and highly paid.[11] Shelley's revolutionary poet seems to have become an advertising executive.

Gardner's theories of intelligence and creativity have their roots in idealist philosophies that place the primacy of mind over culture and society. By so doing, he accepts and naturalises ways of thinking about creativity that are historically contingent. Once loosened from the liberal assumption that creative practices ensure that the benign qualities of human nature are made visible, however, it becomes apparent that 'natural' creativity has very different political articulations. There are at least two ways of looking at this. On the one hand, the idealisation of the creative individual has become harnessed to the culture of competition and individuality that characterises corporate employment, and is thus only really beneficial to the professional classes. Alternatively, and this is a point argued by British educationalist Ken Robinson, a creative education values a wider conception of intelligence than is traditionally afforded, and is thus more socially inclusive.[12]

Creative Dialogues

The idealisation of the creative subject is based on the liberal assumption that ideas change the world. The challenge to this idealist philosophy has traditionally come from Marxists, who have argued that society changes when material circumstances change. They regard idealism as an inadequate account of social progress because it fails to take account of how human thought and ideas are responsive to wider social and economic factors. In other words, people's ideas change when their material circumstances change, rather than the other way round. From this perspective, the idealist position is productive only of human consciousness, whereas Marxists argue that the struggle for social freedom is not to be found inwardly in ideas or the imagination, but is achieved though collective acts in which dominant and oppressive structures of power are challenged.[13]

In relation to applied drama, there is further to go with this debate. It is rare to find either materialism or idealism in their 'pure' forms, if such things exist, and in practice the boundaries between these two political positions are often blurred. Creativity in the arts is complex and, although critical of the politics of individualism, many Marxist critics also acknowledge that artistic creativity is dependent in some way on the development of individual abilities.[14] It is important, especially for those practitioners whose intention is social change, to consider the relationship between idealism and materialism in relation to creative practice, as each defines different objectives for the work and asserts a different social vision. A practitioner influenced by idealist philosophies would emphasise the imagination and creative freedom of the individual, whereas materialists would be more likely to use drama to expose the social forces that govern people in different situations and to consider how theatre and performance contribute to constructing social reality. In order to examine some of the ways in which drama is mediated through these two critical lenses, I have chosen to focus on the theories and creative practices of Augusto Boal, known collectively as 'theatre of the oppressed' (TO).

Depending on how you look at his work, Augusto Boal is either an inspirational and revolutionary practitioner or a Romantic idealist, and this makes his work particularly interesting. He famously described theatre in Marxist terms as a rehearsal for the revolution, and his dramatic strategies are designed to encourage 'actors and non-actors' to learn about the world. Although his theatre is orientated towards social change and experimentation, Boal has consistently argued that 'it is not the place of theatre to show the correct path' and this has led to considerable debate about his ideological position.[15] Richard Schechner has claimed that Boal's refusal to offer solutions to social problems places him firmly with the postmodernists, whereas Michael Taussig has argued that Boal is a traditional humanist because he believes that human nature has the power to transcend cultural difference.[16] As a contribution to the debate about Boal's influence and commitment, Jane Milling and Graham Ley have offered a meticulous analysis of Boal's misreadings and interpretations of Aristotle, Shakespeare, Machiavelli, Brecht and Hegel. The strength of their essay lies in detailing Boal's intellectual contradictions in his manifesto for radical theatre, *Theatre of the Oppressed* (1979), which Milling and Ley systematically examine through close readings of Boal's sources, authorities and adversaries. Milling and Ley point out that Boal's theatre of commitment is built on an inattentiveness to historicism in his account of theatre and on decontextualised political theory.[17] Taken together, this means that although Boal's conception of creativity is consistently orientated towards making a better society, it is sometimes unclear from his theoretical writings exactly what kind of society is envisioned.

It is hardly surprising that, as a politician and theatre director, Boal is a better polemicist than he is an academic. My interest here is in exploring how the practices he advocates illuminate his political position, a debate which turns on his conceptualisation of the creative individual. Boal has offered a codification of the creative subject, and his 'spect-actors' are neither exclusively actors nor spectators, but a combination of the two functions. As such, the 'spect-actor' is *both* able to look at the world *and* act in it, albeit in 'rehearsal' for life. At the end of his influential chapter 'Poetics of the Oppressed' in *Theatre of the Oppressed*, Boal ascribes particular values and characteristics to the spect-actor.

'Spectator' is a bad word! The spectator is less of a man and it is necessary to humanise him, to restore him to his capacity of action in all its fullness. He too must be a subject, an actor on an equal plane with those generally accepted as actors, who must also be spectators. All these experiments of a people's theatre have the same objectives – the liberation of the spectator, on whom theatre has imposed finished visions of the world. . . . The spectators in the people's theatre . . . cannot go on being passive victims of that theatre.[18]

In this passage Boal equates his idea of the spect-actor with 'man' (*sic*) which is, for Boal, an ideal category. In terms reminiscent of Romanticism, the spect-actor possesses a vision and active imagination which have been lost to the passive spectator. The purpose of theatre, therefore, is to restore a lost humanity to the spectator, to counter his uncritical encounters with 'finished visions' of the world that have rendered him inhuman and emasculated. Once freed from social restraint through the liberating power of theatre, Boal anticipates that this renewed self-knowledge will enable individuals to act at their most creative, which he assumed would be a positive force for the good. Boal developed his argument in his later text *The Rainbow of Desire* (1995), which he wrote as a response to his work in the West, where he found 'new oppressions' based on psychological pressures rather than the more visible effects of poverty. Here he appears most interested in self-reflection, recommending the 'faculty for self-observation in an imaginary mirror' found in theatre which, as 'the true nature of humanity', will lead spect-actors to self-knowledge.[19] Boal imbues his spect-actors with special qualities of creativity, autonomy, freedom and self-knowledge, and although his language and terminology is often Marxist in tone, it is on this idealist and Enlightenment construction of human nature that Boal depends for his vision of social change.

Boal does explicitly discuss the distinctions between idealist and materialist politics in his manifesto *Theatre of the Oppressed*, in which he aligns himself with the materialism of Brecht, which he sees in direct opposition to the idealism of Hegel. Milling and Ley have argued that in this book Boal presented a 'primitive communism' in which he sustains sharp divisions between the passive spectator and the active actor to illuminate his perceptions of social inequality. Although Boal's version of theatrical exchange may underline his Marxist credentials, it is actually based on a selective reading of Arnold Hauser's social history of art in which there is a more subtle reading of the dialogic relationship between performers and spectators than Boal has owned. Boal similarly rewrites Brecht's theories to serve his own political inflections, positioning his own participatory practices as having the stronger revolutionary potential.[20] For those with an interest in applying Boal's theatrical strategies to pedagogical encounters, although his interpretations of Brechtian theatre are important, it is Boal's relationship to the work of Paulo Freire which has most direct relevance. It is here that the pedagogical implications of the negotiations and tensions between materialism and idealism in Boal's work are most apparent.

Boal's relationship to the political pedagogies of Freire has been investigated by Carmel O'Sullivan, who has charted Boal's political journey. O'Sullivan argues that, unlike Marx and Freire, Boal's emphasis is not on the exploitative and inequitable values of the capitalist system but on 'corrupt or evil *individuals*' (her italics).[21] She argues that TO is based on examining personal experiences of oppression and, crucially, offering *ideas* that will alter participants' perceptions of the world:

> Whereas Marx recognised that all things are contradictory, and contradiction provides the impulse for activity and change . . . Boal's techniques inherently deny the 'unity of opposites' in an effort to superficially 'solve' individual oppression.[22]

This implies that people can 'think themselves free', and that social change depends on the creative solutions of imaginative individuals more than on collective forms of social action. Or, to put it another way, liberation is created by the idealised spect-actor rather than the inhuman spectator. By individualising social change in this way, O'Sullivan suggests that Boal fails to take adequate account of the ways in which structures of power are created and sustained. This is particularly significant in terms of Freirean pedagogy. As I pointed out in Chapter 3, Freire recognised that it is the dialectical and dependent relationships between the oppressors and oppressed which maintains unequal systems of power. Breaking these inequitable social patterns involves dismantling the social system on which it is built rather than self-liberation through self-reflection which, according to Freire, supports a culture of conformity. O'Sullivan observes that Boal's use of terminology is indicative of his changing political stance 'from radical social transformation to individual empowerment'.[23] She concludes that Boal is more closely aligned to idealism than to the materialism of Freirean praxis.

Although O'Sullivan's analysis of Boal's shifting political position is astute and apposite, she does not take full account of his consistent allegiance to traditional humanism. Boal's optimistic belief in the essential goodness of human nature leads him to accept that individuals are not radically evil but have been corrupted by an iniquitous social system. His theatre has always been explicitly tied to narratives of redemption, placing his faith on the efficacy of creative dialogues between similarly liberated individuals. Boal sees a direct link between freeing the body, freeing the mind and social change, and spect-actors are encouraged to 'know' their bodies as part of this process of liberation, as a way of restoring their lost humanity. In the second edition of *Games for Actors and Non-Actors*, Boal not only implies that a synthesis of mind and body is liberating, but he also recognises the significance of dialogue.

Life is expansive, it expands inside our own body, growing and developing, and it also expands in territory, physical and psychological, discovering spaces, forms, ideas, meanings, sensations – this should be done as dialogue: receiving from others what others have created, giving them the best of our own creation.[24]

What this redemption narrative misses – or does not accept – is a view of selfhood as discursively or culturally constructed. Boal states clearly that cultural differences are superficial, but in practice his belief in a common humanity can prove to be an obstacle to social change. This is acknowledged in a fascinating interchange between TO practitioners in North America, where Rhonda Payne suggested that in this context one of the limitations of forum theatre is its emphasis on individual change at the expense of social change. The discussion offered the example of a play performed by women from Burkino Faso about their conditions at an international conference where 'liberated European' spect-actors stepped in with suggestions that were entirely inappropriate to the African context. The spect-actors' suggestions not only revealed a lack of contextual understanding, but their ill-informed contributions 'had no basis in the reality of the people who were there in the play'.[25] This suggests that the efficacy of TO strategies, particularly forum theatre, depends on a degree of shared experience between spect-actors and a common understanding of the social situation that is portrayed.

My suggestion is that Boal's work lies between the two theoretical poles of idealism and materialism. It is clear, however, that Boal is neither a relativist nor a moderate liberal, and my argument rests on the view that the spirit of his robust commitment to social change has Marxist sympathies, but is actually based on abstract and idealised conceptions of the creative actor. This suggests that an uncritical reading of Boal's theories of creative exchange has the potential to obscure the significance of context to applied drama. It is left to those who use his techniques, therefore, to consider the political implications of context and to consider how the creative dialogue enabled by TO strategies might illuminate different situations. Practitioners with a range of political perspectives apply Boal's methods to many different situations and problems, and this means that developing a coherent and creative praxis involves recognising that all dramatic dialogues are not only contextually and contingently located but also variously politically situated.

Creativity in Context

At the end of the last section, I suggested that Boal's techniques and strategies are most successful when the situations presented have immediate concern for all the spect-actors. Without shared knowledge and experience between the participants, as Mady Schutzman rightly points out, there are limitations to a system in which 'the oppressed' is consistently regarded as 'the other' – one of the negative effects of the belief that human nature transcends cultural and social difference.[26] Where there is some degree of homogeneity between the spect-actors, however, these problems are potentially side-stepped. In order to tease out these ideas a little further, I shall discuss in this section an example of theatre practice influenced by Boal. I have chosen to focus on the work of the British theatre company Cardboard Citizens, which was founded in 1991 by Adrian Jackson, Boal's English translator.

One of the most significant aspects of Cardboard Citizens' work is that many of the company members have direct experience of homelessness themselves, which not only lends the company credibility in complex situations, but also suggests that the performers and homeless audiences share an understanding of life on the streets. The company describes itself as 'the only professional company in the UK consistently working with homeless and ex-homeless people, including refugees and asylum seekers as creators, participants and audiences', and the company's work recognises and values their unique experiences.[27] This detailed attention to context demonstrates Jackson's interpretation of Boal's theories, and represents the company's commitment to changing the lives and material circumstances of this particular client group. The point of this description of practice is to explore the significance of context for creativity, and to examine how the political differences between idealism and materialism are negotiated in a specific performance.

Cardboard Citizens staged a show called *The Man with Size Twelve Feet*, written by Adrian Jackson, during 2002 and early 2003. The play was the company's response to the events of 11 September 2001, and it toured shelters for the homeless as well as more commercial venues. It told the story of Terry, a man who had been in prison on drug-related offences. Terry's story is told through a series of flashbacks, charting his camaraderie with fellow inmates in prison, his rejection by his daughter on his release, and the destructive effects of drug and alcohol addiction on his life. Thematically, the play explores how world politics impact on ordinary people, with the clear political message that globalisation is exploitative and destructive both in the larger world theatre and on the smaller stage of an individual life. At the end of the play, Terry's sense of personal frustration and despair has become politicised, and his final suicidal gesture is to light the match that will burn down the squat in which he is living. He will take with him his former cell mates, Doug and Abudullah, both of whom have tried, and failed, to find solutions to their problems through religion. In his closing monologue Terry describes himself as a suicide bomber, stating that his act of arson will send a message to all who have exploited him in the past. 'Innocent people,' he says, 'have got to die for the truth to come out.' Directly analogous to 11 September, Terry stands for all who fall victim to the destructive effects of globalised power structures.

A few days before Christmas in 2002, I arrived with my colleague at a hostel for the homeless in central London to film the performance as part of a research project. It was staged in a cramped basement, and the audience of around sixteen easily filled the space. The Joker, Terry O'Leary, explained to the audience that we would be filming the performance, pointing out that as residents of the hostel they were used to cameras following their movements (she pointed to a security camera in the corner of the room), and so they had no need to worry about our camcorder in the corner. Although none of the audience seemed concerned by our presence, and the company and the hostel had given us permission to film under clear conditions, were we part of this surveillance? We let the cameras roll, trusting the company's experience and judgement of the situation and on the understanding that we would stop filming at any point if requested. My interest here is in the audience's responses to the play, and in the forum that followed the performance.

This forum followed three distinct stages, facilitated by the Joker's skilful questioning in response to the spect-actors' suggestions. They began by choosing the issue with which they identified most immediately on an emotional and personal level. The forum then moved on to explore the social context in which the protagonist found himself until, finally, there was a discussion of how global forces impact on the lives of individuals. Taken together, this forum mapped a political journey from self-reflection to an exploration of how individuals negotiate societal pressures, and to an examination of the ways in which material circumstances and global politics shape and determine people's lives. In theoretical terms, there was a negotiation between idealism and materialism throughout this forum.

In the first part of the forum, the spect-actors found what Boal described as 'an imaginary mirror' that enabled them to reflect on their own lives. Much of the play's action revolved around the three male characters, with Terry's daughter as the most rounded female character. From the beginning of the forum it was clear that many of the audience identified with Terry himself, although I was told by company members that when the show was staged in a women's hostel the evening before, it was the daughter's situation audience members wanted to explore. This suggests that spect-actors find their own points of entry into the story through identification with individual characters. The Joker began the forum by focusing on the audience's immediate emotional responses to the play, asking them whether they had any sympathy for Terry.

> *First spect-actor*:   No.
> *Joker*:   You haven't?
> *Second spect-actor*:   No.
> *Joker*:   Why haven't you got any sympathy for Terry?
> *Second*:   It's all his own fault, innit, really.
> *Joker*:   It's his own fault? Why?
> *Second*:   He should deal with it.
> *First*:   That's it – it's his own fault, innit.
> *Second*:   He has to deal with it.
> *Joker*:   Deal with what?
> *Second*:   Deal with his drug problem . . . whatever.
> *Joker*:   Right . . . so you think . . .
> *First*:   Instead of going into prison, he comes out of prison, whatever . . . it ain't like . . .
> *Second*:   Yeah. He's clean when he comes out.
> *Joker*:   He's clean when he comes out.
> *First*:   Yeah . . . and he do some shit – then, like, basically, it's like all of us. He go in prison – I've been in prison like so many times and I've come out. . . . I'm still on the gear. Still wrecked. You know what I mean. And it's not as easy as that. . . .
> *Joker*:   It's not as easy as that, is it? I mean, like, have you managed to come out of prison and be clean, and then get back on the gear?
> *First*:   About two weeks.
> *Second*:   (*jokingly*) Liar.

This conversation reveals the spect-actors' negative self-images. Contrary to my earlier interpretation of the play, they blamed Terry for his continuing drug problem and, because they identified with his situation, they included themselves in this judgement. The first spect-actor, a man in his late twenties, admitted that the first thing he does when leaving prison is 'score'. He saw addiction as a matter of personal responsibility, arguing that neither childhood nor background should be blamed for drug abuse. In highly individualised terms, he commented that there was 'so much help out there' and that coming off drugs was basically a matter of 'willpower and motivation'. The Joker, however, responded quickly to the spect-actor's comment about the difficulties of overcoming addiction, thereby challenging both the culture of blame and the spect-actor's negative self-image. The style of the conversation was fast and engaged, with participants picking up on each other's contributions and interrupting freely, suggesting that they shared common experiences. Within the first three minutes of the forum, this audience was already using the play to reflect on their own experiences – the combination of the narrative of the play and the facilitation of the forum enabling them to find points of contact between the fictional world of the play and the personal realities of addiction.

The transition moment from individualist interpretations to an examination of societal pressures came when the Joker moved the process forward and encouraged the audience to consider how Terry might have acted differently. Following her prompt, three spect-actors came forward. The dominant suggestion from the audience was that Terry's problems would have been alleviated if he could have avoided peer pressure to take drugs, and that staying with his daughter would have helped this process of rehabilitation. The scene where Terry arrived on his daughter's doorstep asking for accommodation was a good example of a 'forum-able' scene, as it held a clear central debate. The daughter was understandably angry with her father, but at that stage in the play Terry intended to mend his ways. In the script, their relationship deteriorates to the point where Terry insults and threatens the daughter's boyfriend, and is rejected by her. One of the spect-actor's suggestions was that Terry might change the situation by being nicer to his daughter, and he was persuaded to enter the acting area. His intervention was witty, and he asked to see his daughter alone, without her student boyfriend Peter whom he dubbed 'Pete the Plum'. In the scene that followed, in role as Terry, he apologised for his past behaviour and tried to convince his daughter that he really intended to stay off drugs. It was a sensitive scene, and at the moment that she seemed about to soften, the spect-actor playing Terry asked if he could stay with her. At this point, the spect-actor diffused the moment of tension by bursting into laughter and leaving the stage. This prompted a discussion amongst other audience members about the difficulty of accepting change, of letting an old life go, even if it was, in the living, very painful. It was an insight which represented a significant shift in thinking from the earlier discussion. Rather than the participants seeing themselves as isolated individuals with sole responsibility for authoring their lives, there was a growing awareness of the significance of social relations in defining a sense of identity and belonging. Seen in this way, breaking old patterns of behaviour is more than a matter of individual choice, will-power or thinking about yourself in new ways. It involves establishing new kinds of relationships with others and, crucially, being accepted and judged differently by others in society.

The final stage in the forum's political journey came almost as the evening was ending. After various attempts to reform Terry's behaviour were suggested, another audience member articulated his response to the play in a way that showed that he recognised the central political theme of the play. Identifying himself as a refugee from an Islamic country, he offered an interpretation which made connections between Terry's inability to change and global politics. This Terry was not a victim of his own self-destructive behaviour but was caught in a chain of global events that inevitably led him to suicide. This unending chain included 11th September, the West's 'war' on terrorism and the international displacement of the vulnerable – a pattern of events that gave Terry an overwhelming sense of powerlessness. It would not be unreasonable to suppose that this man had been similarly trapped in this web. Like those who stayed in the hostel with him, he was interpreting the play through the lens of his own experiences. But unlike them, he did not think that Terry should learn to overcome his problems, nor that his problems would be resolved when society saw him differently. It was the world that should change, and then his life would be able to change too.

The contrasting interpretations of the dramatic situation offered by the spect-actors not only reflected their own experiences but also illustrated the differences between idealist principles and materialist politics. Those whose world-view had been influenced by idealist narratives of self-creativity based their suggestions on the assumption that individuals can change their own stories, whereas materialist analyses would expect personal change to follow changes in global politics. What I saw in practice was how these two different perspectives might co-exist in the same piece of forum theatre. Nothing had been resolved for Terry, of course. But what else had happened in the course of the performance and forum? The audience had entered the fictional world of the play, and for many it confirmed a view that, if they so chose, there was at least the possibility of changing their own life-stories. Others found that the play articulated the social effect of world politics, in which they found themselves caught. The contributions of those who advocated personal change were confessional and emotionally open. The more political interjections were analytical, focused and angry. Somewhere between these two positions there was an interesting negotiation between two world-views that enabled the spect-actors to shift their perspectives and look at the situation differently. The political dynamic of this particular forum, therefore, lay in finding creative ways to think differently *and* act productively in a wider social and global context. Cardboard Citizens offer theatre workshops which enable homeless people to develop their artistic creativity, but the dialogue in this forum was orientated towards finding ways of living creatively in an uncertain, complex and often dangerous world.

Creative Spaces

The work of Cardboard Citizens illustrates the importance of understanding the context in which practice in applied drama takes place. Hal Foster has suggested that artists should be 'familiar not only with the structure of each culture well enough to map it, but also with its history well enough to narrate it' and stressed the importance of reflexivity in interventionist art-making as a way of claiming some sense of critical distance, and to avoid forming 'a hierarchy of suffering whereby the wretched can do little wrong'.[28] Because practice in applied drama is intimately and complexly tied to the contexts in which it takes place, the ways in which space is constructed takes on a particular significance. In this section I shall consider how we can think about the significance of space in relation to creativity and social intervention.

The great theatrical symbol of a modernist utopia is the empty space, designed to liberate the soul and the imagination by insulating actors and audiences from the restrictions of history, the regulations of place and the materiality of everyday life. One of the concrete realisations of the ideal of the empty space is the black box theatre which, as David Wiles has pointed out, 'is also bound up with the modernist goal of transforming society, which may seem paradoxical in view of the way it cuts itself off from any contact with an implicitly corrupt and false social world outside'.[29] Although actually working in a black box theatre may seem a rare luxury to some practitioners in applied drama, the symbolism of the empty space as a place of creativity and social transformation calls attention to the various ways in which places and spaces are constructed and experienced. The idealisation of the empty space, and the assumption that temporary isolation from other social practices leads to social transformation, rests on the belief that a space that has been stripped of the obvious signs of social interaction is ideologically neutral and without cultural inscription. The idea that participants emerge from an empty space transformed as individuals and ready to transform society is dependent on idealist constructions of the creative imagination, a modernist interpretation of Romanticism. It takes the following familiar logic: the imagination is most free when it is least influenced by society, so those whose imaginations are most liberated will create better societies. Although this image may appear appealingly democratic, it ignores the social context in which the drama takes place and the many ways in which spaces are interpreted, experienced and lived.

An alternative conception of space is to be found in an essay by Victor Turner that has assumed major importance in performance theory. Turner argued that 'the seedbeds of cultural creativity' are found 'betwixt and between' the normal regulatory structures of life. It is in liminal spaces, he suggests, that 'new models, symbols, paradigms etc. arise'.[30] This is a persuasive and, in some ways, seductive image to relate to creativity in applied drama, which is often thought to work best on the margins of society or in-between cultural spaces rather than in the mainstream. When taken at face value, it implies that play, disorder and 'letting off steam' will lead participants to new and creative insights into the world. Because liminal spaces appear to operate outside normal societal constraints, it might be assumed that creativity is most liberated when it is unplanned, dislocated from everyday realities, or even (*pace* Gardner) when participants achieve a state of being that borders on the insane.

Not only does my experience of working with people in many different educational and community contexts make me suspicious of the perception that chaos and creativity are natural allies, I also feel that this would be a misreading of Turner's argument. Liminal spaces are culturally specific contexts in themselves, and can only be described in these terms because their attributes of openness and ambiguity are different from, and contrast with, the laws, customs and conventions of everyday life. In short, liminal spaces have to be 'betwixt and between' *something* in order to be spaces at all. Normal life may be temporarily suspended, but the playfulness of liminality masks, rather than obliterates, other forms of convention and custom. This is similar to Derrida's use of words crossed out, where the erased word and its meaning can still be discerned beneath the line. Correspondingly, the structures and patterns of ordinary life remain evident in the collective memory precisely because they have been deliberately erased in that moment. Creativity, in this conceptualisation, might be located within a specific context (such as a drama workshop or rehearsal), but it also pertains to the everyday and, however obliquely, references it within its practice. In that sense creativity is doubly contextualised rather than decontextualised, and one of the challenges of working (or playing) in this creative space involves negotiating the apparent openness of the drama experiences and the relatively regulated world of the ordinary and the everyday. This acknowledges that creativity requires a degree of disorder, a sense of speculation and an atmosphere in which old rules can be overturned, but that it is also investigative and systematic. As Joan Littlewood observed, 'chaos has to be very well organised'.[31]

The idea that any space can exist outside social practice was challenged by the French cultural theorist Henri Lefebvre, whose study *The Production of Space* was written in 1976 and translated into English in 1991. Lefebvre was critical of idealist conceptions of space, and his central thesis is that space is never empty but always actively socially produced. He furthers an understanding of space as a dynamic social practice that is produced and reproduced through social action and interaction. He contends that space is not simply an abstract concept; it is lived, experienced and embodied physically and is therefore differently interpreted according to culture and history. This means that space is multiply inscribed, and its meanings are continually generated and regenerated as a creative process with 'many aspects and many contributing currents'.[32] This way of thinking about space as a social practice has particular resonance for applied drama, not least because the work often takes place in environments or institutions (prisons or care homes for the elderly, for example) that already carry very specific meanings. Making what Mihaly Csikszentmihalyi has described as a 'congenial' environment for creativity in such contexts presents particular challenges.[33]

Lefebvre offers three categorisations of space that illuminate the different ways in which people relate to space. *Representations of space* are conceived conceptually, usually constructed by professionals as a way of codifying or ordering space according to specific ways of thinking and structures of power. *Representational spaces*, by contrast, are those of everyday life, spaces that are embodied and which articulate the complex symbolisations and images of lived experience. *Spatial practices* are the patterns which structure the social world, and relate to people's perceptions of the world and the different social purposes space fulfils. Although, as Wiles has pointed out, theatre would be generally associated with the middle category – representational space – this would not fully explain the complex relationship between participants and space that is evident in applied drama. Because much applied drama takes place in very specific contexts and institutional settings, all three categorisations of space Lefebvre outlined – conceived, lived and perceived – are interconnected in its practice.

In institutional settings, space is conceived according to the structures of disciplinary power and the rules governing the ways in which space is often used to define relations between people. These spaces are, to use Lefebvre's words, 'informed by effective knowledge and ideology'.[34] This means that work in these contexts is often framed by the ways in which space is used to regulate or order people's movement and behaviour. My visit to the hostel for the homeless to see the work of Cardboard Citizens offers a good example of how representations of space are negotiated and reconstructed in relation to theatre practice. On my arrival at the hostel, the ways in which space was regulated became clear. Gaining admission required me to use the video entry-phone, wait in an entrance hall painted a calming shade of pink, while my identity was checked, sign in – and only then was I allowed into the performance space, travelling through several locked doors and observed by many surveillance cameras. I have no doubt that my feelings about this experience, and my interpretation of the space, would have been very different from that of the residents of the hostel. A related example is offered by Jenny Hughes, writing about theatre-making in Styal, a women's prison. Hughes' experience of working with the women meant that she was extremely sensitive to the 'double' contexts of the drama workshop and prison life, and she understood that the women would need to 'block out the effects' of the prison culture in order to work creatively on the drama project. As a result, Hughes described one project on which she allowed time at the beginning and at the end of each day as 'safety valves' – time which enabled the participants to warm up and wind down and discuss any issues that had been raised during the work. Hughes used her knowledge of the potential conflict between the two contexts to support the women in moving into the representational space of the workshop and in easing them back into the more regulated representation of space within the prison environment when the drama was over. Michael Balfour has also highlighted the delicate position of the facilitator or practitioner, and suggests that an imaginative escape from the corrective regimes of the prison is essential for successful creative practice.[35]

Transforming highly regulated spaces into creative performance and workshop spaces is not just an interesting artistic challenge. It involves reconstructing how space is conceived, temporarily overlaying its codes with alternative spatial practices. Fluidity between represented space (abstract, codified, regulated) and representational space (embodied, open, symbolic) depends, according to Lefebvre, on an understanding of how spatial practices are perceived. Lefebvre resisted the binary opposition of mind/body, arguing that it is the critical understanding of how spatial practices have been constructed and internalised that makes social intervention possible. Spatial practice, he argued, is discursive, and understanding how space is perceived leads to what he called a 'spatial competence' which makes its meanings open to change. As Lefebvre commented, 'any social space may be subjected to formal, structural or functional analysis'.[36] Related to drama, this requires practitioners to understand how discourses of power and authority are constructed and reproduced in space and, therefore, how they can be rewritten for the duration of the drama and beyond.

Applied drama is principally concerned with enabling people to move beyond the ordinary and everyday and use the aesthetics of drama, theatre and performance to gain new insights into the social and cultural practices of life. Lefebvre's materialist analysis of the social production of space offers a way of thinking about creativity in relation to context and history. In particular, it provides a basis for discussion about how spaces are re-interpreted and reproduced, and where there might be consonance or dissonance between how spaces are conceived institutionally and organisationally, and how they might be experienced and symbolised in the process of making drama. Creative spaces are those in which people feel safe enough to take risks and to allow themselves and others to experience vulnerability. It is creative moments of transition that enable participants to move out of restricted spaces – literally or symbolically – and beyond identities that are fixed and codified by particular spatial practices into new forms of social identification. If spaces for drama are to become 'seedbeds of cultural creativity', they will enable participants to experiment with the production and reproduction of space collaboratively, recognising that its meanings can be complexly symbolised and layered. This way of thinking about creativity moves the focus of attention away from the inner qualities of the autonomous individual, and towards the significance of responsive, reciprocal and compassionate relationships between participants within the specific context in which the work is taking place. It accepts that creativity is fostered through networks of social relationships which, in turn, raises ethical questions about how congenial environments of trust might be formed.

7 Human Rights in Performance

Agendas and Advocacy

It has been argued that the language of human rights has filled the vacuum left by the demise of grand political narratives after the Cold War. This view would seem to be borne out by experience and, as the radical students of 1968 start drawing their pensions, idealistic young theatre workers are far more likely to be interested in human rights issues than in starting revolutions. Theatre in search of social change has responded to new world orders, and the successors of mid-twentieth-century theatre activists are more likely to be found working for non-governmental organisations in the developing world rather than mobilising workers in their local factories. This shift from overtly revolutionary politics to more local explorations of injustice is often seen within the wider context of international standards of human rights. Despite the many contradictions and debates about how a human rights agenda might be legitimately furthered, it remains one of the abiding utopian ideas over which there is general international consensus.

As I suggested in the previous chapter, there is a move towards a new political language in socially committed theatre-making in which idealism is tempered by an understanding of the material circumstances of participants and the local and regional conditions in which the work takes place. The balance between abstract idealism and more local expressions of justice appears to be satisfied by recourse to the vocabulary of human rights, taking us beyond the polarisation between universalists and relativists and into more transcultural ideas of morality and humane standards of living. On the surface, the discourse of human rights that has gathered momentum in the post-Cold War era sounds reassuringly principled and humanitarian rather than directly political. Rights-based agendas have claimed a new urgency, and campaigns against torture, discrimination and the effects of poverty, for example, appear entirely uncontroversial. This way of thinking has permeated applied drama, not least because of the strong alliance between applied drama and the charitable trusts and human rights organisations that frequently fund practice.[1] In places where human rights are violated, forms of popular theatre that bring together information and entertainment are seen as effective ways of reaching large audiences, particularly where performances are accompanied by discussion or other forms of community participation. Such locally based work, often part of wider regional campaigns, is intended to meet the objectives of an international human rights agenda.

The new global discourse on human rights has legitimised international intervention in the name of universal social justice, but it is not without its dissenters. Although many people associate human rights exclusively with the courageous work of organisations such as Amnesty International who campaign to end human rights violations, it is important to remember that the formal constitution of universal human rights is constructed according to the principles of a liberal democracy that favour capitalism as a political economy. It is based on a system of individual rights and civic responsibilities in which society is built on a consensus of abstract political virtues such as freedom of speech, tolerance and the right to self-determination, which are enshrined and protected in law. It has been argued, however, that because contemporary notions of human rights have derived from a very specific history of European liberalism, this has had the effect of normalising Western individualism in ways which are at best insensitive to local cultures and at worst another way in which the hegemonic values of powerful nations are colonised.[2]

Within the field of applied drama, critics from the developing world have raised questions about who owns the discourse on human rights, and whether this is simply another way in which transnational corporations create local conditions that are favourable to their own globalised work practices. The relationship between universal human rights and political power has also been challenged by the resurgence of regionalism, and there are different interpretations of human rights regimes in, for example, the Asian Pacific Rim, Europe and the Arab world. The tensions between these different conceptions of human rights are exacerbated by the unequal power-relations of global politics, particularly in contexts in which human rights are seen primarily as a Western agenda. These are major issues, and they face practitioners who apply drama to human rights advocacy on a daily basis. My aim in this chapter is to look at the question of human rights advocacy from a range of different perspectives, and then to consider how some of the debates about globalisation and cultural diversity impact on applied drama in practice. The chapter offers no clear-cut answers but is based on the view that furthering an ethical, rights-based agenda for applied drama involves understanding and negotiating the tricky terrain within which humanitarian politics is situated.

Human Rights and Globalisation

The idea that human rights is a product of Western liberalism has been subject to particular scrutiny from the political Left, where it has been argued that Enlightenment concepts of universal rights are designed to shore up the interests of possessive individualism within a free market economy. Susan George, an activist and writer on global poverty, speaking at the Amnesty International lectures in 2003 made the link between human rights and economics explicit. She used her lecture to argue that the standards of ethics set down in the Universal Declaration of Human Rights can only be met in liberal democracies because they do not strive towards complete equality, as might be expected in state socialism for example, but are centrally concerned with the liberal ideals of individual dignity and the right to self-determination.[3] Historically, this has cemented the link between democracy and economics, not least, said George, because people vote for parties on the basis of their economic policies. Equally pressingly, debates about the impact of globalisation on the spread of human rights have revealed inconsistencies between the practice of human rights and the humanitarian rhetoric of corporate organisations and governments. If economic interests, human rights and democratic politics are complexly interwoven, it follows that all interventions associated with human rights, including those carried out in applied drama, are inevitably caught up in this larger conceptual scheme.

Opinion is divided about whether globalisation is an effective means of furthering a human rights agenda, or whether it is incompatible with humanitarian values. On the one hand, global capitalists argue that increasing the global marketplace is one way to extend human rights. Bill Gates, writing in *The Washington Post* in May 2000, argued that China's 'participation in the global community' and 'increased economic and cultural interaction' would enable the West to address the social and human rights issues evident there.[4] An attractive picture of globalisation is painted as the means whereby the benefits of the world market are brought to the poorest people in the world through the use of new global technologies. Globalisation, allied to free world trade, appears to unite the principle of universality with an expansion of wealth. This perspective has been vehemently challenged, however, by those who consider it to be more concerned with the spread of capitalism than with human happiness. Amongst others, US academic Noam Chomsky has argued that globalisation is incompatible with human rights, and has catalogued an array of practices which reveal how the conduct of the US government falls short of, and contradicts, its libertarian rhetoric. He is particularly critical of the ways in which the doctrine of free trade has been used to further capitalist self-interest, citing the example of tobacco advertising aimed at women and children in Asian countries, which was actively promoted by the USA and enforced with the threat of economic sanctions. Susan George has argued that globalisation is directly opposed to human rights because it increases divisions in wealth, with power and money continually drifting to the top. The ethical question, she suggests, is 'How can we guarantee the human rights of those that globalisation leaves behind?'[5]

The complexity of theatre which aims to promote human rights has been thoughtfully analysed by Syed Jamil Ahmed. Ahmed has written about theatre for development in his home country of Bangladesh, and his work raises questions about the relationship between globalisation and human rights. Ahmed offers an analysis of discourses on development, arguing that international development has been orientated towards 'a bloodless and revolution-free prosperity to the "developing" nations'.[6] He argues that poverty alleviation schemes, with which theatre for development is often associated, have been funded by aid agencies whose human rights agenda is driven by the economic imperatives of capitalist donors of the West, and this means that the work is inevitably allied to globalisation. In Bangladesh, he observes, issues explored in theatre for development are not chosen by the local people themselves but by NGOs in collaboration with those in positions of power. His list of topics represented in theatre for development include 'social injustice, dowry, polygamy, *fatwa*, arbitrary violence, gender discrimination, illiteracy, unjust possession of public resources by the power cliques, superstitious health practices, degradation of the environment and its consequences', all of which easily attract foreign donations.[7] On the face of it, all these issues seem entirely acceptable in part at least, because of their close affinity to an international human rights framework. Ahmed has pointed out that where development workers have not understood the complexities of the local context, however, the issues are frequently presented as crude pieces of agit-prop theatre in which obstacles to human rights protection are either ignored or badly over-simplified. Crucially, local people themselves have not been invited to set the agenda for the plays, and although audiences are invited to 'share their opinions', scope for a more robust political (and Freirean) dialogue is limited. The current process does not lead to changing social structures, Ahmed suggests, and this kind of human rights advocacy succeeds only in domesticating villagers rather than liberating them. As a process of domestication, he argues, it serves the needs of globalising capitalists because it creates a docile workforce who are easily exploited as cheap labour. Ahmed's rueful question about theatre for development, therefore, is 'development for whom'?

Ahmed has painted a bleak picture of some of the effects of theatre for development and, no doubt, the motives of the individual theatre practitioners and aid workers are far less cynical. It seems likely that such theatre workers are themselves caught up in structures of power rather than intentionally perpetrating them, and for this reason Foucault's theories of governmentality are apposite. Foucault argued that power is not sustained through fixed systems of domination, but is played out more subtly through a mixture of self-regulation and coercion. He claimed that power is seen to be lodged with experts, who possess knowledge which may well be used to support benign intentions – humanitarian reforms of health care, prisons, schools and so on – but the effect of their endeavours is often that individuals are constructed, and construct themselves, according to their perceptions of how they think they are expected to behave. This process produces what Foucault calls 'docile bodies', people who conform to the disciplinary knowledge of experts without questioning the power base from which it derived, and they regulate their lives accordingly. 'A body which is docile', Foucault argued, 'may be subjugated, used, transformed, improved.'[8] In such a culture of self-improvement, there is no obvious central locus of power which might be opposed. This way of thinking relates closely to Ahmed's account of theatre for development in Bangladesh because it implies that *both* the development workers *and* villagers collude in their own transformation into 'docile bodies'. Seen in this light, the rhetoric of transformation and empowerment so often associated with applied drama takes on a different meaning. A Foucauldian reading of Ahmed's argument would pose the following question: is theatre being used to transform Bangladeshi villagers into docile bodies in order that they might be empowered to become effective workers for multinational corporations?

Susan George has pointed out that one way to remedy the inequalities associated with globalisation is to evaluate the success of the whole economic system on the basis of experiences of the least privileged rather than the profitability of the few. Chomsky has extended his challenge to the ethics of humanitarian intervention, which he sees used increasingly frequently by powerful nations as a justification for their use of force as well as an important means by which they extend their economic advantage. He points out that powerful nations, including Britain and USA, appear to consider themselves exempt from the principle of universality in relation to human rights, which they invoke as they impose their values elsewhere. Writing before the allied forces' war on Iraq, Chomsky cites many cases of human rights violation in the USA, such as child poverty, enforced prison labour, and the cases of juvenile offenders sitting on death row. He concludes that the universalist ethics of humanitarian politics, when applied to the practice of human rights, seems very politically pliable when in the hands of the rich and powerful.[9]

In relation to theatre, one of the central political questions which Ahmed has identified is concerned with who owns the means of cultural expression in a globalised world. In his utopian 'world without theatre for development', theatre practitioners would be concerned not with 'development' but with 'plain and simple theatre'. His dramatic pedagogy would involve a more equitable process of transcultural collaboration and exchange, with theatre practitioners sharing their knowledge of their own cultural traditions – citing Brecht's and Stanislavsky's theatre as areas of interest to Bangladeshi practitioners. Ahmed calls, therefore, for knowledge to be relocated, ensuring that local practitioners have access to both local and international expertise *in drama* as a form of cultural literacy, a process which would contribute to breaking down the divide between the rural poor and the urban cosmopolitan in Bangladesh.[10] From this point of view, Foucault's deterministic analysis of the power of expert knowledge tells only part of the story. Literacy, as Paulo Freire was well aware, is a social practice that enables people to formulate new insights and ideas, to offer social criticism and to develop relationships. If this is extended to the embodied languages of theatre, bodies rendered docile may start to move. This would shift the focus of international development away from message or issue-based theatre, described by Ahmed as 'top–down', and towards a local and indigenous theatre, where practitioners are able to use their cultural knowledge of different styles of artistic production.

Theatre director Rustom Bharucha commented succinctly that there is a 'policing of human rights by which First World nations legitimate their control of Third World economies on humanitarian grounds'.[11] If applied drama is to avoid contributing to this cultural policing, practitioners need to be aware of the limits of liberalism and the politics of globalisation. The problem lies not only in the hypocrisy of governments, but in the foundational link between human rights, global economics and liberal individualism. This suggests that theatre which is intended to spread human rights necessarily inhabits a contradictory space, in which the tensions between competing values of a world in a permanent state of transition are continually played out. My interest here is not to challenge the general moral aspirations of a human rights framework, but in how we might exercise continual vigilance over the ethical implications of their interpretation and representation in different social and cultural contexts.

Representing Human Rights

The tradition of democratic liberalism states that human rights are universals, an assumption that is based on the idealist philosophy that human nature is universally shared and universally good.[12] From an anthropologic perspective, it has been pointed out that the individualist vocabularies of human rights are inflexible to local cultures because they are based on European conceptions of human nature developed in the eighteenth and nineteenth centuries, a category described by Richard Wilson as 'one of the more offensive ways of imposing the prejudices of "Western culture"'.[13] The concept of the human subject inscribed in human rights legislation is not, however, a static formation, and it has been redefined many times in the last two hundred years. This philosophical history is always orientated towards improving and extending human rights, and the process of redefining the human subject has led to the explicit inclusion of the rights of women and children in law, for example, although it is interesting to note in this context that the United States of America has so far failed to ratify the United Nations Convention on the Rights of the Child (1989). The Western philosophical tradition claims that the human subject on which the discourse of human rights depends is timeless and universal, whereas in reality it is actually responsive to specific social struggles.

In his 1995 lecture for Amnesty International, Jacques Derrida made connections between the construction of the human subject, human rights and language. Reminding his audience that the discourse of human rights emerges from a specific philosophical tradition, he argued that neither philosophical concepts of the human subject nor language exist outside the cultures in which they are practised. Language, he suggested, is 'always pretending to be universal' but the use of any specific language inevitably affirms the values, cultural memories and traditions of the nation or groups of nations within which it is used. Language, he argued, carries the imprint of culture and histories. This has particular political consequences for using languages that have become hegemonic, most obviously the English language. If the use of English as a convenient means of international communication has the effect of erasing or denying local languages, it follows that the sense of belonging to a local culture or national identity will be eroded or lost. In looking for a new way of conceptualising language in relation to human rights, Derrida concludes that:

> When you show some respect for the other, you have to respect another's language and to affirm yours. That is the deep experience of translation – it is not only political, but poetic.[14]

Taking Derrida's insight that human rights are affirmed through linguistic practices which are both political and poetic draws attention to the ways in which human rights are represented. This has two specific implications for applied drama that I should like to explore a little further. The first is concerned with the language of human rights reporting, which raises questions about the impact of narrative in applied drama. The second is related to the aesthetic languages of theatre and the tools of cultural expression in drama as they are applied to human rights issues.

One of Syed Jamil Ahmed's criticisms of theatre for development is that some Western practitioners have little understanding of the contexts in which the work takes place and that, in the process, theatre workers unwittingly impose their own culturally specific values on the rural poor in Bangladeshi communities. This implies that an uncritical belief in human rights as universal and absolute moral principles is, in fact, prejudicial. From an anthropological perspective, Richard Wilson has explained that one of the difficulties of working towards an understanding of human rights in an international context arises precisely because it is built on abstract and legal concepts – freedom of speech, liberty, social justice – and this has meant that human rights issues have tended to be represented in similarly positivist language. He argues that much human rights reporting is couched in legalistic terms, which has the effect of taking stories of abuse out of context. This means that the reports focus on empirical facts, with the consequence that the analysis of the reasons for human rights violation and the motives of the perpetrators is limited. Without a sense of context and narrative, he concludes, questions surrounding the significance of locality and culture are either displaced or erased from official accounts. A more ethical approach, according to Wilson, would not seek to make moral judgements based on universalist abstractions, nor to depersonalise the abusive acts, but to locate the practice or violation of human rights within specific social and community contexts.

> By situating social persons in the communities and contexts, and furnishing thick descriptions of acts of the violent exercise of power, it can be seen how rights themselves are grounded, transformative and inextricably bound to purposive agents rather than being universal abstractions. . . . By embracing a technocratic language, human rights reporting lays itself open to the same critique as could be made of the devalued, dehumanised language of abusive forms of governance.[15]

Chris Brown, an academic who works in international relations, has convincingly argued that this kind of universalism actually impedes the protection of human rights because there is a refusal to admit that its values *are* liberal and Western.[16] Charges of ethnocentrism in these matters are subject to continual debate in non-governmental organisations, where it is acknowledged that the balance between social intervention on an international scale and the imposition of Western political systems is not easily struck.

The debate turns on how human rights become integrated into social practices, and how they shift from the legalistic framework in which they are couched into the vernacular and the everyday. Reciprocally, there are questions about how local practices might influence international human rights debates. Anthropologist Sally Engle Merry has offered an illuminating insight into how 'indigenous peoples' mobilise human rights in order to have 'conversations about justice'. Her study is of native Hawaiians, where she observed that the people did not accept the imposition of a Western or North American version of human rights, but regarded it as 'an open text' which they might appropriate and redefine according to their own local circumstances.[17] By campaigning

for political sovereignty based on Hawaiian cultural practices and languages, the native Hawaiians re-asserted their local rights by recourse to
aspects of international law. In the process, they redefined international
human rights law in ways which have influenced discussions about
indigenous rights at the United Nations. This suggests, Merry concludes,
that it is possible for the global to become localised, and the local to be
globalised. In other words, neither human rights nor cultures have
fixed, determined, knowable essences or boundaries. They are always and
continually in flux, contingent on time and space, and have both
porousness and specificity.

Richard Wilson's critique of the a-cultural rhetoric of human rights
organisations presents a salutary reminder for workers in applied drama.
It would be easy to suggest that drama is exempt from such concerns
because it is necessarily involved in creating narratives and characters
that flesh out human rights reports in ways which Wilson appears to
be advocating. This warrants further investigation. Drama is used as
part of human rights campaigns precisely because it is seen as an effective
means of bringing about change. By definition, therefore, any leaning
towards what Wilson calls 'soggy relativism where any representation is as
good as another' is out of the question.[18] Some rights-based theatre is
designed to offer information – about health care or the rights of
children, for example – and this means that the drama may contain
very precise information. But without working in sustainable partnership
with local communities and other agencies, the work is likely to perpetuate the very inequalities that it seeks to erode. None of the commentators
invoked in this section would do away with an international framework of
human rights, but all acknowledge the limitations of social practices
which impose a highly individualised system of rights and 'freedoms'
in the name of social progress or development. As Wilson identified,
there is a need to recognise that there is a multiplicity of narratives
inherent in both human rights agendas and their violations, and
that a more equitable distribution of power recognises the part local
knowledge, cultural languages and personal experiences have to play in
the process of redefining and relocating the international discourse of
human rights.

Community Networks and Cultural Expressions

So far I have argued that theatre which aims to promote human rights
needs to be rooted in the cultures in which the work takes place rather

than rely on abstract universalism or moral individualism for its efficacy. I am not suggesting, however, that human rights should be entirely locally determined, and I accept that the United Nations charters on human rights represent a compelling system of international social justice. What I am interested in securing are approaches to human rights in drama which go beyond the rather distracting debates between cultural relativists and universalists. The problem with both these perspectives is that they depend on the outdated view that cultures are fixed, internally coherent and holistic units rather than recognising that societies and cultures change, and are in a continual process of reformulation through local, regional and global dialogues. I am interested in questioning the role theatre might have in facilitating such dialogues about human rights, and how drama might be used to narrate local and personal experiences.

In terms of applied drama, this raises a number of questions about how practice might mediate the gap between local and global discourses in relation to human rights advocacy. As it is not unusual for practitioners in applied drama to seek out situations in which human rights are violated, this has particular implications for our field. In order to interrogate this further, I have chosen to focus on theatre that confronts the rights of women subjected to family violence, in part because as an issue it is fraught with ambiguities and local complexities. Like so many others, I am also aware of its effects at first hand and witnessing this kind of abuse has given me some insights into how difficult it is for men and women to disclose that it is going on. There is obviously no doubt that family violence is wrong, and that it is a violation against human rights and dignity. But as one experienced NGO in Sri Lanka pointed out to me, to work from the simple premise that women should just not put up with family abuse is not only likely to ignore the complex and powerful emotions at stake, it may also pay scant attention to factors such as the women's economic status or local constructions of honour, duty and family responsibilities. Raising awareness of family violence as a matter of social injustice and as a violation of human rights, rather than primarily as a private or personal problem is, therefore, particularly difficult. As examples of practice, I have chosen two campaigns for the prevention of violence against women in the family, both funded by the United Nations Development Fund for Women (UNIFEM). The main focus for this discussion will be a project developed in Malawi, but I shall also refer to work developed by Philippine Educational Theater Association (PETA), one of the most experienced and highly respected companies in the world. Each illuminates different aspects of the negotiation between international standards of human rights and respect for local culture, and they also articulate some shared solutions to the ethical challenges of humanitarian intervention through theatre.

The Malawi project was undertaken by the Story Workshop Educational Trust, a 'nonprofit-making media group creating entertainment for social change in Malawi'.[19] Based in Malawi's second city, Blantyre, the organisation has a history of intercultural dialogue about human rights issues, which has influenced the work both politically and artistically. In part, this exchange has come about because much of the work is funded by international humanitarian organisations and, although almost everyone working at Story Workshop is Malawian, it is significant that the founder of Story Workshop is American and a small number of European theatre practitioners have worked with the company for extended periods. There is, of course, a delicate balance to be struck here, and this is reflected in the company's creative output. There is a strong commitment to sustaining Malawi's traditional cultural forms, but the medium of communication is primarily radio and the main focus of Story Workshop is the production of two radio soap operas that are broadcast across Malawi. This approach is consistent with James Clifford's much quoted observation that contemporary identities:

> no longer presuppose continuous cultures or traditions. Everywhere individuals and groups improvise local performances from (re)collected pasts drawing on foreign media, symbols and languages.[20]

Story Workshop's creative output is similarly inflected by a range of symbolic forms; their soap operas have become a major form of popular entertainment in Malawi where many people are illiterate and very few have access to television. The two radio soaps, *Zimachitike* and *Tilitonse*, aim to address issues of rural development and civic education. They were inspired by the long-running BBC radio soap *The Archers*, which was started in the 1950s to provide information for farming communities, and the two soaps also built on the success of radio dramas produced by the Malawi Broadcasting Corporation in the early 1990s. *Zimachitike* and *Tilitonse* have a huge following, and villagers will gather around a radio to catch the latest episodes. The convention of soaps is that strong and recognisable characters drive a linear plot, and audiences learn to like (and dislike) particular characters and either identify with them, argue with them or empathise with the dramatic situations they portray. This means that soaps are particularly well placed to contribute to civic education programmes, as popular characters are able to articulate information in ways which are palatable to audiences. David Kerr, a theatre academic who has worked extensively in Africa, has pointed out that there are similarities between radio drama and the oral traditions of Africa, and the form, as well as the content, account for its popularity.[21]

The success of *Zimachitike* and *Tilitonse* was significant for *Tingathe!*, the theatre project funded by UNIFEM in order to draw attention to the problems of family violence within a Malawian context. *Tingathe!* was devised as a piece of live theatre by Action Theatre, Story Workshop's community outreach company, and it involved the same performers who appear in the soaps. Radio has made celebrities of these performers, and when they perform live with Action Theatre their popularity not only guarantees large audiences (it is not unusual to see 2000 people at a performance), they will often also adopt the same role they play in the soap opera. As audiences already know the characters well, the cast are able to take some short-cuts in performance, and this enables the audience to focus quickly on the particular issues the plays seek to explore. It also means that the audiences' perceptions of the celebrity performers and their dramatic roles are interestingly layered. Audiences are often complicit in the illusion that soap characters are 'real people' and this means that performers themselves become intimately connected with the genre. Furthermore, as Frances Harding has observed, audiences for African theatre often perceive the performers' identities in the context of their extended repertoire *as* performers.

> Performers and their acts are judged by spectators at multiple levels: as part of the repertoire of the performer, as part of the performer's whole performance on any one occasion and, in comparison with other like artefacts, as part of a *genre*.[22]

As a genre, soap opera sets up certain expectations of character and familiar patterns of plot that can be both sustained and disrupted in live theatre. Action Theatre has exploited the productive tension between the real and the imaginary that exists in all live theatre, but which is all the more acute in this delicious interpretation of performative identities.

When I visited Story Workshop in 2002, the company was in the process of devising *Tingathe!*, a play which told the story of family violence against a fictional woman. Action Theatre perform in ChiChewa, the national language most widely spoken in Malawi, and at the time there were two *mzungus* (white people) working with the cast, Louise

Keyworth as director and Kathryn Pugh as her assistant. In the devising process, the significance of this intercultural dialogue became apparent, both in the play's form and its content. Story Workshop's policy of including the performative traditions of Malawi within their creative output is regarded as an important educational tool in an increasingly urbanised society, and local songs, proverbs, parables and folk-tales are integrated into their live theatre as well as their radio programmes. The Malawian actors had considerable local knowledge of these forms of performance as well as having extensive ability to improvise both musically and dramatically. They were also able to bring their understanding of how symbolism and metaphor worked in different forms of local performance, which the English directors obviously lacked. The directors, by contrast, had been trained in the tradition of European theatre, and their experiences gave them access to processes of rehearsal and devising which were unfamiliar to the actors. The combination of these different experiences and cultural backgrounds contributed to a rich melting pot of genres and styles on which the company could draw. Not only was this artistically exciting, but the process of collaboration and intercultural dialogue also revealed some of the ways in which dramatic genres imply different ways of thinking about the world.

There was one particular moment in rehearsal which demonstrated to me that the blurring of genres can create new insights into the local and international politics of human rights. The story revolved around a woman, Mrs Mbewe, who had been beaten in her home by her husband, and when I arrived in Malawi the company was at the point in the devising process where it needed to discuss how the plot should develop and, more particularly, what should happen to the abused woman. If she were to leave her husband, she would be ostracised by her community, becoming economically destitute and homeless. If she stayed, the beatings would doubtless continue as the husband was showing no remorse for his actions and was even justifying them. The actors agreed that this was likely to be the reality of the situation in Malawi, but they were genuinely surprised to hear that family violence is also prevalent in England. In the discussions about her fate, the cast felt that it was important that the audience sympathised with the abused woman. This had inevitably given rise to discussions about dramatic form. As director, Louise had suggested that they experimented with naturalism as a form of representation – the subject of this play afforded a good opportunity for these highly skilled professional actors to learn to use Stanislavsky's method. As a result of working on the physical and psychological objectives of their roles in different situations, they built characters to whom they hoped the audience would be able to respond emotionally. Contrary to local expectations that live theatre is comic entertainment, this play was intended to be serious and sombre in mood. To this end the cast used three tempos to control the pace and dramatic atmosphere – angry and explosive; heavy and painful; tense and anxious. It was decided that the mood would be re-enforced in performance by the Joker, who would establish a contract with the audience at the beginning of the play. This was a risk, as it was a form of live theatre which was culturally unfamiliar.

The crunch came on the second day I attended rehearsals. The central problem – whether or not Mrs Mbewe should leave her husband – had been resolved by a phone call to Pamela Brooke, the American founder and director of Story Workshop, who strongly advised that she should leave. The company was uncomfortable about this decision and, as an observer in the process, so was I. I was concerned that this decision was based on an Anglo-American feminist answer to family violence and, although I would generally subscribe to this position at home, I feared that in the context of Malawi the resolution did not take full account of how the woman would be treated by her local community if she were to leave her husband. But it was a decision, and the company set about trying to make it work both theatrically and politically. They decided to dramatise the dilemma the woman faced, and invite the audience to discuss her situation after the performance. At the centre of the performance space they constructed a crossroads, which provided a simple theatrical metaphor for the woman's troubled decision. Standing at this powerful central point, the cast improvised a song using the traditional Malawi form of 'call and response' that underscored a soliloquy spoken by Mrs Mbewe. It was the meeting point of different theatrical genres, and each had a different dramatic purpose. The soliloquy was designed to elicit audiences' imaginative sympathy for – or empathy with – her emotional turmoil as an individual, and the song suggested a strong collective voice. The soliloquy and song shared the same words, but the aesthetic created a deeper political dialectic. Soliloquy is a theatrical interpretation of the tradition of Western individualism, whereas the 'call and response' song invokes the oral and communitarian culture of African performance. In rehearsal this combination of individualism and communitarianism was a powerful and moving way of representing the play's political problem. The cast were aware that audiences would know what would happen to her if she left her violent husband, and they thought it likely that some audience

FIGURE 2   THE PERFORMANCE OF *TINGATHE!* (PHOTOGRAPHED BY LOUISE KEYWORTH)

members would be complicit in ostracising someone in her position. But they hoped that, in performance, the sympathy she had gained as a character would make her actions comprehensible. Having left Malawi before the performance took place, I am dependent on Louise Keyworth's description of the event:

> The first performance of *Tingathe!* was in a small town outside Blantyre, renowned for its poverty-driven crime. A local man had recently killed and dismembered two women there. We arrived at the open area next to the market. We felt very exposed and the team was apprehensive about performing a controversial piece that was experimental in a part of town we usually all avoided.
>
> Curious, crowds gathered, pushed and shouted as we set up the arena. We dug holes in the ground for the stakes then tied them with rubber to keep the audience out – comprising passers-by and those doing nothing in particular. People asked questions: is it really their favourite characters Chithope and Nabanda from *Zimachitike*? Are they going to perform? And who are the two white women banging hammers and doing manual work? The atmosphere felt full of aggression. Kat let go of a stretched rubber-band that flew back and knocked her over. The onlookers' laughter was loud and disconcerting.
>
> When we started the arena was surrounded by around a thousand people. Typically in Malawi, audiences laugh when something serious is

performed. The Joker challenged the audience directly as Mr Mbewe hit his wife for the first time. It went quiet for two reasons, I think. Firstly, the Joker's words had an effect: 'Why do you laugh my friends? We are not here to make you laugh, see the seriousness . . . etc.' Secondly, the naturalistic acting style was unfamiliar to most audiences in Malawi. The laughter swapped to tutting and the culturally familiar sound of surprise (a fast, low 'Aah-ahh!'). Their noises became angry and disapproving at the violent moments and verbal abuse. The atmosphere became serious and the previous sense of aggression faded. Women stood alone, thinking, concentrating – different to the usual groups of girlfriends watching something together.

At the end fifteen people entered the arena for the audience-participation section. They were asked if Mrs Mbewe should have left her husband and to stand on the spot that represented their view. The options were 'Yes', 'No' and 'Don't know'. At first most people were equally spilt between 'Yes' and 'No'. One older women stood at 'Don't know'. The participants hot-seated the characters. The older woman, who was undecided, spoke eloquently and addressed everyone listening. She said the decision was tricky and although violence is wrong Mrs Mbewe's life would be more difficult for cultural reasons. A lively discussion ensued, facilitated by the Joker. At the end of it, participants had the option of moving to a different floor cloth if they'd changed their mind. Twelve moved to 'Don't know', leaving one person on 'Yes' and one on 'No'. The participation at the end of the piece made Mrs Mbewe's choice ambiguous. We all left without resolving the story, deliberately.[23]

This description suggests that the audience's expectations were disrupted by the use of elements of dramatic form which were culturally unfamiliar. The change in the audience's reactions – from laughter at the husband's beating to an intense silence – implies an empathetic engagement with the play which was profoundly personal, emphasised by the observation that women in the audience moved to watch alone. By showing the emotional effects of family abuse on an individual in the performance, and by presenting an unresolved and unresolvable dilemma in the participatory programme, the audience were invited to respond sympathetically to Mrs Mbewe as an individual and to question their cultural values towards family violence and examine community responsibilities towards the abused woman. The play had contextualised the human rights 'issue' of family violence, and the ambiguity inherent in the dramatic form recognised its political and cultural complexities. In this instance the intercultural dialogue enabled the company to blur artistic genres, with the effect of making accepted values strange, as if they were viewed from another place.

Tingathe! affords a good opportunity to analyse the political and artistic potential for intercultural dialogue in theatre which seeks to promote human rights. Intercultural dialogue has been described by Rustom Bharucha as a process of 'seeking the familiar in the unfamiliar, the unfamiliar in the familiar'. Such an exchange of cultural capital is not easily equitable and involves not only aesthetic choices but, in Bharucha's words, the ability to 'negotiate different systems of power'.[24] By focusing on the dialogue between European and Malawian practitioners in this analysis of practice I have, however, given the misleading impression that Malawian culture is homogeneous and internally cohesive, which is very far from the case. As a way of conceptualising the differences within cultures Bharucha has made a useful distinction between *inter*culturalism and *intra*culturalism, terms he uses to differentiate 'intercultural relations *across* national boundaries, and the intracultural dynamics between and across specific communities and regions *within* the boundaries of the nation-state'.[25] This insight offers a way of analysing how different cultural dynamics found within national boundaries might affect the processes of social change. As no culture is a fixed and stable entity, there are always points of cultural continuity and discontinuity within cultures which means that change takes place. For this process to be productive, Bharucha argues, there needs to be a negotiation of the intracultural space between 'the stabilities of cultural diversity and the indeterminacies of cultural difference'.[26]

The significance of intraculturalism to the process of human rights mobilisation might be observed in the campaign against family violence to which PETA made a major contribution. The project, which took place in 1998–9, was called *Breaking Silence*, and is well documented in a book of the same name. It arose from long-term partnerships within the Philippines between PETA, the National Family Violence Prevention Programme (NFVPP) and the Women's Crisis Centre and offers a clear example of the effect and effectiveness of multi-agency work. Describing family violence as 'the gravest form of human rights violation' because it turns the safe space of home into a place of danger, the campaigning organisations identified the need for a change in *culture* if women were to be supported in disclosing cases of abuse.[27] Their intention was to use theatre to challenge the attitude that family violence is a private matter by bringing the issue into the public domain and inviting people to talk about it within the safe space of participatory workshops. Research undertaken in advance of the project revealed the nature and extent of family abuse in the Philippines, but significantly it also provided statistical information about the problem on an international scale. Acknowledging that family violence is a global problem helped place the attitude found in parts of the Philippines – that domestic violence is just 'part of family life' – in a wider social context. This research process also provided important information that PETA needed to develop a piece of theatre which would both encourage reciprocity and dialogue between audience and performers, and present a clear message that family violence is a matter of public responsibility as it is a violation of international standards of human rights.[28]

One of the striking aspects of the campaign to which PETA made a major contribution was that it acknowledged that combating family violence is an extremely complex and multi-layered process because there are different attitudes towards it within any given culture or community. In order to address these intracultural differences, the campaign was structured to offer considerable support and information to women in a variety of ways. The NFVPP worked alongside local and community-based organisations (NGOs, local government agencies, universities, religious groups and youth organisations) in order to address the various and different struggles against family violence experienced across the country. As a direct result of their theatrical intervention, there was an increase in the numbers of abused women seeking help and advice from appropriate agencies. Not only does this multi-agency approach recognise that family violence is not an issue which can be seen in isolation from other cultural values, it also acknowledges that, although theatre is a good form of communication and social mobilisation, on its own it is an incomplete weapon against social injustice.

These projects show that even the most humanitarian interventions are not borderfree but are located on *inter-* and *intra*-cultural routes of dialogue and exchange. Effective campaigns relate human rights principles to the vernacular and to the everyday practices of life, a process that Richard Wilson has suggested offers the potential to turn the idealistic intentions of an international human rights framework to social action by recognising the cultural contradictions inherent in particular local contexts. Cultures are continually reformulated through creative practice, leading to optimistic encounters between the specificity of local cultures and normative vocabulary of human rights. Drama has the potential to trouble absolutes and, at best, the aesthetics of production can encourage a reflexivity and a sharing of experience that can contribute to the process of unfixing habitual patterns of thought and behaviour.

Performing Rights

Any perspective on human rights would be disingenuous and incomplete without some serious reflection on its implications at home as well as internationally. I am conscious that all the examples of practice I have offered so far in this chapter refer to work outside my own British context, for which I might be justly criticised for giving the impression that human rights violations happen 'elsewhere' and that everything in the European garden is rosy. This is not only very far from the actual case but also offers a narrow picture of human rights as a collection of social issues rather than, as I have argued, integral to a system of liberal governance. As a conclusion to this chapter, I should like to take the discussion of the application of drama to human rights in a slightly different direction. I shall take up Derrida's challenge to construct a poetics of human rights in relation to applied drama by re-examining one of the recurring themes in this book: the dialectic between identity and alterity, self and other.

In his lecture entitled 'On Writing Rights', Homi Bhabha described the politics of human rights as a 'process of making connections' between divergent perspectives. Citing Adrienne Rich's poem *Movement*, he argued that constructing an equitable ethic of human rights involves re-imagining the construction of human identity not as a series of fixed oppositions (self/other; minority/majority) but as a process of movement between different cultural milieux. Not only does Bhabha make a significant point about how the 'human' of human rights is not a universal but a cultural category, he also suggests that the process of moving towards equality involves individuals confronting their own demons, desires and motivations. This recognises that individuals inhabit dialogical spaces in which they continually negotiate and renegotiate a sense of who they are and who they might become, in narrative and through conversation. It brings together the ethics of human rights – its legal and formal frameworks – with the aesthetics of self-construction. Describing narrative as 'a moving sign of civic life', he suggests that it is the 'right to narrate' which enables people to recognise their own experiences, reinterpret history and change the direction of the future. His words have such resonance with the themes in this book that they are worth quoting at length.

> By the 'right to narrate', I mean to suggest all those forms of creative behaviour that allow us to represent the lives we lead, question the conversations and customs that we inherit, dispute and propagate the

ideas and ideals that come to us most naturally, and dare to entertain the most audacious hopes and fears for the future....Suddenly in painting, dance, or cinema you rediscover your senses, and in that process you discover something profound about yourself, your historical moment, and what gives value to a life in a particular town, at a particular time, in particular social and political conditions.[29]

Bhabha's emphasis on narrative and contextuality is important here, as it shows that human rights are not experienced solely as social 'issues' but are played out in the dialogic space of everyday existence. The practice of the arts enables experiences to be framed and, I am suggesting, practising drama has the potential to bring life into sharp relief by inviting participants to step outside themselves, to embody the narratives of others. This is a process which often involves seeing themselves as outsiders and experiencing life from different perspectives. The interweaving of ethics and aesthetics implies a journey or movement, in which we are asked not only to consider where we are, but to question which way we are going.

Bhabha's concept of the right to narrate locates human rights in the performative practices of everyday life where an awareness of social justice is articulated in people's behaviour and attitudes towards others. It also draws attention to political questions about who has access to the means of cultural expression and where this right to narrate is denied. Both perspectives are articulated in a disturbing account of work in British prisons by theatre practitioner Martin Glynn. Glynn described how he sought to enable black male inmates to explore and narrate their own social realities in dramatic form but was confronted with hostility, racism and opposition by white prison officers. Prisons are notoriously difficult places to show emotional vulnerability or take risks, and the repressive environment which surrounds life in the penal regime is not conducive to the more sensitive aspects of theatre-making. Glynn's intention – to encourage disaffected black inmates to find an outlet for 'self-examination and creative expression' – was motivated by a need to connect with those whose voices were unheard and 'invisible' in the penal regime but with whom he felt he shared a social, cultural and political bond.[30] He is extremely critical of the ways in which the prison service is unquestioningly based on white values and norms, which at best does little to promote black-led thought or recognise the complexity and diversity of black experience, and at worst is actively racist. The role of black artists within this system is doubly problematic, as Glynn's account of his painful encounters with officials in prison institutions testifies. His essay encapsulates and examines many aspects of human rights that have been explored in this chapter – the significance of language to cultural affirmation and mutual respect; the ways in which normative vocabularies of institutions are inevitably partisan; the potential for the neglect of human rights in a system in which there is no reflection on the social and cultural specificity of its regime and regulations. What he adds to this analysis is an awareness of the need for self-reflection in order to understand how his own beliefs impact on the work, and to recognise how his psychological strengths and weaknesses affect its progress. This self-knowledge contributes to, and feeds into, the process of setting boundaries within drama workshops and to defining the parameters of acceptable behaviour with all those involved in the work. As Glynn's account clearly illustrates, this may be an uncomfortable experience. One of the insights from psychoanalytic theory is that prejudice is often the unconscious projection of one's own needy feelings onto others, and this means that tackling some of the more subtle forms of human rights infringement can feel intensely personal and disturbing.

In some ways every social encounter is a performative negotiation of human rights. Derrida's concept of a poetics of human rights recognises that there is an aesthetic dimension to ethical social interactions, and that human rights are practised only when the dialectic between self and other is troubled and the fixed polarity is challenged. In this context, therefore, one of the social purposes of drama is to practise human rights by both embodying the position of an imagined other and re-affirming an assured sense of selfhood. These aspirations are not contradictory: they are not allied to an uncritical cultural pluralism and nor do they represent an individualised liberal tolerance. It is quite the reverse. A poetics of human rights is about taking collective responsibility for the performance of rights, and recognising the creative opportunities afforded by envisioning social change. This approach to human rights is inherently dramatic and performative because it unites the personal with the political, the public with the private, thought and action, and asks all of us to make a daily commitment redefining where we are and improving human rights for the future.

Part IV
Epilogue

8 The Gift of Theatre

The major characteristic of the experience of the gift is, without doubt, its ambiguity.

Pierre Bourdieu, 'Marginalia – Some Additional Notes on the Gift' (1997) p. 231

Becoming Ethical

In the opening scene of Rebecca Prichard's play *Yard Gal* the stage directions state that the two characters, Boo and Marie, stare at the floor to avoid looking at the audience as each waits for the other to begin the play. When they do eventually start to speak, it is to goad each other on:

Boo: Wh' you looking at me for?
Marie: Uh?
Boo: Wha' you looking at me for man?
Marie: Ain't you gonna start it?
Boo: I ain't starting it start what?
Marie: Fuck you man, the play.
Boo: I ain't tellin' them shit.
Marie: What?
Boo: I ain't telling them shit. If you wanna make a fool of yaself it's up to you. I ain't telling them shit.
Marie: You said you's gonna back me up! You said you's gonna back me up tellin' the story.[1]

Yard Gal was written as a result of the playwright's residency at Bulwood Hall women's prison in 1997, and was commissioned by Clean Break

Theatre Company as part of its work with women prisoners and ex-offenders. First staged at the Royal Court Theatre Upstairs in London, the play's opening implies a question-mark over whether these young women will choose to tell their stories to this audience, whether they will decide to reveal the circumstances that led to Boo's imprisonment to 'them'. This ambiguity was emphasised in the first production by playing the lines with humour, the actors' body language and banter suggesting that there was a difference between what the characters actually said – 'I ain't tellin' them shit' – and what they would like to do, which was to enact their stories for a live and captive audience.

I have chosen this theatrical moment to begin this chapter because it raises a number of ethical questions that I should like to revisit and to explore a little further. One of the noticeable qualities of the script is that the characters acknowledge the presence of the audience, introducing themselves in a way which assumes that there are differences between their narratives and experiences and those of the theatre-going audience.

> *Boo*:   We's from Hackney. People talk a lot of shit about Hackney when they ain't never been there, and they talk a lot of shit about yards when they ain't never met none. So me and Maria we come to tell you a story that is FI' REAL.[2]

There is a sense that these characters, though fictional, are putting the record straight about 'real' young women in the criminal justice system by inviting the audience to witness their stories. By referencing the theatricality of the play there is a sense that Prichard is also gesturing towards the context of her residency in which the play was researched. The dialogue acknowledges the understandable ambivalence many feel about revealing their personal narratives so publicly in drama, and the device of re-enacting apparently autobiographical narratives to a live audience also has the effect of honouring the voices of the prisoners who worked with the playwright during her residency. This blurring of fiction and reality implies that there are personal and social benefits for both the young women and for the play's audiences. The characters offer a commentary on the stories they enact that demonstrates how reflecting on experience in drama can lead to new insights and ways of thinking. For the audience, the act of witnessing the narratives of struggle and friendship enables them to see 'yard gals' in a different light. Although the yard gals initially view the audience with suspicion, they act generously towards the audience by inviting them into their world through their stories. Taken together, this play raises ethical questions about whose stories are told in drama, about the context and ownership of autobiographical stories, about the power of narrative to effect social change and, by extension, about the relationships of trust and reciprocity between practitioners and participants in applied drama – all key themes in this book.

Throughout this book I have been concerned with furthering a praxis which, like *Yard Gal*, both bears witness to a plurality of voices and experiences and maintains a commitment to a radical social democracy. Finding a balance (rather than a compromise) between equality and difference is not a matter of moral relativism, where all values are seen to be equally legitimate. Rather, I am interested in developing a praxis which, whilst based on secure principles, does not seek to discriminate against a plurality of perspectives and multiple ways of living. In this respect, the distinction between ethics and morality made by Chantal Mouffe is illuminating. She describes ethics as 'a domain which allows for competing conceptions of the good life', and morality as 'a domain where a strict proceduralism can be implemented and impartiality reached leading to the formulation of universal principles'.[3] Critical of the implication that morality is remote from political concerns, Mouffe's advocacy of a revitalised democracy is based on the view that there needs to be constant vigilance over what constitutes contemporary notions of 'the good life' if its ethical limits are to be explored and contested. With this in mind, it is the ethics of practice in applied drama that is the subject of this final chapter. What does it mean to act ethically in contexts where there are 'competing conceptions of the good life' amongst participants and practitioners in applied drama?

One practical answer to this question might be found in the various guidelines for conduct laid down by professional associations in, for example, drama therapy and for educational research. These tend to emphasise the need to secure the participants' informed consent to practise and research, and require prescribed levels of confidentiality and competence.[4] The application of drama to community settings is, however, often unregulated and although standards of professionalism are obviously extremely important, the terms and conditions of codes and contracts are often only invoked when they are seriously transgressed. It is helpful, therefore, to look beyond these standards and for practitioners to consider what is involved in realising ethical partnerships with social agencies or organisations, with funders and, most importantly, with the participants themselves. These can be difficult sets of negotiations as there are sometimes different interests at stake, which makes the need for an ethics of praxis all the more acute.

An ethic of praxis that acknowledges and interrogates the 'competing conceptions of the good life' which Mouffe described has been offered by Patti Lather in her *Applying Derrida: (Mis)Reading the Work of Mourning in Educational Research* (2003). Lather has critiqued her own assumptions about a praxis based on ideas of 'transformative intellectuals' who work towards 'empowering' or 'emancipating' others, assumptions originally put forward in 1986 and reprinted in her much cited book *Getting Smart* (1991). This easy symmetry between moral action and social transformation, she argues, is no longer compatible with a post-Marxist era in which straightforward equations between 'uncovering [the] hidden forces' of power and social enlightenment have been troubled.[5] Drawing on the ethical preoccupations of Jacques Derrida, Lather offers a way of salvaging many of the political aspirations of Marxism without resorting to the 'dream of cure, salvation and redemption' so often invoked by the rhetoric of theatre practitioners working in community arts.[6] In place of redemption narratives, Lather argues for an ethical praxis that 'disrupts horizons' and, in terms similar to those I identified in Chapter 3, for pedagogies which map 'new possibilities for playing out relations between identity and difference, margins and centres'.[7]

I should like to respond to Lather's challenge to re-inscribe praxis, and to Mouffe's call for an ethic of social responsibilities based on a 'never-ending interrogation of the political by the ethical', by returning to the metaphor of the gift. My intention in this final chapter is to draw together some thoughts about the ethics of practice in applied drama through this theoretical lens. Before I revisit the concept of the gift as a political metaphor that unites the themes of this book, however, I shall attempt to offer a brief summary of some of the distinct arguments in previous chapters as a way of refocusing on the book's core debates.

Re-visiting the Scene

The central debate in this book is political. The task I set myself in writing this book was to find ways of conceptualising and articulating practice which maintains and renews the radicalism that has been traditionally associated with community-based theatre, but does not rely on the 'dream of cure, salvation and redemption' that Lather identified as politically limiting in the new world (dis)order. In raising questions about the values of applied drama, it has not been my intention to suggest that applied drama/theatre is a new discipline with fixed boundaries. On the contrary, I have suggested that the theories and practices of applied drama are continually on the move and always renegotiated in practice. Consequently, my attempt to map and narrate the theoretical terrain of applied drama is based on the premise that, because it involves a process of encounter and engagement, applied drama is more helpfully conceptualised as a diasporan rather than a disciplinary space.

In diaspora space, the boundaries that define and confine knowledge, meaning-making and understanding are subject to continual critical scrutiny, and the ways in which power is constructed are closely examined. Rather than seeking a single canonical reference point or a single set of dramatic practices, it is an approach to theatre-making that embraces diverse forms of cultural learning and many different theatre forms. The concept of diaspora space also has the potential to offer ways of thinking about how boundaries are encountered and transgressed, how those on the margins can move to the centre, and how the global asserts itself into the local. As a framework for analysis, this recognises that the process of locating and mapping narrating enables us to more fully appreciate where, temporarily and contingently, the horizons and limits of practice in applied drama may lie. Aesthetic and performative encounters within diaspora spaces also require the capacity to move around and negotiate different locations, not as the meeting place of fixed identities or positions, but as an open state of becoming. With this in mind, it is worth revisiting the place where I started, and looking at the scene from a different point of view.

The premise with which I began this book was that there are major theoretical concepts which impact on applied drama – community, citizenship, identity, human rights, creativity, the effects and efficacy of narrative – all of which invite us to consider important questions about the wider role and significance of theatre in society. In many ways, the application of drama to community contexts forces us to confront questions about the ethics and efficacy of performance which are relevant to all theatre practices but often remain at the level of rhetoric or advocacy elsewhere. I have argued that, at best, the dynamic of live theatre challenges the predictability and sameness of globalisation, and offers creative re-interpretations of what it means to live well and to live ethically. Although the politics of social participation may be felt most acutely and directly when drama is explicitly applied to different community settings, all theatre has the potential to stretch the ethical imagination.

What becomes particularly apparent when drama is applied to different contexts and settings is that there is always a need to be vigilant about whether the practice is accepted as a generous exercise of care or whether, however well intentioned, it is regarded as an unwelcome intrusion. It is easy for trust to become dependency, for generosity to be interpreted as patronage, for interest in others to be experienced as the gaze of surveillance. As a way of engaging further with this complex debate, I shall return to the metaphor of the gift.

The Metaphor of the Gift

Because it is concerned with how values are articulated in diverse social and cultural practices, gift theory also has the potential to offer an ethical alternative to the kind of salvation narratives critiqued by Lather. The application of gift theory to applied drama is a way of acknowledging the positive attributes of empathy, generosity and care for others that characterises much good practice. Equally significant, however, are the less positive characteristics of the gift such as self-interest or the system of debts and social obligations, which are sometimes associated with the act of giving. It is the ethical problems and uncertainties raised by the metaphor of the gift which makes its application to drama particularly illuminating. I shall begin by discussing the less positive attributes of the gift, which dominated much early writing in gift theory, before considering the principles of reciprocity and generosity with which it is also associated. As the quotation with which I began this chapter suggests, the experience of the gift is fraught with paradoxes.

The theme of the gift, which has become important to discussions of value in gender studies, economics, philosophy and anthropology and to interdisciplinary debates about ethics, found an early articulation in the work of the French social anthropologist Marcel Mauss. Mauss's essay *The Gift* was first published in 1924 and has formed a touchstone for subsequent discussions. In this essay, Mauss noted that the etymology of *gift* in Germanic languages has given rise to both the words 'present' and 'poison'. He traces this history to gifts of drink offered between ancient Germans and Scandinavians, where the recipients were never quite sure whether their drinks would be poisoned or not. Mauss uses this example to indicate the state of uncertainty associated with the gift, which might be experienced as either pleasure or displeasure. With this in mind, Mauss documented the use and symbolism of gifts in societies he considered archaic, and was amongst the earliest in anthropology to identify the coercive function of gift-giving. In his discussion of the elaborate potlatch ceremonies in communities such as the Kwakiutl in the north-west Pacific, he noted that the aim of gift-giving was to overwhelm rivals with presents, which they were both obliged to reciprocate and which were so 'generous' that they could not possibly repay them. The potlatch symbolised, for Mauss, gift-giving at its most self-interested. His intention in this work was to isolate how aspects of the gift become tied to economic self-interest and thence to a nexus of other social obligations. He described his study of:

> presentations which are in theory voluntary, disinterested and spontaneous, but are in fact voluntary and interested. The form usually taken is that of the gift generously offered; but the accompanying behaviour is formal pretence and social deception, while the transaction itself is based on obligation and self-interest.[8]

Despite the many counter-arguments and objections to Mauss's thesis that have since been offered, his observations about the relationship between disinterestedness and self-interest continue to exert a powerful influence on gift theory.

Mauss's legacy has relevance for applied drama insofar as it problematises the relationship between gift-givers and recipients. It serves as a useful reminder that not all acts of giving are made unconditionally and that, as I pointed out in Chapter 2, self-interest plays a part in many exchanges. This is particularly relevant where the balance of power or material wealth between donor and recipient is already unevenly distributed. As I have argued throughout this book, the desire for equity and social participation is a major preoccupation for theatre practitioners in applied drama. What a reading of gift theory adds to this debate is a way to question the ethics and motives of the various agencies and individuals that contribute to practice. What do we, as practitioners, expect in return for our labours? Artistic satisfaction? The participants' acquisition of skills or abilities? Do we ask participants to adopt new ways of thinking or different political values? Do we expect them to change their behaviour in particular ways? In turn, how far might our own perspectives alter as a result of the work? What about the funders? Do they have expectations of a return? None of these questions can be answered glibly. The paradox of the gift is that, because it can be seen simultaneously as both a present and a poison, it is sometimes worth remembering the unpalatable truth that a present, however well intentioned, may be thought to be poisonous by those who live in a different context and whose vision of a good life differs from our own.

Although Mauss's analysis of the ethics of gift-exchange remains influential, his critics have pointed out that he paid scant attention to forms of giving which are less binding and socially contractual. More recently, concern for an ethic of social welfare has ensured that the more positive attributes of the gift have been well theorised, most conspicuously by the French social theorists and philosophers Hélène Cixous, Jacques Derrida and Pierre Bourdieu. In his work *Given Time* (1992) Derrida challenges the circle of obligation described by Mauss and, in the opening pages, re-inscribes the gift as a more open and generous expression of desires and responsibilities. He is interested in developing a new theoretical tradition for the gift which 'interrupts the system as well as the symbol' of debt, counter-giving, credit and the social obligations associated with reciprocal patterns of exchange. He suggests that one of the problems is that as soon as the gift becomes identified as a gift, it has already acquired a symbolism that distorts its value. For Derrida, a gift is made voluntarily and unconditionally: not as an economic exchange, as capitalism invariably requires, but as an ethical alternative to self-interest. He suggests that when the gift acquires symbolic value, it is already caught up in a chain of exchange.

> For the symbol immediately engages one in resituation. To tell the truth, the gift must not even appear or signify, consciously or unconsciously *as* gift for the donors, whether individual or collective subjects. For the moment the gift would appear as gift...it would be engaged in a symbolic, sacrificial, or economic structure that would annul the gift in the ritual circle of debt.[9]

For Derrida, the gift is always ethical, but the paradox is that it is inevitably destroyed when it becomes embroiled in cycles of reciprocity.

Because the gift is annulled when it is recognised as a gift, Derrida describes it not as an impossibility, but as 'the impossible'. This means that although it is possible to conceive of the gift in terms that are entirely selfless and generous, the practice of giving always locates it in particular systems of value. Cycles of giving and counter-giving, therefore, are based on common principles of value, where the codes are shared and understood. Derrida suggests that changing the values of society or the dynamics of a relationship requires this symmetry and homogeneity to break, a process that might be achieved if the gift is relocated in the ethical gap between the impossible (a 'pure' gift) and the thinkable (an ethical culture). Such asymmetrical patterns of giving are acts of resistance, challenging those reciprocal relations between donor and recipient which are driven by a political economy based on market exchange. By refusing to reduce the gift to reciprocity, Derrida replaces the homogeneity of a fixed system of economic exchange with the heterogeneity of generosity, in which the gift becomes associated with shifting roles, spontaneity, desire, loss and risk.

In place of the narratives of redemption and salvation, the metaphor of the gift offers a way of examining both the positive qualities of social interaction and those based on less equitable principles. It also points to the political complexities of cultural exchange and the ethical promises and pitfalls associated with social intervention. It is precisely because the gift is unstable, because it has the potential to interrupt established patterns of social interaction and disrupt old certainties that it provides such a powerful metaphor for the ethics of applied drama. In following Derridean thought, Lather similarly calls for a praxis based on 'undecidability, incompleteness and dispersion rather than the comforts of transformation and closure'.[10] Applied to drama, this theoretical reading of the gift relationship acknowledges the risks, contradictions and uncertainties of theatre-making in community settings. It also offers an opportunity to renew a commitment to openness, in which practitioners recognise that their role is not to *give* participants a voice – with all the hierarchical implications that phrase invokes – but to create spaces and places that enable the participants' voices to be heard.

Acts of Giving

As Derrida implies, a significant element of gift-giving practices that is under-emphasised by theories of contractual exchange is the role of the emotions. Gifts are not, of course, always reducible to the political values of the marketplace and there are many aspects of gift-giving which differ from commercial forms of transaction. Many people enjoy giving and receiving, and although gift-giving practices tell conflicting narratives, there is also a need to recognise that the practice of giving is not always logical, safe and rational but is also (following Derrida) spontaneous, risky and emotional. It is the aspect of the gift that relates to the emotions which has particular relevance for artistic practice, and which I should like to explore a little further in relation to applied drama.

In her essay on the social and emotional significance of the gift, Lee Anne Fennell suggests that gifts are set apart from ordinary commodities because they are specifically chosen for someone else as part of a process of sustaining and deepening personal relationships. In terms similar to those I discussed in Chapter 4, she uses the phrase 'empathetic dialogue' to describe the most positive aspect of gift-giving in which both donor and recipient gain emotional pleasure. A successful gift, she argues, involves the donor putting herself in the recipient's place and imagining not only what they would like, but also what they would like to receive from this particular person. In turn, the recipient imagines the donor's 'empathetic efforts' to find the right gift, and it acquires sentimental value that has little to do with its market value. Fennell suggests that this form of empathetic dialogue is based on desire:

> The desire to identify with another; the desire to have one's true prefer- ences divined by another (even when those preferences may not even be clear to oneself); the desire to surprise and be surprised.[11]

Giving gifts, she concludes, is part of a 'specialised communication' through which donors are able to express feelings that may not be easily put into words.

Fennell's version of gift-giving is intentionally idealised, and relies on mutual affection between donor and recipients. Her insights into the role of the imagination, positive identification with others and empathy suggest that there is an artfulness about giving and receiving. The parallels between Fennell's optimistic gift relationship and applied drama are clear – both encourage relationships of empathy and imagina- tive identification with the lives of others and there are many examples of such positive interactions in this book. In both instances, the process of giving is intended to affect or benefit others in some way as well as giving satisfaction to the donor. Both the experience of making theatre and the experience of the gift are special forms of communication through which personal relationships and feelings are dramatised, often through fictionalising or symbolising emotions in ways which may be both spontaneous and planned, risky and rewarding.

It is significant to the ethics of applied drama that the positive aspects of gift-giving Fennnell describes are not solely based on private acts of friendship. Generous gift relationships have wider social and public significance, and this has been well theorised, particularly by feminist educationalists and philosophers.[12] Writing from a philosophical perspective, Annette Baier has identified the significance of the emotions in the fabric of society. Baier's central thesis is that interpersonal rela- tionships inspire feelings of trust, neediness and interdependency that are central to public life because they provide the bedrock for a society based on an ethic of care. She argues that caring emotions have been effectively privatised and individualised in Western societies, and she questions how far the 'virtues' of independence, autonomy and self-sufficiency have provided an ethical basis for social welfare. In a veiled reference to Mauss, she comments on the inadequacy of theories of the gift which fail to recognise that it symbolises powerful emotional bonds that are socially productive:

> Only those determined to see every proper moral transaction as an exchange will construe every gift as made in exchange for an IOU, and every return gift made in exchange for a receipt.[13]

For Baier, the social significance of the emotions is that feelings of empathy and affection lead to practical action. In this way she links the gift to the practice of citizenship, recognising that emotional involvement with others is generative of a caring ethic which, in turn, has wider social implications. She suggests that one of the consequences of failing to acknowledge the social role of the emotions has been to render caring roles invisible (historically the lot of women). Her ethic of care is intended to relocate the emotions in a political context, and her thesis is orientated towards redressing this omission.

What I have suggested here is a way of thinking about the gift which takes it out of Mauss's negative cycle of debt, recognising its contextuality, its relationship to desire, its spontaneity and other positive social and emotional effects. As I have represented this argument, however, it does not entirely satisfy questions about how the gift might be given and received by those with different or competing conceptions of the good life. Throughout this book I have stressed that communities are not always homogeneous, that feelings of affection are not always mutual, and that dramatic experiences can be differently construed and interpreted. Furthermore, because gifts – whether possessions of sentimental value or experiences in drama – always carry the imprint of those who gave them, their meanings may change over time. When relationships become stale or unhappy this is often reflected in how gifts are given and received and, as people stop taking time to imagine what another would like, the element of desire, spontaneity, or surprise is lost. Gifts which were once thought of with hostility or affection may acquire new interpretations, and looking back on experiences in drama may change their meaning and significance. In other words, there is a temporality about the feelings attached to gifts which suggests that all meanings are contingent on context and situation.

I have used the metaphor of the gift to indicate some of the fragilities and ambiguities inherent in acts of giving, however generously they may be intended. The analogy between the gift and applied drama suggests that the ethical principles on which practice is based require continual negotiation and re-evaluation. Becoming ethical is an on-going process – a continual journey of action, reflection and evaluation – in which values and beliefs may be challenged and tested over time and in response to new situations and different people. This is not an easy business, and the practice of care can be tough as well as rewarding. This is the paradox of the gift relationship, and there is no easy resolution to this aporia.

The Art of Giving

I recently attended a production staged by young people in a London theatre as part of a festival of theatre organised by Big Foot Theatre Company. The festival aims to raise the aspirations of talented young people who attend mainstream schools throughout London, and the production I saw was the culmination of four weeks of intensive work-shops with theatre professionals. At the end of the stunningly beautiful performance, the artistic director stood up in front of the audience of delighted parents and confessed, with some humour, that he had been utterly horrible to their children. Of course this was not true, and it was easy to see the admiration and affection that had built up between cast and director. But it did hint at the struggles he had encountered, the difficulties of bringing together a disparate group of individuals into an ensemble of thoughtful and expressive performers.

In all its many guises, practice in applied drama is undertaken by those who want to touch the lives of others, who hope that participants and audiences will extend their perception of how life is, and imagine how it might be different. Although other forms of theatre-making may share these experiences and aspirations, what is emphasised in applied drama is its concern to encourage people to use the experience of participating in theatre to move beyond what they already know. Applied drama has a reflexive ethos, a tradition of creative and critical questioning, and the process of interpretation and re-interpretation is central to all its various practices. Writing about painting, Merleau-Ponty described this dynamic between creativity and perception. He suggested that, in the arts, meanings are never transparent nor easily interpreted, which is why it is important to look beyond the immediate and obvious and into the blanks the painter leaves between the brush-stokes, or the silences between the words.[14] These gaps are expressive: they invite multiple interpretations and offer an aesthetic space in which meanings are made.

The artistic practices of applied drama are rich, imaginative and diverse, and the contexts in which it takes place often present very specific challenges. These encounters between art-form and context mean that the ethical boundaries of practice are likely to be constantly challenged. Becoming ethical, therefore, is an on-going negotiation rather than an encounter of fixed positions, where ideas and values may be altered, revised or reaffirmed through the process of making art. It thrives on the heterogeneity of diverse contexts because it is through the encounter of difference that the ethical limits of citizenship might be recognised and explored. In these ways and in many others, applied drama can make a contribution to building a more generous and multi-faceted world by making a creative space in which fixed and inequitable oppositions between the local and the global, self and other, fiction and reality, identity and difference, might be disrupted and challenged. The gift of applied drama is that it offers an opportunity for an ethical praxis that disrupts horizons, in which new insights are generated and where the familiar might be seen, embodied and represented from alternative perspectives and different points of view. In the words of Merleau-Ponty, describing the 'embodied agency' of the artist's eye, 'this gift is earnt by exercise'.[15]

Notes

Notes to Chapter 1: An Introduction to Applied Drama

1. Joan Littlewood, *Joan's Book: Joan's Peculiar History as She Tells It* (London: Minerva Press, 1995), pp. 702–6.
2. Ibid., p. 740.
3. Websites cited: www.cssd.ac.uk; www.man.ac.uk; www.gu.edu.au/centre/atr/; www.minedu.govt.nz accessed 29 December 2003.
4. Judith Ackroyd, 'Applied Theatre: Problems and Possibilities', *Applied Theatre Journal*, 1 (2000): www.gu.edu.au/centre/atr/ accessed 16 April 2004.
5. Quoted in S. Grady, 'Accidental Marxists? The Challenge of Critical and Feminist Pedagogies for the Practice of Applied Drama', *Youth Theater Journal*, 17 (2003), 68.
6. See G. Bolton, 'Drama in Education and TIE: a Comparison', in T. Jackson (ed.), *Learning Through Theatre* (London: Routledge, 1993), pp. 39–50.
7. I am indebted to Philip Taylor for stimulating this discussion. See Philip Taylor, 'Musings on Applied Theatre: Towards a New Theatron', *Drama Magazine*, 10: 2 (2003), pp. 37–42.
8. Bjørn Rasmussen, 'Applied Theater and the Power Play – an International Viewpoint', *Applied Theatre Journal*, 1 (2000): www.gu.edu.au/centre/atr/ accessed 16 April 2004.
9. There are many different sources for this discussion. For a sociological analysis see, for example, Pierre Bourdieu, *The Rules of Art*, trans. S. Emanuel (Cambridge: Polity Press, 1996), pp. 135–8. C. Taylor, *Sources of the Self: The Making of the Modern Identity* (Cambridge: Cambridge University Press, 1989) offers a reading of how the artist became integrated into the Western consciousness.
10. J. Neelands, *Beginning Drama, 11–14* (London: David Fulton Press, 1998), p. 23.
11. B. Kershaw, *The Radical in Performance: Between Brecht and Baudrillard* (London: Routledge, 1999), p. 31.
12. Pierre Bourdieu, *Distinction: A Social Critique of the Judgement of Taste*, trans. R. Nice (London: Routledge & Kegan Paul, 1984), p. 34.
13. Tony Kushner, 'How Do You Make Social Change?' *Theater*, 31: 3 (2001), p. 62.
14. These related and international histories are described in S. Craig (ed.), *Dream and Deconstructions: Alternative Theatre in Britain* (Ambergate: Amber Lane Press, 1980); T. Shank, *Beyond the Boundaries: American*

Alternative Theatre (Ann Arbor, MI: University of Michigan Press, 2002); R. Samuel, E. MacColl and S. Cosgrove, *Theatres of the Left, 1880–1935: Workers' Theatre Movements in Britain and America* (London: Routledge & Kegan Paul, 1985); R. Stourac, and K. McCreery, *Theatre as a Weapon: Workers' Theatre in the Soviet Union, Germany and Great Britain, 1917–1934* (London: Routledge & Kegan Paul, 1986); S. Capelin, *Challenging the Centre: Two Decades of Political Theatre* (Brisbane: Playback Press, 1995); K. P. Epskamp, *Theatre in Search of Social Change* (The Hague: Centre for the Study of Education in Developing Countries, 1989).
15. For two contrasting readings of this history in relation to drama education, see D. Hornbook, *Education and Dramatic Art* (Oxford: Basil Backwell, 1989) and G. Bolton, *Acting in Classroom Drama* (Stoke-on-Trent: Trentham Books, 1998). For a more general analysis of the place of the arts in progressive education see J. Donald, *Sentimental Education* (London: Verso, 1992).
16. For analyses and discussion of the history and politics of twentieth-century and contemporary community theatre, see B. Kershaw, *The Politics of Performance: Radical Theatre as Cultural Intervention* (London: Routledge, 1992); E. Van Erven, *Community Theatre: Global Perspectives* (London: Routledge, 2001); R. Fotheringham (ed.), *Community Theatre in Australia* (Sydney: Currency Press, 1992); S. C. Haedicke and T. Nellhaus (eds), *Performing Democracy: International Perspectives on Community-Based Performance* (Ann Arbor: University of Michigan Press, 2001).
17. Kershaw, *The Radical in Performance*, pp. 6–7.
18. Victor Turner, *The Anthropology of Performance* (New York: Performing Arts Journal Press, 1986), pp. 72–4.
19. Richard Schechner, 'Performers and Spectators Transported and Transformed', in P. Auslander (ed.), *Performance: Critical Concepts in Literary and Cultural Studies*, vol. 1 (London: Routledge, 2003), p. 270.
20. Tim Etchells, *Certain Fragments* (London: Routledge, 1999), p. 59.
21. J. Willett (ed.), *Brecht on Theatre: The Development of an Aesthetic* (London: Methuen, 1964), p. 51.
22. bell hooks, *Teaching to Transgress: Education as the Practice of Freedom* (London: Routledge, 1994), p. 59.
23. Michel Foucault and Gilles Deleuze, 'Intellectuals and Power', in D. F. Bouchard (ed.), *Language, Counter-memory, Practice: Selected Essays and Interviews by Michel Foucault* (New York: Cornell University Press, 1977), pp. 205–6.
24. Ibid., p. 207.

Notes to Chapter 2: The Practice of Citizenship

1. Peter Sellars, 'The Question of Culture', in M. Delgado and C. Svich (eds), *Theatre in Crisis: Performance Manifestos for a New Century* (Manchester: Manchester University Press, 2002), p. 142.

2. In *The German Ideology* of 1845, Marx and Engels argued that the citizen of bourgeois theory masked deeper social divisions and inequalities.

3. 'Don't Play Truant to Join Bush Demo, Pupils Warned', *Guardian*, 17 November 2003. For a discussion of how citizenship became absorbed into formal education see J. Beck, *Morality and Citizenship in Education* (London: Continuum, 1998).

4. See, for example, B. Shepard and R. Hayduk (eds), *From ACT UP to the WTO: Urban Protest and Community Building in the Era of Globalisation* (London: Verso, 2002); C. Orenstein, 'Agitational Performance, Now and Then', *Theater*, 31: 3 (2002), pp. 139–51; J. Cohen-Cruz, 'The Motion of the Ocean: the Shifting Face of US Theater for Social Change since the 1960s', *Theater*, 31: 3 (2002), pp. 95–107; G. McKay (ed.), *DiY Culture: Party and Protest in Nineties Britain* (London: Verso, 1998).

5. Chantal Mouffe (ed.), *Dimensions of a Radical Democracy* (London: Verso, 1992), p. 4. She is indebted to the work of Hannah Arendt (1958), who was the first author to conceptualise citizenship as political participation.

6. T. H. Marshall and T. Bottomore, *Citizenship and Social Class* (London: Pluto Press, 1992), p. 8.

7. This point is made by Nancy Fraser and Linda Gordon (1994), who observe that although the rhetorical traditions of the United States emphasise civil citizenship, citing 'individual liberties' and 'freedom of speech' as good examples, the idea of collective responsibility for public welfare is largely absent from this aspect of political discourse.

8. Marshall and Bottomore, *Citizenship and Social Class*, p. 18.

9. B. S. Turner (ed.), *Citizenship and Social Theory* (London: Sage, 1993), p. 2.

10. Mouffe, *Dimensions of a Radical Democracy*, p. 237.

11. J. Thompson, *Applied Theatre: Bewilderment and Beyond* (Oxford: Peter Lang, 2003).

12. I have written elsewhere of the circularity of risk and trust in relation to applied drama. See H. Nicholson, 'Drama Education and the Politics of Trust', *Research in Drama Education*, 7: 1 (2002), pp. 81–93.

13. Chantal Mouffe, *The Democratic Paradox* (London: Verso, 2000), p. 104.

14. Tim Prentki and Jan Selman described popular theatre as motivated by 'an urgent need for change in the society and conditions in which many live' (*Popular Theatre in Political Culture*, Bristol: Intellect Books, 2000, pp. 9–10).

15. J. Willett (ed.), *Brecht on Theatre: The Development of an Aesthetic* (London: Methuen, 1964), p. 108.

16. Forum theatre is discussed in more detail in Chapter 6.

17. A. Boal, *Legislative Theatre* (London: Routledge, 1998), p. 20.

18. Mouffe, *The Democratic Paradox*, p. 52.

19. Paul Dwyer (2004) traces different versions of Boal's story about the woman in Lima, and concludes that it has been variously inflected to suit Boal's purposes.

20. Paul Heritage, 'The Courage to be Happy', *The Drama Review*, 38: 3 (1994), pp. 25–34. Boal explained his campaigning tactics to Richard Schechner and Sudipto Chaterjee in an interview in *The Drama Review* in 1998.

21. McKay, *DiY Culture*, pp. 133–4.
22. Ibid., p. 130. For other discussions of popular protest see B. Kershaw, 'Ecoactivist Protest: the Environment as Partner in Protest?', *The Drama Review*, 46: 1 (2002), pp. 188–130. Other examples of the elision between direct action and performance are discussed in J. Cohen-Cruz (ed.), *Radical Street Performance: An International Anthology* (London: Routledge, 1998).
23. B. Kershaw, *The Radical in Performance: Between Brecht and Baudrillard* (London: Routledge, 1999), particularly Chapters 1 and 2.
24. S. J. Ahmed, 'When Theatre Practitioners Attempt Changing an Ever-changing World: a Response to Tim Prentki's *Save the Children? Change the world*', *Research in Drama Education*, 9: 1 (2004), p. 96.
25. James J. Thompson, 'Ugly, Unglamorous and Dirty: Theatre of Relief/Reconciliation/Liberation in Places of War', *Research in Drama Education*, 7: 1 (2000), pp. 108–13.
26. A. Comte, *The Positive Philosophy of Auguste Comte*, vol. 11, trans. H. Martineau (London: John Chapman, 1953), p. 479.
27. D. Miller, 'Are They *My* Poor? The Problem of Altruism in a World of Strangers', in J. Seglow (ed.), *The Ethics of Altruism* (London: Frank Cass, 2004), p. 109.
28. See N. K. Badhwar, 'Altruism versus Self-interest: Sometimes a False Dichotomy', in E. F. Paul, D. Miller and J. Paul (eds), *Altruism* (Cambridge: Cambridge University Press, 1993), pp. 90–117, for an analysis of the beneficial impact of altruism on the giver.
29. S. Linden, *I Have Before Me a Remarkable Document Give to Me by a Young Lady from Rwanda* (London: Aurora Metro Press, 2004), p. 23.
30. J. Thompson, *Applied Theatre: Bewilderment and Beyond* (Oxford: Peter Lang, 2003), p. 22.
31. A. Tanyi-Tang, 'Theatre for Change: an Analysis of Two Performances by Women in Mundemba Sub-Division', *Research in Drama Education*, 6: 1 (2001), pp. 23–38; A. Tanyi-Tang, 'Unpeeling the Onion of Privilege', in J. O'Toole and M. Lepp (eds), *Drama for Life: Stories of Adult Learning and Empowerment* (Brisbane: Playlab Press, 2000), pp. 67–76.
32. K. Graham, 'Altruism, Self-Interest and the Indistinctiveness of Persons', in J. Seglow (ed.), *The Ethics of Altruism* (London: Frank Cass, 2004), p. 61.
33. Ibid., p. 60.
34. S. Žižek, *Welcome to the Desert of the Real* (London: Verso, 2002), p. 19.
35. Ibid., p. 66.
36. R. Bharucha, *The Politics of Cultural Practice: Thinking Through Theatre in an Age of Globalisation* (London: Athlone Press, 2000), p. 26.
37. This is discussed by feminist philosopher Jane Flax (1993), who relates this reading of subjectivity to human rights and altruism.
38. S. Sevenhuijsen, *Citizenship and the Ethics of Care*, trans. L. Savage (London: Routledge, 1998), p. 57.

Notes to Chapter 3: Pedagogies, Praxis and Performance

1. P. Lather, 'Post-Critical Pedagogies: a Feminist Reading', in C. Luke and J. Gore (eds), *Feminisms and Critical Pedagogy* (London and New York: Routledge, 1992), p. 121.
2. P. Lather, *Getting Smart: Feminist Research and Pedagogy with/in the Postmodern* (London: Routledge, 1991), p. 57.
3. Ibid., p. 11.
4. I am indebted to theatre director and applied theatre practitioner Fiona Lesley for furthering my understanding of the implications of this metaphor to our field.
5. See H. K. Bhabha, *The Location of Culture* (London: Routledge, 1994) for a post-colonial analysis of this term.
6. See the work of North American critical pedagogues H. A. Giroux (*Between Borders*, 1997), P. McLaren (1995), P. Lather (1992), and C. Doyle (1993), who applied deconstructive thought to education.
7. D. Conquergood, 'Performance Studies: Interventions and Radical Research', in H. Bial (ed.), *The Performance Studies Reader* (London: Routledge, 2004), p. 311.
8. Ibid., p. 312.
9. Ibid., p. 311.
10. A. M. A. Freire and D. Macedo (eds), *The Paulo Freire Reader* (London: Continuum, 2001), p. 61.
11. This strategy is discussed on the Action Aid website. www.actionaid.org.
12. In writing about applied theatre, Philip Taylor attributes the development of the term 'praxis' to Freire himself (*Applied Theatre*, p. 35). This is factually incorrect. It is a term which was popularised by Marx but was derived from the Greek, where *praxis* signified the free action of citizens. Marx's conceptualisation of praxis was based on the idea that the bourgeois consciousness was ideologically limited, and that this was an obstacle to the revolution. Critical of the Enlightenment perception that the ideas of free-thinking intellectuals would change the world, Marx insisted that thought is the product of material reality, not outside it. In *The German Ideology*, Marx and Engels reversed the conventional dialectic between life and consciousness, stating that '[l]ife is not determined by consciousness, but consciousness by life' (1974, p. 47). If this were the case, it would be possible, therefore, to reshape human consciousness.
13. Freire, and Macedo (eds), *The Paulo Freire Reader*, p. 64.
14. S. Grady, 'Accidental Marxists? The Challenge of Critical and Feminist Pedagogies for the Practice of Applied Drama', *Youth Theatre Journal*, 17 (2003), p. 70.
15. H. Foster, *Recodings: Art, Spectacle, Cultural Politics* (Port Townsend: Bay Press, 1985), p. 153.

16. B. Kershaw, *The Radical in Performance: Between Brecht and Baudrillard* (London: Routledge, 1999), p. 70.
17. Kate Donelan's research is important to this discussion because it raises questions about how the local and the global are complexly interwoven. See K. Donelan, '"Overlapping Spheres" and "Blurred Spaces": Mapping Cultural Interactions in Drama and Theatre with Young People', *Drama Australia*, 28: 1 (2004), pp. 15–32.
18. R. Edwards and R. Usher, *Globalisation and Pedagogy: Space, Place and Identity* (London: Routledge, 2000), p. 124.
19. D. Conquergood, 'Of Caravans and Carnivals: Performance Studies in Motion', *The Drama Review*, 148 (1995), pp. 137–8.
20. See J. McKenzie, *Perform or Else: From Discipline to Performance* (London: Routledge, 2001), pp. 49–53; V. Turner, *From Ritual to Theatre: The Human Seriousness of Play* (New York: Performing Arts Journal Publications, 1982).
21. McKenzie, *Perform or Else*, p. 72. He also includes an analysis of the role of unions, which is not included here.
22. For a fuller discussion, see Michel Foucault, 'Technologies of the Self', in P. Rabinow (ed.), *Ethics: Essential Works of Foucault, 1954–1984* (London: Penguin Books, 1994), pp. 223–52.
23. http://dramafortraining.com accessed 28 May 2004.
24. Edwards and Usher, *Globalisation and Pedagogy*, p. 132.
25. See, for example, the feminist pedagogies of Patti Lather (1991) and the Marxian pedagogy of Henry A. Giroux (*Between Borders*, 1997).
26. P. Freire, *Cultural Action for Freedom* (Harmondsworth: Penguin Books, 1972), p. 29.
27. Ibid., pp. 35 and 37.
28. L. Delpit, *Other People's Children* (New York: The New Press, 1995), p. 19.
29. M. Cox (ed.), *Shakespeare Comes to Broadmoor* (London: Jessica Kingsley, 1992), p. 56.
30. See A. Kempe, N. McCaffrey and V. Wordfold, 'Ain't no Cotchin' in the Jo: Working with Young Offenders', *Journal of National Drama*, 9: 2 (2002), pp. 31–8 for a discussion of the relationship between drama and language codes amongst imprisoned young people in Britain.
31. See A. Kempe, 'The Role of Drama in the Teaching of Speaking and Listening as the Basis for Social Capital', *Research in Drama Education*, 8: 1 (2003), pp. 65–78.
32. Freire, *Cultural Action for Freedom*, pp. 36–7.
33. E. Ellsworth, 'Why Doesn't This Feel Empowering?', in C. Luke and J. Gore (eds), *Feminisms and Critical Pedagogy* (London: Routledge, 1992), pp. 90–119.
34. For an analysis of how professional experts have regulated and controlled the lives of those in institutions, see Michel Foucault, *Discipline and Punish*, trans. A. Sheridan (Harmondsworth: Penguin Books, 1991), pp. 170–7.
35. Lather, 'Post-Critical Pedagogies, pp. 120–2.

36. Creative Partnerships aims to encourage creative approaches to teaching and learning across the curriculum, and recognises that creativity is just as important to education as is literacy and numeracy. See www.creative-partnerships.com.

37. L. Coghlan, *A Feeling in My Bones*, ed. A. Kempe (Walton-on-Thames: Nelson Thornes, 1992). Andy Kempe also offered advice on working with children with special needs.

38. P. Bundy, 'Aesthetic Engagement in the Drama Process', *Research in Drama Education*, 8: 2 (2003), pp. 171–81.

39. T. Eagleton, *The Ideology of the Aesthetic* (Oxford: Basil Blackwell, 1990), p.13.

40. A. Brah, *Cartographies of Diaspora* (London: Routledge, 1996), p. 11.

Notes to Chapter 4: Narrative and the Gift of Storytelling

1. W. Benjamin, 'The Storyteller', in *Illuminations*, trans. H. Zonn (London: Fontana Collins, 1992), pp. 83–107.

2. P. Ricoeur, *Oneself as Another*, trans. K. Balmey (Chicago: University of Chicago Press, 1992), p. 170.

3. K. Gallagher, 'Emergent Conceptions in Theatre Pedagogy and Production', in K. Gallagher and D. Booth (eds), *How Theatre Educates: Convergences and Counterpoints* (Toronto: University of Toronto Press, 2002), p. 12.

4. A. Brah, *Cartographies of Diaspora* (London: Routledge, 1996), p. 247.

5. P. Ricoeur, *The Rule of Metaphor* (London: Routledge, 1977), p. 236. See also K. Donelan (2004) for the application of this conception of narrative to drama education.

6. S. Stamp, 'Holding On: Dramatherapy with Offenders', in J. Thompson (ed.), *Prison Theatre: Perspectives and Practices* (London: Jessica Kingsley, 1998), pp. 89–108.

7. J. Thompson, *Applied Theatre: Bewilderment and Beyond* (Oxford: Peter Lang, 2003), p. 183.

8. Sithmparanathan, Keynote Lecture, International Conference on Community Theatre, Batticaloa, Sri Lanka, 26 July 2003.

9. I am grateful to James Thompson for his insights on the longevity of globalisation in this region, and for locating globalisation in relation to its history of colonialism. It is significant in this context that the region was colonised by Westerners bearing gifts of musical instruments.

10. S. Freud, *The Interpretation of Dreams* (Harmondsworth: Penguin Books, 1976), p. 232.

11. S. Freud, 'Group Psychology and the Analysis of the Ego', *The Complete Psychological Works of Sigmund Freud*, vol. XVIII (1920–2) (London: The Hogarth Press, 1955), p. 108.

12. H. Cixous and C. Clement, *The Newly Born Woman*, trans. B. Wing (Minneapolis: University of Minnesota Press, 1975), p. 148.
13. J. Willett, (ed.), *Brecht on Theatre: The Development of an Aesthetic* (London: Methuen, 1964), p. 277.
14. Ibid., pp. 92–3.
15. T. Brenan, 'Introduction', in T. Brenan (ed.), *Between Feminism and Psychoanalysis* (London: Routledge, 1989), p. 10.
16. A. Campbell, *Anansi*, ed. A. Kempe (Walton-on-Thames: Thomas Nelson, 1992), p. 12.
17. A. MacIntyre, *After Virtue: A Study in Moral Theory* (London: Duckworth, 1981), p. 216.
18. This point has been particularly well theorised in relation to drama education by Joe Winston in his *Drama, Narrative and Moral Education* (London: Falmer Press, 1998).
19. Campbell, *Anansi*, p. 22.
20. M. Boler, 'The Risks of Empathy: Interrogating Multiculturalism's Gaze', *Cultural Studies*, 11: 2 (1997), pp. 261, 263. See also M. Nussbaum, *Poetic Justice* (Boston, MA: Beacon Press, 1995) for a discussion of the moral authority of sympathy in relation to the practice of reading.
21. A. Boal, *Theatre of the Oppressed* (London: Pluto Press, 1979), p. 113.
22. Boler, 'The Risks of Empathy', p. 261.
23. A. Kempe and L. Warner, *Starting with Scripts*, 2nd edn (Cheltenham: Nelson Thornes, 2002), p. vii; E. Goffman, *The Presentation of Self in Everyday Life* (London: Penguin Books, 1959).
24. J. O'Toole, *The Process of Drama* (London: Routledge, 1992).
25. See G. Bolton and D. Heathcote, *So You Want to Use Role Play? A New Approach* (Stoke-on-Trent: Trentham Books, 1999).
26. See, for example, feminist readings of the performance of gender by Judith Butler (1990); readings of performance given by Elin Diamond (1997) and Peggy Phelan (1993); and an analysis of education by Madelaine Grumet (1988).
27. P. Phelan, *Unmarked: The Politics of Performance* (London: Routledge, 1993), p. 163.
28. Goffman, *The Presentation of Self in Everyday Life*.
29. For an interesting and lively debate on drama and moral education, see the exchange between Brian Edmiston and Joe Winston in *Research in Drama Education*, 5: 1 (2000). One of the points of dispute is over Edmiston's claims that participants are transformed in particular ways as a result of working with him in drama.

Notes to Chapter 5: Community Narratives

1. I. M. Young, 'The Ideal of Community and the Politics of Difference', in L. J. Nicholson (ed.), *Feminism/Postmodernism* (London: Routledge, 1990), p. 302.

2. B. Anderson, *Imagined Communities* (London: Verso, 1983).
3. A. Brah, *Cartographies of Diaspora* (London: Routledge, 1996), p. 93.
4. V. Amit, 'An Anthropology without Community?', in V. Amit and N. Rapport, *The Trouble with Community* (London: Pluto Press, 2002), p. 58.
5. Ibid., p. 165.
6. Brah, *Cartographies of Diaspora*, pp. 116–18.
7. E. Probyn, 'Travels in the Postmodern: Making Sense of the Local', in Nicholson (ed.), *Feminism/Postmodernism*, p. 187.
8. M. Pearson and M. Shanks, *Theatre/Archaeology* (London: Routledge, 1991), p. 96; Sally Mackey (2002) has also reflected on the significance of landscape and place to theatre-making and performative practices in applied drama.
9. A. Portelli, 'What Makes Oral History Different', in R. Perks and A. Thomson (eds), *The Oral History Reader* (London: Routledge, 1998), p. 69.
10. Personal Narratives Group (eds), 'Truths', *Interpreting Women's Lives: Feminist Theory and Personal Narratives* (Bloomington: Indiana University Press, 1989), p. 261.
11. P. Tait, *Converging Realities* (Sydney: Currency Press, 1994), p. 33.
12. J. Sangster, 'Telling our Stories: Feminist Debates and the Use of Oral History', in Perks and Thomson (eds), *The Oral History Reader*, p. 90.
13. B. Kershaw, *The Radical in Performance: Between Brecht and Baudrillard* (London: Routledge, 1999), p. 160.
14. B. McConachie, 'Approaching the "Structure of Feeling" in Grassroots Theater', in T. Nellhaus and S. C. Haedicke (eds), *Performing Democracy: International Perspectives on Community-Based Performance* (Ann Arbour: University of Michigan Press, 2001), p. 55.
15. Portelli, 'What Makes Oral History Different', p. 66.
16. C. Steedman, *Landscape for a Good Woman* (London: Virago Press, 1986), p. 6.
17. R. Schechner, 'Performers and Spectators Transported and Transformed', in P. Auslander (ed.), *Performance: Critical Concepts in Literary and Cultural Studies*, vol. 1 (London: Routledge, 2003), p. 280.
18. Programme notes for *A Woman's Place*, directed by Sarah Sansom.
19. Schechner, 'Performers and Spectators Transported and Transformed', p. 270.
20. Ibid., p. 283.
21. R. Schechner, *Between Theatre and Anthropology* (Philadelphia: University of Philadelphia Press, 1985), pp. 35–6.
22. Kershaw, *The Radical in Performance*, p. 173.
23. Personal interview, December 2003.
24. Brah, *Cartographies of Diaspora*, p. 95.
25. Amit, 'An Anthropology without Community?', pp. 60–2.
26. K. Soper, *Troubled Pleasures* (London: Verso, 1990), p. 154.

27. Probyn, 'Travels in the Postmodern', p. 187.
28. A. Boal, *Games for Actors and Non-actors*, trans. A. Jackson (London: Routledge, 1992), p. 40.
29. Boal, *Games for Actors and non-actors*, trans. A. Jackson, 2nd edn (London: Routledge, 2002), p. 56. This view is also put forward by Australian theatre director Welsey Enoch (2004), who describes the importance of place and home to his sense of identity.
30. P. Auslander, *From Acting to Performance* (London: Routledge, 1997), p. 105.
31. P. Schweitzer, 'Many Happy Retirements', in M. Schutzman and J. Cohen-Cruz, *Playing Boal* (London: Routledge, 1994), p. 80.
32. A. D. Basting, '"God is a Talking Horse": Dementia and the Performance of Self', *The Drama Review*, 45: 3 (2001), pp. 78–94.
33. A. Dawson, 'The Mining Community and the Ageing body: Towards a Phenomenology of Community?', in V. Amit (ed.), *Realizing Community* (London: Routledge, 2002), p. 23.
34. Ibid., p. 35.
35. J. Freidman, '*Muscle Memory*: Performing Embodied Knowledge', in R. Candida Smith (ed.), *Art and the Performance of Memory* (London: Routledge, 2002), p. 166.
36. P. Auslander, 'Boal, Blau, Brecht: The Body', in Schutzman and Cohen-Cruz *Playing Boal*, pp. 124–33.
37. M. Foucault, 'Nietzsche, Genealogy, History', in D. F. Bouchard (ed.), *Language, Counter-memory, Practice: Selected Essays and Interviews by Michel Foucault* (New York: Cornell University Press, 1977), p. 146.
38. Ibid., p. 148.
39. S. Freud, 'A Note on the Mystic Writing Pad [1925]', in A. Richards (ed.), *Sigmund Freud: On Metapsychology* (Harmondsworth: Penguin, 1991), p. 429.
40. J. Derrida, *Archive Fever*, trans. E. Prenowitz (Chicago: University of Chicago Press, 1995), p. 36.
41. M. Merleau-Ponty, *The Phenomenology of Perception*, trans. C. Smith (London: Routledge, 2002), pp. 161–2.

Notes to Chapter 6: Creativity and Social Intervention

1. P. Shelley, 'A Defence of Poetry', in A. D. F. Macrae (ed.), *Selected Prose and Poetry of P. B. Shelley* (London: Routledge, 1991), p. 233. Raymond Williams (1993) was an influential critic of Romanticist views of the artist, and the history of Romanticism has been analysed by Marilyn Butler (1981).
2. See, for example, C. Battersby, *Gender and Genius: Towards a Feminist Aesthetics* (London: The Women's Press, 1989) and T. Eagleton, *The Ideology of the Aesthetic* (Oxford: Basil Blackwell, 1990).

3. For Gardner's theory of multiple intelligences see H. Gardner, *Frames of Mind* (New York: Basic Books, 1983).
4. H. Gardner, *Extraordinary Minds* (London: Weidenfeld and Nicolson, 1997), p. 54.
5. A. Craft, B. Jeffrey and M. Leibling (eds), *Creativity in Education* (London: Continuum, 2001), p. 48.
6. See, for example, K. Robinson, *Out of Our Minds* (Oxford: Capstone Press, 2001), who draws on Gardner's work. Arthur J. Cropley (2001) has outlined a taxonomy of domain-specific forms of creativity that is similar in focus to that of Gardner.
7. Gardner, *Frames of Mind*, pp. 226–9.
8. B. Roper and D. Davies, 'Howard Gardner: Knowledge, Learning and Development in Drama and Arts Education', in *Research in Drama Education*, 5: 2 (2000), p. 225.
9. www.pz.harvard.edu/Research/GoodWork.htm
10. Craft, Jeffrey and Leibling (eds), *Creativity in Education,* p. 6.
11. R. Florida, *The Rise of the Creative Class* (New York: Basic Books, 2002).
12. Robinson (2001) is particularly interested in the significance of creativity in education, arguing that an education that encourages creativity is essential to economic progress.
13. A. Callincos, *The Revolutionary Ideas of Marx* (London: Bookmarks, 1995) offers an analysis of Marx's attitude to the social role of the artist and intellectual.
14. See, for example, A. Hauser, *The Sociology of Art*, trans. K. Northcott (London: Routledge, 1982), p. 23; T. Adorno, *Aesthetic Theory*, trans. C. Lenhardt (London: Routledge, 1984), p. 245.
15. A. Boal, *Theatre of the Oppressed* (London: Pluto Press, 1979), p. 141.
16. M. Taussig and R. Schechner, 'Boal in Brazil, France and the USA', in M. Schutzman and J. Cohen-Cruz (eds), *Playing Boal* (London: Routledge, 1994), pp. 28–30.
17. J. Milling and G. Ley, 'Boal's Theoretical History', *Modern Theories of Performance* (Basingstoke: Palgrave Macmillan, 2001), pp. 147–72.
18. Boal, *Theatre of the Oppressed*, p. 155.
19. A. Boal, *The Rainbow of Desire*, trans. Adrian Jackson (London: Routledge, 1995), pp. 13–14.
20. Milling and Ley, 'Boal's Theoretical History', pp. 159–69.
21. C. O'Sullivan, 'Searching for the Marxist in Boal', *Research in Drama Education*, 6: 1 (2001), p. 92.
22. Ibid., p. 90.
23. Ibid., p. 94.
24. A. Boal, *Games for Actors and Non-actors*, trans. A. Jackson, 2nd edn (London: Routledge, 2002), p. 2.
25. M. Schutzman, 'Canadian Roundtable: An Interview', in M. Schutzman and J. Cohen-Cruz (eds), *Playing Boal* (London: Routledge, 1994), p. 221.

26. Ibid., pp. 220–1. Frances Babbage (1995) also acknowledged this risk in her introduction to an issue of *Contemporary Theatre Review* (3: 1) devoted to the work of Boal.
27. Cardboard Citizens, *The Man with Size Twelve Feet*, programme notes (2002).
28. H. Foster, *The Return of the Real* (Cambridge, MA: MIT Press, 1996), pp. 202–3.
29. D. Wiles, *A Short History of Western Performance Space* (Cambridge: Cambridge University Press, 2003), p. 257.
30. V. Turner, *From Ritual to Theatre: The Human Seriousness of Play* (New York: Performing Arts Journal Publications, 1982), p. 28.
31. Quoted in R. Run Rel, 'Theatre Workshop: Its Philosophy, Plays and Production', unpublished PhD thesis, University of Texas, Austin.
32. H. Lefebvre, *The Production of Space*, trans. D. Nicholson-Smith (Oxford: Basil Blackwell, 1991), p. 110.
33. M. Csikszentmihalyi, *Creativity: Flow and the Psychology of Discovery and Invention* (New York: HarperCollins, 1996).
34. Lefebvre, *The Production of Space*, p. 42.
35. J. Hughes, 'Resistance and Expression: Working with Women Prisoners and Drama', in J. Thompson (ed.), *Prison Theatre: Perspectives and Practices* (London: Jessica Kingsley, 1998), p. 59; M. Balfour (ed.), *Theatre in Prison* (Bristol: Intellect Books, 2004), p. 13.
36. Lefebvre, *The Production of Space*, p. 148.

Notes to Chapter 7: Human Rights in Performance

1. For examples, see *Theatre Matters*, ed. R. Boon and J. Plastow (Cambridge: Cambridge University Press, 1998).
2. Noam Chomsky (in his *The Umbrella of US Power*, 1999) is particularly critical of the ways in which US policy-makers have used human rights as a way of furthering their own power.
3. S. George, 'Globalizing Rights?', in M. J. Gibney (ed.), *Globalizing Rights* (Oxford: Oxford University Press, 2003), pp. 15–33.
4. B. Gates, 'Yes, More Trade with China', *New York Times*, 23 May (2000), reproduced www.microsoft.com/billgates; visited 19 September 2004.
5. George, 'Globalizing Rights?', p. 24.
6. J. S. Ahmed, 'Wishing for a World without "Theatre for Development": Demystifying the Case of Bangladesh', *Research in Drama Education*, 7: 2 (2002), p. 208.
7. Ibid., p. 211.
8. D. F. Bouchard (ed.), *Language, Counter-memory, Practice: Selected Interviews with Michel Foucault* (New York: Cornell University Press, 1977), p. 136.

9. N. Chomsky, ' "Recovering Rights": A Crooked Path', in M. J. Gibney (ed.), *Globalizing Rights* (Oxford: Oxford University Press, 2003), pp. 45–80.
10. Ahmed, 'Wishing for a World without "Theatre for Development"', pp. 217–18.
11. R. Bharucha, *The Politics of Cultural Practice: Thinking Through Theatre in an Age of Globalisation* (London: Athlone Press, 2000), p. 21.
12. See R. A. Wilson (ed.), *Human Rights, Culture and Context* (London: Pluto Press, 1997).
13. Ibid., p. 5.
14. J. Derrida, *The Amnesty Lectures on Human Rights*, Channel 4 TV (1995).
15. Wilson, *Human Rights, Culture and Context*, p. 155.
16. Ibid., p. 104.
17. S. E. Merry, 'Legal Pluralism and Transnational Culture', in ibid., p. 30.
18. Ibid., p. 156.
19. www.storyworkshop.org/; visited 19 September 2004.
20. J. Clifford, *The Predicament of Culture: Twentieth-Century Ethnography* (Cambridge, MA: Harvard University Press, 1988), p. 14.
21. D. Kerr, *African Popular Theatre: From Pre-Colonial Times to the Present Day* (Oxford: Currey Press, 1995), pp. 177–8.
22. F. Harding, *The Performance Arts in Africa: A Reader* (London: Routledge, 2002), p. 3.
23. Personal correspondence with Louise Keyworth.
24. Bharucha, *The Politics of Cultural Practice*, pp. 19, 26.
25. Ibid., p. 6.
26. Ibid., p. 66.
27. T. V. Barrameda and L. Espellardo, *Breaking Silence: A Nationwide Informance Tour for the Prevention of Violence Against Women in the Family* (Quezon City: PETA, 2000), p. 10.
28. Ibid., p. 30.
29. H. Bhabha, 'On Writing Rights', in M. J. Gibney (ed.), *Globalizing Rights* (Oxford: Oxford University Press, 2003), pp. 162–83.
30. M. Glynn, ' "Silent Voices": Working with Black Male Inmates – A Perspective', in J. Thompson (ed.), *Prison Theatre: Perspectives and Practices* (London: Jessica Kingsley, 1998), pp. 171–82.

Notes to Chapter 8: The Gift of Theatre

1. R. Prichard, *Yard Gal* (London: Faber, 1998), p. 5.
2. Ibid., p. 6. Hackney is a particularly deprived area of London.
3. C. Mouffe, *The Democratic Paradox* (London: Verso, 2000), p. 92.
4. See, for example, the ethical codes of the UK National Association of Drama Therapists at www.nadt.org/.
5. P. Lather, *Applied Derrida: (Mis)reading the Work of Mourning in Educational Research*, www.coe.ohio-state.edu/plather (2003), p. 4; visited 9 August 2004.

6. A good example of how redemption narratives are applied to community practice is offered in the introduction to the book *Theatre and Empowerment*, ed. Richard Boon and Jane Plastow (2004).

7. Lather, *Applied Derrida*, p. 5.

8. M. Mauss, *The Gift*, trans. I. Cunnison (London: Cohen and West, 1954), p. 1.

9. J. Derrida, *Given Time: Counterfeit Money*, trans. P. Kamuf (Chicago: University of Chicago Press, 1992), p. 23.

10. Lather, *Applied Derrida*, p. 7.

11. L. A. Fennell, 'Unpacking the Gift: Illiquid Goods and Empathetic Dialogue', in M. Olsteen (ed.), *The Question of the Gift* (London: Routledge, 2002), p. 86.

12. See, for example, N. Noddings, *Caring: A Feminine Approach to Ethics and Moral Education* (Berkeley: University of California Press, 1984) and C. Gilligan, *In a Different Voice: Psychological Theory and Women's Development* (Cambridge, MA: Harvard University Press, 1982). For an analysis of an ethic of care in relation to drama education, see J. Winston, *Drama, Narrative and Moral Education* (London: Falmer Press, 1998).

13. A. C. Baier, *Moral Prejudices* (Cambridge, MA: Harvard University Press, 1994), p. 109.

14. M. Merleau-Ponty, *The Prose of the World*, trans. J. O'Neill (Evanston: Northwestern University Press, 1973), p. 43.

15. Ibid., p. 286.

Bibliography

Ackroyd, J., 'Applied Theatre: Problems and Possibilities', *Applied Theatre Journal*, no. 1 (2000): http://www.gu.edu.au/centre/atr/ accessed 16 April 2004.

Adorno, T., *Aesthetic Theory*, trans. C. Lenhardt (London: Routledge, 1984).

Ahmed, J., 'When Theatre Practitioners Attempt Changing an Ever-changing world: a Response to Tim Prentki's *Save the Children? Change the World*', *Research in Drama Education*, 9: 1 (2004), pp. 96–100.

Amit, V., 'An Anthropology without Community?', in V. Amit and N. Rapport, *The Trouble with Community* (London: Pluto Press, 2002), pp. 73–160.

Amit, V. and Rapport, N., *The Trouble with Community* (London: Pluto Press, 2002).

Anderson, B., *Imagined Communities* (London: Verso, 1983).

Arendt, H., *The Human Condition* (Chicago: University of Chicago Press, 1958).

Auslander, P., 'Boal, Blau, Brecht: the Body', in M. Schutzman and J. Cohen-Cruz (ed.), *Playing Boal* (London: Routledge, 1994), pp. 124–33.

Auslander, P., *From Acting to Performance* (London: Routledge, 1997).

Babbage, F., 'Introduction to Working without Boal: Digressions and Developments in Theatre of the Oppressed', *Contemporary Theatre Review*, 3: 1 (1995), pp. 1–8.

Badhwar, N. K., 'Altruism versus Self-interest: Sometimes a False Dichotomy', E. F. Paul, D. Miller and J. Paul (eds), *Altruism* (Cambridge: Cambridge University Press, 1993), pp. 90–117.

Baier, A. C., *Moral Prejudices* (Cambridge, MA: Harvard University Press, 1994).

Balfour, M. (ed.), *Theatre in Prison* (Bristol: Intellect Books, 2004).

Barrameda, T. V. and Espellardo, L., *Breaking Silence: A Nationwide Informance Tour for the Prevention of Violence against Women in the Family* (Quezon City: PETA, 2002).

Basting, A. D., ' "God is a Talking Horse": Dementia and the Performance of Self', *The Drama Review*, 45: 3 (2001), pp. 78–94.

Battersby, C., *Gender and Genius: Towards a Feminist Aesthetics* (London: The Women's Press, 1989).

Beck, J., *Morality and Citizenship in Education* (London: Continuum, 1998).

Benjamin, W., 'The Storyteller', *Illuminations*, trans. H. Zonn (London: Fontana Collins, 1992), pp. 83–107.

Bhabha, H. K., 'On Writing Rights', in M. J. Gibney (ed.), *Globalizing Rights* (Oxford: Oxford University Press, 2003), pp. 162–83.

Bhabha, H. K., *The Location of Culture* (London: Routledge, 1994).

Bharucha, R., *The Politics of Cultural Practice: Thinking Through Theatre in an Age of Globalisation* (London: Athlone Press, 2000).

Boal, A., *Theatre of the Oppressed* (London: Pluto Press, 1979).

Boal, A., *Games for Actors and Non-actors*, trans. A. Jackson (London: Routledge, 1992).

Boal, A., *The Rainbow of Desire*, trans. Adrian Jackson (London: Routledge, 1995).

Boal, A., *Legislative Theatre* (London: Routledge, 1998).

Boal, A., *Games for Actors and Non-actors*, trans. A. Jackson, 2nd edn (London: Routledge, 2002).

Boler, M., 'The Risks of Empathy: Interrogating Multiculturalism's Gaze', *Cultural Studies*, 11: 2 (1997), pp. 253–73.

Bolton, G., 'Drama in Education and TIE: a Comparison', in T. Jackson (ed.), *Learning through Theatre* (London: Routledge, 1993), pp. 39–50.

Bolton, G., *Acting in Classroom Drama* (Stoke-on-Trent: Trentham Books, 1998).

Bolton, G. and Heathcote, D., *So You Want to use Role Play? A New Approach* (Stoke on Trent: Trentham Books, 1999).

Bond, E., *Saved* (London: Methuen Drama, 1965).

Boon, R. and Plastow, J., *Theatre and Empowerment: Community Drama on the World Stage* (Cambridge: Cambridge University Press, 2004).

Boon, R. and Plastow, J., *Theatre Matters: Performance and Culture on the World Stage* (Cambridge: Cambridge University Press, 1998).

Bouchard, D. F. (ed.), *Language, Counter-memory, Practice: Selected Interviews with Michel Foucault* (New York: Cornell University Press, 1997).

Bourdieu, P., 'Marginalia – Some Additional Notes on the Gift', trans. R. Nice, in A. D. Schrift (ed.), *The Logic of the Gift: Towards an Ethic of Generosity* (London: Routledge, 1997), pp. 231–41.

Bourdieu, P., *Distinction: A Social Critique of the Judgement of Taste*, trans. R. Nice (London: Routledge & Kegan Paul, 1984).

Bourdieu, P., *Language and Symbolic Power*, trans. G. Raymond and M. Adamson (Cambridge: Polity Press, 1992).

Bourdieu, P., *The Rules of Art*, trans. S. Emanuel (Cambridge: Polity Press, 1996).

Brah, A., *Cartographies of Diaspora* (London: Routledge, 1996).

Brenan, T. (ed.), *Between Feminism and Psychoanalysis* (London: Routledge, 1989).

Bundy, P., 'Aesthetic Engagement in the Drama Process', *Research in Drama Education*, 8: 2 (2003), pp. 171–81.

Burn, A., Franks, A. and Nicholson, H., 'Looking for Fruits in the Jungle: Head Injury, Multi-modal Theatre and the Politics of Visibility', *Research in Drama Education*, 6: 2 (2001), pp. 61–178.

Butler, J., *Gender Trouble: Feminism and the Subversion of Identity* (London: Routledge, 1990).

Butler, M., *Romantics, Rebels and Revolutionaries* (Oxford: Oxford University Press, 1981).

Callincos, A., *The Revolutionary Ideas of Marx* (London: Bookmarks, 1995).

Campbell, A., *Anansi*, ed. A. Kempe (Walton-on-Thames: Thomas Nelson, 1992).

Capelin, S., *Challenging the Centre: Two Decades of Political Theatre* (Brisbane: Playback Press, 1995).

Chomsky, N., ' "Recovering Rights": A Crooked Path', in M. J. Gibney (ed.), *Globalizing Rights* (Oxford: Oxford University Press, 2003), pp. 45–80.

Chomsky, N., *The Umbrella of US Power: The Universal Declaration of Human Rights and the Contradictions of US Policy* (New York: Seven Stories Press, 1999).

Churchill, C., *Faraway* (London: Nick Hern Books, 2000).

Cixous, H. and Clement, C., *The Newly Born Woman*, trans. B. Wing (Minneapolis: University of Minnesota Press, 1975).

Clifford, J., *The Predicament of Culture: Twentieth-Century Ethnography* (Cambridge, MA: Harvard University Press, 1988).

Coghlan, L., *A Feeling in My Bones*, ed. A. Kempe (Walton-on-Thames: Nelson Thornes, 1992).

Cohen-Cruz, J. (ed.), *Radical Street Performance: An International Anthology* (London: Routledge, 1998).

Cohen-Cruz, J., 'The Motion of the Ocean: The Shifting Face of US Theater for Social Change since the 1960s', *Theater*, 31: 3 (2002), pp. 95–107.

Coleridge, S. T., *Biographia Literaria* (London: J. M. Dent, 1975).

Comte, A., *The Positive Philosophy of Auguste Comte*, vol. 11, trans. H. Martineau (London: John Chapman, 1953).

Conquergood, D., 'Of Caravans and Carnivals: Performance Studies in Motion', *The Drama Review*, 148 (1995), pp. 137–41.

Conquergood, D., 'Performance Studies: Interventions and Radical Research', in H. Bial (ed.), *The Performance Studies Reader* (London: Routledge, 2004), pp. 311–22.

Cox, M. (ed.), *Shakespeare Comes to Broadmoor* (London: Jessica Kingsley, 1992).

Craft, A., Jeffrey, B. and Leibling, M. (eds), *Creativity in Education* (London: Continuum, 2001).

Craig, S. (ed.), *Dream and Deconstructions: Alternative Theatre in Britain* (Ambergate: Amber Lane Press, 1980).

Cropley, A. J., *Creativity in Education and Learning* (London: Routledge, 2001).

Csikszentmihalyi, M., *Creativity: Flow and the Psychology of Discovery and Invention* (New York: HarperCollins, 1996).

Dawson, A., 'The Mining Community and the Ageing Body: Towards a Phenomenology of Community?', in V. Amit (ed.), *Realizing Community* (London: Routledge, 2002), pp. 21–37.

Delpit, L., *Other People's Children* (New York: The New Press, 1995).

Derrida, J., *Archive Fever*, trans E. Prenowitz (Chicago: University of Chicago Press, 1995).

Derrida, J., *Given Time: Counterfeit Money*, trans. P. Kamuf (Chicago: University of Chicago Press, 1992).

Derrida, J., *The Amnesty Lectures on Human Rights*, Channel 4 TV (1995).

Diamond, E., *Unmaking Mimesis* (London: Routledge, 1997).

Donald, J., *Sentimental Education* (London: Verso, 1992).

Donelan, K., ' "Overlapping Spheres" and "Blurred Spaces": Mapping Cultural Interactions in Drama and Theatre with Young People', *Drama Australia*, 28: 1 (2004), pp. 15–32.

Doyle, C., *Raising Curtains on Education: Drama as a Site for Critical Pedagogy* (Westport, CT: Bergin & Garvey, 1993).

Dwyer, P., 'Augusto Boal and the Woman in Lima: A Poetic Encounter', *New Theatre Quarterly*, May (2004), pp. 155–63.

Eagleton, T., *The Ideology of the Aesthetic* (Oxford: Basil Blackwell, 1990).

Edmiston, B., 'Drama as Ethical Education', *Research in Drama Education*, 5: 1 (2000), pp. 63–84.

Edwards, R. and Usher, R., *Globalisation and Pedagogy: Space, Place and Identity* (London: Routledge, 2000).

Ellsworth, E., 'Why Doesn't This Feel Empowering?', in C. Luke and J. Gore (eds), *Feminisms and Critical Pedagogy* (London and New York: Routledge, 1992), pp. 90–119.

Enoch, W., 'Home Coming: Points of Reference for Learning and Making Drama', *Drama Australia*, 28: 1 (2004), pp. 7–12.

Epskamp, K. P., *Theatre in Search of Social Change* (The Hague: Centre for the Study of Education in Developing Countries, 1989).

Erven, E. van, *Community Theatre: Global Perspectives* (London: Routledge, 2001).

Etchells, T., *Certain Fragments* (London: Routledge, 1999).

Fennell, L. A., 'Unpacking the Gift: Illiquid Goods and Empathetic Dialogue', in M. Olsteen (ed.), *The Question of the Gift* (London: Routledge, 2002), pp. 85–102.

Flax, J., *Disputed Subjects: Essays on Psychoanalysis, Politics and Philosophy* (London: Routledge, 1993).

Florida, R., *The Rise of the Creative Class* (New York: Basic Books, 2002).

Foster, H., *Recodings: Art, Spectacle, Cultural Politics* (Port Townsend: Bay Press, 1985).

Foster, H., *The Return of the Real* (Cambridge, MA: MIT Press, 1996).

Fotheringham, R. (ed.), *Community Theatre in Australia* (Sydney: Currency Press, 1992).

Foucault, M., 'Intellectuals and Power', in D. F. Bouchard (ed.), *Language, Counter-Memory, Practice: Selected Essays and Interviews by Michel Foucault* (New York: Cornell University Press, 1977), pp. 205–6.

Foucault, M., 'Nietzsche, Genealogy, History', in D. F. Bouchard (ed.), *Language, Counter-memory, Practice: Selected Essays and Interviews by Michel Foucault* (New York: Cornell University Press, 1977), pp. 139–64.

Foucault, M., 'Technologies of the Self', in P. Rabinow (ed.), *Ethics: Essential Works of Foucault, 1954–1984* (London: Penguin Books, 1994), pp. 223–52.

Foucault, M., *Discipline and Punish*, trans. A. Sheridan (Harmonsworth: Penguin Books, 1991).

Fraser, N. and Gordon, L., 'Civil Citizenship against Social Citizenship?', in B. van Steenbergen (ed.), *The Condition of Citizenship* (London: Sage Publications, 1994), pp. 90–107.

Freidman, J., 'Muscle Memory: Performing Embodied Knowledge', in R. Candida Smith (ed.), *Art and the Performance of Memory* (London: Routledge, 2002), pp. 156–80.

Freire, A. M. A. and D. Macedo (eds), *The Paulo Freire Reader* (London: Continuum, 2001).

Freire, P., *Cultural Action for Freedom* (Harmondsworth: Penguin Books, 1972).

Freire, P., *Pedagogy of the Oppressed* (Harmondsworth: Penguin Books, 1970).

Freud, S. (1991), 'A Note on the Mystic Writing Pad [1925]', in A. Richards (ed.), *Sigmund Freud: On Metapsychology* (Harmondsworth: Penguin, 1991), pp. 427–34.

Freud, S., 'Group Psychology and the Analysis of the Ego', in *The Complete Psychological Works of Sigmund Freud*, vol. XVIII: *1920–1922* (London: The Hogarth Press, 1955), pp. 67–143.

Freud, S., *The Interpretation of Dreams* (Harmondsworth: Penguin Books, 1976).

Gallagher, K., 'Emergent Conceptions in Theatre Pedagogy and Production', in K. Gallagher and D. Booth (eds), *How Theatre Educates: Convergences and Counterpoints* (Toronto: University of Toronto Press, 2003), pp. 3–13.

Gardner, H., *Extraordinary Minds* (London: Weidenfeld and Nicolson, 1997).

Gardner, H., *Frames of Mind* (New York: Basic Books, 1983).

Gates, B., 'Yes, More Trade with China', *The Washington Post*, 23 May 2000; www.microsoft.com/billgates, visited 19 September 2004.

George, S., 'Globalizing Rights?', in M. J. Gibney (ed.), *Globalizing Rights* (Oxford: Oxford University Press, 2003), pp. 15–33.

Gilligan, C., *In a Different Voice: Psychological Theory and Women's Development* (Cambridge, MA: Harvard University Press, 1982).

Giroux, H. A., *Between Borders: Pedagogy and the Politics of Cultural Studies* (New York: Routledge, 1994).

Giroux, H. A., *Education and Cultural Studies: Towards a Performative Practice* (New York: Routledge, 1997).

Giroux, H. A., *Pedagogy and the Politics of Hope* (Boulder, CO: Westview Press, 1997).

Glynn, M., ' "Silent Voices": Working with Black Male Inmates – A Perspective', in J. Thompson (ed.), *Prison Theatre: Perspectives and Practices* (London: Jessica Kingsley, 1998), pp. 171–82.

Goffman, E., *The Presentation of Self in Everyday Life* (London: Penguin Books, 1959).

Grady, S., 'Accidental Marxists? The Challenge of Critical and Feminist Pedagogies for the Practice of Applied Drama', *Youth Theater Journal*, 17 (2003), pp. 65–81.

Grady, S., *Drama and Diversity* (New York: Heinemann Press, 2000).

Graham, K., 'Altruism, Self-Interest and the Indistinctiveness of Persons', in J. Seglow (ed.), *The Ethics of Altruism* (London: Frank Cass, 2004), pp. 49–67.

Grumet, M., *Bitter Milk* (Amherst: University of Massachusetts Press, 1988).

Guardian Editorial, 'Don't Play Truant to Join Bush Demo, Pupils Warned', *Guardian Educational Supplement*, 17 November 2003; http://education. guardian.co.uk/schools/story/, visited 9 October 2004.

Haedicke, S. C. and Nellhaus, T. (eds), *Performing Democracy: International Perspectives on Community-Based Performance* (Ann Arbour: University of Michigan Press, 2001).

Harding, F., *The Performance Arts in Africa: A Reader* (London: Routledge, 2002).

Hauser, A., *The Sociology of Art*, trans. K. Northcott (London: Routledge, 1982).

Heritage, P., 'The Courage to be Happy', *The Drama Review*, 38: 3 (1994), pp. 25–34.

hooks, b., *Teaching to Transgress: Education as the Practice of Freedom* (London: Routledge, 1994).

Hornbook, D., *Education and Dramatic Art* (Oxford: Basil Backwell, 1989).

Hughes, J., 'Resistance and Expression: Working with Women Prisoners and Drama', in J. Thompson (ed.), *Prison Theatre: Perspectives and Practices* (London: Jessica Kingsley, 1998), pp. 43–64.

Jellicoe, A., *Community Plays: How to Put Them On* (London: Methuen, 1987).

Kane, S., *Blasted and Phaedre's Love* (London: Methuen, 1996).

Kant, I., *The Critique of Judgement*, trans. J. C. Meredith (Oxford: Clarendon Press, 1952).

Kay, J., *Other Lovers* (Newcastle upon Tyne: Bloodaxe Books, 1993).

Kempe, A., 'The Role of Drama in the Teaching of Speaking and Listening as the Basis for Social Capital', *Research in Drama Education*, 8: 1 (2003), pp. 65–78.

Kempe, A. and Warner, L., *Starting with Scripts*, 2nd edition (Cheltenham: Nelson Thornes, 2002).

Kempe, A., McCaffrey, N. and Wordfold, V., 'Ain't no Cotchin' in the Jo: Working with Young Offenders', *Journal of National Drama*, 9: 2 (2002), pp. 31–8.

Kerr, D., *African Popular Theatre: From Pre-Colonial Times to the Present Day* (Oxford: Currency Press, 1995).

Kershaw, B., 'Ecoactivist Protest: the Environment as Partner in Protest?', *The Drama Review*, 46: 1 (2002), pp. 118–30.

Kershaw, B., *The Politics of Performance: Radical Theatre as Cultural Intervention* (London: Routledge, 1992).

Kershaw, B., *The Radical in Performance: Between Brecht and Baudrillard* (London: Routledge, 1999).

Kushner, T., 'How Do You Make Social Change?', *Theater*, 31: 3 (2001), pp. 62–93.

Lather, P., *Getting Smart: Feminist Research and Pedagogy with/in the Postmodern* (London: Routledge, 1991).

Lather, P., 'Post-Critical Pedagogies: a Feminist Reading', in C. Luke and J. Gore (eds), *Feminisms and Critical Pedagogy* (London and New York: Routledge, 1992), pp. 120–37.

Lather, P., *Applied Derrida: (Mis)reading the Work of Mourning in Educational Research* (2003), www.coe.ohio-state.edu/plather, visited 9 August 2004.

Lefebvre, H., *The Production of Space*, trans. D. Nicholson-Smith (Oxford: Basil Blackwell, 1991).

Linden, S., *I Have Before me a Remarkable Document Give to Me by a Young Lady from Rwanda* (London: Aurora Metro Press, 2004).

Littlewood, J., *Joan's Book: Joan's Peculiar History as She Tells It* (London: Minerva Press, 1995).

Mackey, S., 'Drama, Landscape and Memory: to Be Is to Be in Place', *Research in Drama Education*, 7: 1 (2002), pp. 9–26.

Macrae, A. D. F. (ed.), *Selected Prose and Poetry of P. B. Shelley* (London: Routledge, 1991).

Marshall, T. H. and Bottomore, T., *Citizenship and Social Class* (London: Pluto Press, 1992).

Marx, K. and Engels, F., *The German Ideology* (London: Lawrence and Wishart, 1974).

Mauss, M., *The Gift*, trans. I. Cunnison (London: Cohen and West, 1954).

McConachie, B., 'Approaching the "Structure of Feeling" in Grassroots Theater', in S. C. Haedicke and T. Nellhaus (eds), *Performing Democracy: International Perspectives on Community-Based Performances* (Ann Arbor: The University of Michigan Press, 2001), pp. 29–57.

McKay, G. (ed.), *DiY Culture: Party and Protest in Nineties Britain* (London: Verso, 1998).

McKenzie, J., *Perform or Else: From Discipline to Performance* (London: Routledge, 2001).

McLaren, P. L., *Critical Pedagogy and Predatory Culture: Oppositional Politics in a Postmodern Era* (London: Routledge, 1995).

McLaren, P. L. and Lankshear, C. (eds), *Politics of Liberation: Paths from Freire* (London: Routledge, 1994).

Merleau-Ponty, M., *The Phenomenology of Perception*, trans. C. Smith (London: Routledge, 2002).

Merleau-Ponty, M., *The Prose of the World*, trans. J. O'Neill (Evanston: Northwestern University Press, 1973).

Merry, S. E., 'Legal Pluralism and Transnational Culture', in R. A. Wilson (ed.), *Human Rights, Culture and Context* (London: Pluto Press, 1997), pp. 28–48.

Miller, D., 'Are They *My* Poor? The Problem of Altruism in a World of Strangers', in J. Seglow (ed.), *The Ethics of Altruism* (London: Frank Cass, 2004), pp. 106–27.

Milling, J. and Ley, G., 'Boal's Theoretical History', *Modern Theories of Performance* (Basingstoke: Palgrave Macmillan, 2001), pp. 147–72.

Mouffe, C. (ed.), *Dimensions of a Radical Democracy* (London: Verso, 1992).

Mouffe, C., *The Democratic Paradox* (London: Verso, 2000).

Neelands, J., *Beginning Drama 11–14* (London: David Fulton Press, 1998).

Nicholson, H., 'Aesthetic Values: Drama Education and the Politics of Difference', *Drama Australia*, 23: 2 (1999), pp. 81–90.

Nicholson, H., 'Drama Education and the Politics of Trust', *Research in Drama Education*, 7: 1 (2002), pp. 81–93.

Nicholson, H., 'The Performance of Memory', *Drama Australia*, 27: 2 (2003), pp. 79–92.

Noddings, N., *Caring: A Feminine Approach to Ethics and Moral Education* (Berkeley: University of California Press, 1984).

Nussbaum, M., *Poetic Justice* (Boston, MA: Beacon Press, 1995).

Orenstein, C., 'Agitational Performance, Now and Then', *Theater*, 31: 3 (2002), pp. 139–51.

O'Sullivan, C., 'Searching for the Marxist in Boal', *Research in Drama Education*, 6: 1 (2001), pp. 85–98.

O'Toole, J., *The Process of Drama* (London: Routledge, 1992).

Pearson, M. and Shanks, M., *Theatre/Archaeology* (London: Routledge, 1991).

Personal Narratives Group (eds), *Interpreting Women's Lives: Feminist Theory and Personal Narratives* (Bloomington: Indiana University Press, 1989).

Phelan, P., *Unmarked: The Politics of Performance* (London: Routledge, 1993).

Popular Memory Group, 'Popular Memory: Theory, Politics, Method', in R. Perks and A. Thomson (eds), *The Oral History Reader* (London: Routledge, 1998), pp. 75–86.

Portelli, A., 'What Makes Oral History Different', in R. Perks and A. Thomson (eds), *The Oral History Reader* (London: Routledge, 1998), pp. 63–74.

Prentki, T. and Selman, J., *Popular Theatre in Political Culture* (Bristol: Intellect Books, 2000).

Prichard, R., *Yard Gal* (London: Faber & Faber, 1998).

Probyn, E., 'Travels in the Postmodern: Making Sense of the Local', in L. J. Nicholson (ed.), *Feminism/Postmodernism* (London: Routledge, 1990), pp. 176–89.

Rasmussen, B. (2000) 'Applied Theater and the Power Play – An International Viewpoint', *Applied Theatre Journal No. 1*, http://www.gu.edu.au/centre/atr/ (2000), visited 16 April 2004.

Ricoeur, P., *Oneself as Another*, trans. K. Balmey (Chicago: University of Chicago Press, 1992).

Ricoeur, P., *The Rule of Metaphor* (London: Routledge, 1977).

Robinson, K., *Out of Our Minds* (Oxford: Capstone Press, 2001).

Roper, B. and Davies, D., 'Howard Gardner: Knowledge, Learning and Development in Drama and Arts Education', *Research in Drama Education*, 5: 2 (2000), pp. 217–34.

Runkell, R., 'Theatre Workshop: Its Philosophy, Plays and Production', unpublished PhD thesis, University of Texas (1996).

Samuel, R., MacColl, E. and Cosgrove, S., *Theatres of the Left, 1880–1935: Workers' Theatre Movements in Britain and America* (London: Routledge & Kegan Paul, 1985).

Sandler, J. (ed.), *Freud's On Narcissism: An Introduction* (New York: Yale University Press, 1991).

Sangster, J. (1998) 'Telling Our Stories: Feminist Debates and the Use of Oral History', in R. Perks and A. Thomson (eds), *The Oral History Reader* (London: Routledge, 1998), pp. 87–100.

Schechner, R., 'Performers and Spectators Transported and Transformed', in P. Auslander (ed.), *Performance: Critical Concepts in Literary and Cultural Studies*, vol. 1 (London: Routledge, 2003), pp. 263–90.

Schechner, R. and Chaterjee, S., 'Augusto Boal, City Councillor: Legislative Theatre and the Chamber in the Streets', *The Drama Review*, 42: 4 (1998), pp. 75–90.

Schechner, R., *Between Theatre and Anthropology* (Philadelphia: University of Philadelphia Press, 1985).

Schutzman, M., 'Canadian Roundtable: an interview', in M. Schutzman and J. Cohen-Cruz (eds), *Playing Boal* (London: Routledge, 1994), pp. 198–226.

Schweitzer, P. (1994) 'Many Happy Retirements', in M. Schutzman and J. Cohen-Cruz (eds), *Playing Boal* (London: Routledge, 1994), pp. 64–80.

Sellars, P., 'The Question of Culture', in M. Delgado and C. Svich (eds), *Theatre in Crisis: Performance Manifestos for a New Century* (Manchester: Manchester University Press, 2002), pp. 127–43.

Sevenhuijsen, S., *Citizenship and the Ethics of Care*, trans. L. Savage (London: Routledge, 1998).

Shank, T., *Beyond the Boundaries: American Alternative Theatre* (Ann Arbor: University of Michigan Press, 2002).

Shepard, B. and Hayduk, R. (eds), *From ACT UP to the WTO: Urban Protest and Community Building in the Era of Globalisation* (London: Verso, 2002).

Soper, K., *Troubled Pleasures* (London: Verso, 1990).

Soper, K., *What is Nature? Culture, Politics and the Non-human* (Oxford: Basil Blackwell, 1995).

Spivak, G., *In Other Worlds: Essays in Cultural Politics* (London: Methuen, 1987).

Stamp, S., 'Holding On: Dramatherapy with Offenders', in J. Thompson (ed.), *Prison Theatre: Perspectives and Practices* (London: Jessica Kingsley, 1998), pp. 89–108.

Steedman, C., *Landscape for a Good Woman* (London: Virago Press, 1986).

Stourac, R. and McCreery, K., *Theatre as a Weapon: Workers' Theatre in the Soviet Union, Germany and Great Britain, 1917–1934* (London: Routledge & Kegan Paul, 1986).

Tait, P., *Converging Realities* (Sydney: Currency Press, 1994).

Tanyi-Tang, A., 'Theatre for Change: An Analysis of Two Performances by Women in Mundemba Sub-Division', *Research in Drama Education*, 6: 1 (2001), pp. 23–38.

Tanyi-Tang, A., 'Unpeeling the Onion of Privilege', in J. O'Toole and M. Lepp (eds), *Drama for Life: Stories of Adult Learning and Empowerment* (Brisbane: Playlab Press, 2000), pp. 67–76.

Taussig, M. and Schechner, R., 'Boal in Brazil, France and the USA', in M. Schutzman and J. Cohen-Cruz (eds), *Playing Boal* (London: Routledge, 1994), pp. 17–34.

Taylor, C., *Sources of the Self: The Making of the Modern Identity* (Cambridge: Cambridge University Press, 1989).

Taylor, P., 'Musings on Applied Theatre: Towards a New Theatron', *Drama Magazine*, 10: 2 (2003), pp. 37–42.

Taylor, P., *Applied Theatre: Creating Transformative Encounters in the Community* (Portsmouth, NH: Heinemann, 2003).

Thompson, J., *Applied Theatre: Bewilderment and Beyond* (Oxford: Peter Lang, 2003).

Thompson, J., 'Ugly, Unglamorous and Dirty: Theatre of Relief/Reconciliation/ Liberation in Places of War', *Research in Drama Education*, 7: 1 (2002), pp. 108–13.

Thompson, P., *The Voice of the Past: Oral History* (Oxford: Oxford University Press, 1978).

Turner, B. S. (ed.), *Citizenship and Social Theory* (London: Sage Publications, 1993).

Turner, V., *From Ritual to Theatre: The Human Seriousness of Play* (New York: Performing Arts Journal Publications, 1982).

Turner, V., *The Anthropology of Performance* (New York: Performing Arts, 1986).

Wiles, D., *A Short History of Western Performance Space* (Cambridge: Cambridge University Press, 2003).

Willett, J. (ed.), *Brecht on Theatre: The Development of an Aesthetic* (London: Methuen, 1964).

Williams, R., *Culture and Society* (London: The Hogarth Press, 1993).

Wilson, R. A. (ed.), *Human Rights, Culture and Context* (London: Pluto Press, 1997).

Winston, J., 'A Response to Brian Edmiston's Article: Drama as Ethical Education', *Research in Drama Education*, 5: 1 (2000), pp. 112–14.

Winston, J., *Drama, Narrative and Moral Education* (London: Falmer Press, 1998).

Wittgenstein, L., *Philosophical Investigations*, trans. G. E. M. Anscombe (Oxford: Basil Blackwell, 1963).

Young, I. M., 'The Ideal of Community and the Politics of Difference', in L. J. Nicholson (ed.), *Feminism/Postmodernism* (London: Routledge, 1990), pp. 300–23.

Žižek, S., *Welcome to the Desert of the Real* (London: Verso, 2002).

Index